TRANSFORMING HEALTH

Christian Approaches to Healing and Wholeness

Edited by Eric Ram

Director of Global Health Programs
World Vision International

MARC WORLD VISION INTERNATIONAL

TRANSFORMING HEALTH
Christian approaches to healing
and wholeness

Eric R. Ram, editor

ISBN 0-912552-89-1

Published by MARC, a division of World Vision International, 121 East Huntington Drive, Monrovia, California 91016-3400, U.S.A.

Printed in the United States of America. Editing and page layout: Ken Graff. Cover design: Richard Sears. Cover photos: Karen Homer, Terry Madison, Randy Miller, Bruce Strong, David Ward.

By exploring the many dimensions of health and wholeness, this book makes a valuable contribution to the search for a Christian response to God's calling to heal our broken world. It challenges us as members of the ecumenical and global community to a renewed commitment to healing that restores the forces of life and reconciles people in caring communities, a living signal of the coming of the kingdom of God.

Dr. Konrad Raiser, Secretary General
World Council of Churches
Geneva, Switzerland

Contents

Contributing Authors

E. Anthony Allen, M.D., M.Div., MRCPSYCH., is part-time research and development consultant for the community whole-person health program of Bethel Baptist Church in Kingston, Jamaica, West Indies. He also practices psychiatry with a special emphasis on holistic health. He is a theologian with a strong interest in social action.

Peter A. Boelens, M.D., M.P.H., began a medical clinic in 1970 in Cary, Mississippi, under the auspices of the Luke Society, Inc. He expanded the clinic into social work, dentistry, education classes, thrift shops and Bible classes, and founded the Christian Economic Corporation to provide local job opportunities. In the 1960s he served as a medical evangelist in South Korea, where he held mobile medical clinics and helped establish 15 indigenous churches.

Paul Brand, F.R.C.S. (Eng), C.B.E., pioneered research on leprosy and pain during eighteen years as a medical missionary in India. He served as chief of the Rehabilitation Branch of the United States Public Health Service Hospital, Carville, Louisiana, and clinical professor of surgery and professor of orthopedic surgery at Louisiana State University Medical School. He has authored and co-authored a number of books.

Gordon Chavunduka, Ph.D., a sociologist with a diploma in agriculture, is currently vice-chancellor of the University of Zimbabwe. In 1980, he established the first association of traditional healers of Zimbabwe and became its first president. The Government of Zimbabwe soon afterward established a medical council for traditional medicine and appointed Professor Chavunduka as its first chairman. He has published nine books and several articles.

François Choffat is a practicing homeopathic doctor from Switzerland who is trained both in allopathic and homeopathic systems of medicine. He specializes in the patient's participation in prevention and treatment of illness. He has worked in a number of sub-Saharan countries in the area of preventive medicine and public health. He co-founded a professional school on research and teaching of homeopathic medicine in the French part of Switzerland.

Lawrence Mar Ephraem is the Auxiliary Bishop and the Chief Vicar General of the Archdiocese of Trivandrum in South India. His training includes missiology and sociology. He was director of St. John's Leprosy Hospital, Pirappencode, when he started developing a community health program called Health for One Million. He has served in leadership roles for the Catholic Hospital Association of India and the Catholic Bishops' Conference of India.

Annette de Fortín is trained as a medical doctor, a nurse, an educator and a public health specialist. Currently she is the director of World Vision Guatemala. She has worked in both governmental and Christian organizations and has shown how the two work together effectively. Her complete recovery from the Guillain Barré disease, which affects the nervous system, has given her a new perspective to her ministry of healing, especially among the poor and the marginalized.

Karin Granberg-Michaelson, M.T.S., is the former communications director for the international office of the YWCA in Geneva. She has written *Healing in the Land of the Living* and *Healing Community*.

Wesley Granberg-Michaelson, M.Div., is general secretary of the Reformed Church in America. He is the former executive secretary in the World Council of Churches unit on Justice, Peace and Creation. His most recent book is *Redeeming the Creation - The Rio Earth Summit: Challenges for the Churches*.

Christoffer Grundmann, B.D., M.Th., lectures in ecumenics and missions at Hamburg University in Germany. His research work focuses on healing in general and the Christian ministry of healing in particular. He is the moderator of the healing project of the International Association for Mission Studies (IAMS) and heads a sub-group on health, healing and coping with diseases in a forthcoming international project on the missiology of Western culture.

Eliza Kuppozhackel is a member of the International Congregation of the Medical Mission Sisters. She has training in social work, yoga, stress management and oriental medicine. She has developed the Center for Healing and Integration to help promote low-cost, natural, non-drug therapies. In collaboration with the Catholic Hospital Association of India, she directs a national training program of integrated health approaches for community health workers. She has contributed articles to health magazines and written a book on herbal medicine.

Alemu Mammo, Ph.D., M.P.H., has extensive training in community health, disease control and infectious disease epidemiology and has served in several capactities in the Africa region of World Vision International related to training, project design and delivery of primary health care services. He initiated, designed and implemented a successful child survival and development program in the Maasai Land of Kenya.

Sevanand Melookunnel is a Jesuit priest from Kerala State of India. While working as a pastor among tribal people in Bihar State, he became fascinated with herbal medicine and learned a great deal from local experts. He began promoting simple treatments for common diseases to help poor people manage their own health problems. Working at present in the Catholic Hospital Association of India, he gives training sessions, prepares teaching materials and promotes family health kits. He has written a book entitled *Home Remedies*.

Zilda Arns Neumann is a medical doctor from Brazil with specialized training in pediatrics, public health and health education. In 1979 she coordinated the UNICEF International Year of the Child in the Brazilian State of Paraná. From 1980 to 1982, she was the head of infant and maternal health for that state's department of health. In 1983 she co-founded the Pastoral of the Child of the National Conference of the Bishops of Brazil.

Theodore H. Perera, B.D., is a Methodist minister with training in pastoral psychiatry. After 17 years of itinerant ministry, he was released by the Sri Lanka Methodist Conference to labor in the ministry of healing. In March 1971, he founded *Dev Suwa Sevawa* (Ministry of Divine Healing). He has written four books on healing; a fifth is under publication.

Eric R. Ram, Ph.D., is director of global health programs for World Vision International and director of its international liaison office in Geneva. He had been the director of the Christian Medical Commission in Geneva for 11 years. He has served as an advisor and a consultant to UNICEF and WHO and was chairman of ICVA Working Group on Health and Development for six years. He is from India, where he developed widely known models of community-based primary healthcare.

Joe W. de Graft Johnson Riverson, M.B., B.C.H., B.A.O., D.C.H., D.T.M.H., D.T.P.H., F.W.A.C.P., is a medical doctor with graduate training in child health, tropical medicine and tropical public health. He served in a number of hospitals in Ghana. He joined World Vision Ghana in 1984 to implement a nationwide health and nutrition program and became field director in 1990. He has written one book and more than twenty papers and articles.

Murray Robertson, B.D., has pastored Spreydon Baptist Church in Christchurch, New Zealand, since 1968. Under his leadership, the church grew into one of the largest in the country. It has an extensive ministry of local evangelism, community ministries for the poor and needy, and a significant commitment to world mission. Rev. Robertson has also worked for many years with ministry groups such as the New Zealand Baptist Union and Tertiary Students Christian Fellowship.

Stanley L. Rowland, the Africa director of community health evangelism for Medical Ambassadors International, has advanced training in hospital administration and theology. He founded a multimillion dollar company that gave computer design support to hospitals in the U.S.A. He introduced community health evangelism to Campus Crusade for Christ and coordinated the strategy's implementation in Africa. He wrote *Multiplying Light and Truth Through Community Health Evangelism.*

Hugh Sansom, O.B.E., is a meteorologist by profession, retired in 1970 as Deputy Director-General of the East African Meteorological Department. From 1971 to 1986, he worked with the Church Missionary Society and various aspects of church administration. Since 1986, he has been mainly engaged in writing. He co-authored a biography of David Watson and is editor of "Healing and Wholeness," the periodical of Burrswood Christian Centre for Medical and Spiritual Care in southeast England.

Eleazor Oliver Sarmiento, M.D., F.P.C.S., B.Th., is president and founder, Medical Ambassadors Philippines. He served as a medical missionary at the Good News Clinic and Hospital, Banaue, Ifugao, Philippines and a resident Physician in Surgery, Philippines General Hospital. He continues work as a consultant in surgery. He has written papers on the biblical basis of primary health care and on the care of earthquake victims and burn patients.

Gareth David Tuckwell, M.R.C.S, L.R.C.P, M.B., D. Obst., R.C.O.G., M.R.C.G.P., is medical director of Burrswood Christian Centre for Medical and Spiritual Care. He also leads the daily worship services of the Burrswood community. He has extensive experience in medical education, both as student and teacher, and has served in several hospital positions as a physician and surgeon.

Fabio Villalobos is economic development facilitator for World Vision Colombia. He joined WV in 1984, serving as an area project coordinator and facilitator for community development projects. He has pursued initiatives in home vegetable gardening and hydroponic cultivation and currently supports agricultural groups growing rice near Tolima, Colombia. He holds a certificate in agricultural engineering from the University of Tolima. He serves as pastor for youth and elderly people at a local church.

John Wilkinson is a graduate in medicine and divinity of the University of Edinburgh. After thirty years as an ordained medical missionary in Kenya, he returned to Scotland in 1975. He has been a medical consultant for the National Health Service and the Board of World Mission of the Church of Scotland. He has written *Health and Healing: Studies in New Testament Principles and Practice*, *Christian Ethics in Healthcare* and *Making Men Whole: The Theology of Medical Missions*.

Introduction

Jesus healed different people in different situations by different methods: speaking a word, asking a question, applying mud on the eyes. What means does God use today to bring about health, healing and wholeness?

As director of global health programs and international liaison for World Vision International, I see a growing emphasis on holistic health care among Christians in every corner of the world. This is encouraging. Followers of Christ who are health care professionals must help meet the daunting challenge of bringing health and hope to the world.

More than twenty health care colleagues around the world have joined me in sharing ideas, programs and results in *Transforming Health: Christian Approaches to Healing and Wholeness*. In these pages, many of us reflect on the biblical mandate for wholeness, healing, and evangelism. We contemplate Jesus as healer of the whole person and see him motivating and directing our work. We consider Western and traditional ways of healing. We discuss the integrated nature of spirit, mind and body, and how the church can reunite the roles of priest and doctor.

Directly or indirectly, we relate our personal stories of living out God's calling as medical and health professionals who are also Christians. We tell exciting stories of people becoming healed and meeting the Healer. We discuss how primary health care and the gospel come to communities of needy and marginalized people. We show men and women reaching out with Christ's love in practical ways, working toward the highest of goals. (It should be noted in passing that in several chapters of this book, the generic "he" is retained. The intent is clarity, not gender bias.)

Many of us are writing about holistic health programs we have pioneered or are coordinating: a psychiatrist and theologian with a thriving church-based health program in Jamaica; the founder and president of Medical Ambassadors Philippines; the coordinators of Health for One Million in South India, a national children's health program in Brazil and a child survival program among Maasai people in Kenya.

We come from diverse places of ministry within the worldwide body of Christ. Among us are several well-known medical doctors, a Methodist minister in Sri Lanka, a Jesuit priest from India, a Baptist pastor from Australia, a leading health and missiology researcher from Germany, a sociologist from Zimbabwe, and a hydroponic agriculture specialist from Colombia.

But in all this diversity, there is unity of purpose. We have seen Jesus' example. In our own way and according to the mandate our Lord has given us, each of us seeks to follow him in bringing wholeness and healing to our hurting world.

Jesus began his ministry—and shaped ours—in the synagogue at Nazareth. He read from Isaiah:

> The Spirit of the Lord is on me, because he has anointed me to preach good news to the poor. He has sent me to proclaim freedom for the prisoners and recovery of sight for the blind, to release the oppressed, to proclaim the year of the Lord's favor (Luke 4:18-19).

Transforming Health: Christian Approaches to Healing and Wholeness is divided into four parts:

- Healing and Wholeness
- Making Health a Reality
- Building Healing Communities
- Breaking New Ground

Part one, **Healing and Wholeness**, stakes out the ground in biblical and conceptual terms. In "Wholeness, Salvation and the Christian Health Professional," E. Anthony Allen argues that the biblical view of salvation is transformational, not just a matter of evidence or law. Being saved means being transformed. As healing is total transformation, salvation and healing are two sides of the same coin.

Paul Brand, in "The Laws of Health and Wholeness," points out that regardless of their training or cultural bias, Christian physicians, when they discuss holistic health, affirm that true health and healing includes body, mind and spirit .

Part two, **Making Health a Reality**, describes and evaluates several successful health-related programs but also includes biblical reflections and insights. Lawrence Mar Ephraem and Zilda Arns Newmann, respectively, depict community people working to promote healing and wholeness in two massive but community-based programs: Health for One Million in India and the Pastoral of the Child in Brazil.

E. Anthony Allen makes a second contribution, this time using a case-study approach to describe the Whole-Person Healing Center in a Baptist church in Jamaica. In "Christian Witness Through Community Health," Stan Rowland describes community health evangelism in Uganda, India, and Modesto, California, as well as community health education in Muslim countries.

Part three, **Building Healing Communities**, describes some examples of community-centered health efforts. In "Healing: the Church's Birthright," Karin and Wesley Granberg-Michaelson explore why community is central to health. They note that *shalom* is not individual but corporate. It always includes a right relationship to all creation. Its purpose is the praise and glory of God. After the authors consider specific examples of healing—and healthy—communities, they challenge the church to apply several basic principles they have observed.

The watchword of "Therapeutic Conversation and Prayer: Making Persons Whole" by Theodore Perera is, "Don't seek healing. Seek the Lord Jesus Christ." After 45 years in the ministry of divine healing, he affirms the role of the church in holistic health care. Jesus the Healer still asks the sick if they want to get well (John. 5:6) and sends out his disciples to preach and heal (Matt. 10:1).

Part four, **Breaking New Ground**, presents some thought-provoking approaches to health and healing. In "Traditional Medicine in Africa," G. L. Chuvunduka cites the recommendation from the World Health Organization that health professionals take traditional medicine seriously. In Africa, the traditional healer is not the stereotypical medicine man, but rather an essential primary health worker who addresses a wide range of social issues in addition to medical issues.

In "Christians practicing herbal medicine in India," Sevanand Melookunnel emphasizes that giving people power to manage their own health problems is a key concept in community health care. He shows how herbal medicines promote health where other means are not available or appropriate.

Also included is testimony from a member of the Medical Mission Sisters in India. As a Christian health care professional, Eliza Kuppozhackel has adapted the age-old method of pranic healing for use in her work.

I have mentioned only a few of the treasures to be found in this ground-breaking book. God the Healer is truly at work today in both ordinary and extraordinary ways. I commend this book to everyone who is involved in health and healing, whatever may be their place in the community of faith.

Eric Ram
Geneva, February 1995

Part one

Healing and Wholeness

1

Wholeness, salvation and the Christian health professional

E. Anthony Allen

> The ways people think, feel, relate and manage
> their lifestyles can maim and even kill. Spiritual
> crises can kill. But divine healing and renewed
> hope can transcend normal healing processes.
> And divine forgiveness, reconciliation, deliver-
> ance, restoration and renewal bring healing.
> Where God reigns there is healing. Wholeness
> comes not by "treating," but by healing.

Semantics is praxis. The meanings of the language we use tell us
about our actions. Confusion abounds in Western-influenced
health care systems and within the church about the meaning of the
words health on the one hand, and salvation as a religious term on
the other.

Christian health professionals have been faced with a use of
language that demonstrates a critical dilemma. The dilemma is one
of identity. In other words: what is a Christian health professional?
Is he or she a split personality, a person who coincidentally happens to be both a Christian and a health professional? Is he or she a
living contradiction? At times, I have had people ask me how I can
manage to be both a Christian and a psychiatrist.

As a pre-teen, I was encouraged by my family and church
to make a decision to accept Christ. This was because I had the
temerity to ask: What exactly is the meaning of the word salvation?

7

Fortunately, my childlike faith allowed God to sustain me through the extent of the explanation and the struggles of life until I started training to become a health professional. My high school and early university years involved leadership in the Student Christian Movement and participation in the InterVarsity Christian Fellowship. As a medical student, I had to face the question, What is health? Sure enough, I thought I had the answers during my hospital training, as well as the answer to, What is salvation?

But then the confusion started. I began to feel split apart. On Sundays, I would visit the hospital and witness to patients as part of my student group. On Mondays, in the same wards, I would be helping to treat bodies. I would feel obliged not to dare think about, or mention, anything spiritual lest I offend the team or miss the really important symptoms or signs. In fact, with this conditioning, it hardly occurred to me to think in spiritual terms at all in my role as a health care trainee.

In the midst of all of this, I had a strong urge to care spiritually for people and to see their lives really turn around. So, I began thinking about becoming a pastor.

The confusion worsened during internship. Once, while I was trying to save the life of a young woman in the final stages of renal failure, a student nurse put the screens around the dying patient and prayed her into eternity. Was that audacity or being a Christian health professional? During my psychiatric residency the business of being a health professional who had a zeal to help people really change their lives (that is, to witness to the gospel), was becoming even more frustrating. While doing backbreaking work under inadequate conditions I was only helping the very ill to cope or the less ill to merely return to their former level of coping or to achieve limited growth. The idea of what salvation meant in practical terms became more elusive.

Eventually, I decided to enter the Christian ministry. This was partly in order to discover what exactly was this salvation that I had experienced through childlike faith but had difficulty sharing as a Christian health professional. Fortunately, God had other plans for me than to leave medicine completely. He helped me to resolve some of my confusion and become a more aware and fulfilled Christian health professional.

I share this personal example with my colleagues in health care to illustrate the problems that many of us must share. I took the drastic step that I did, not only to clarify my theology, but also because I more strongly felt a call of God to working out a ministry. This has resulted in my current work with churches as a community whole-person health consultant; God has also used me to influence the setting up of church-based healing ministries in Jamaica. Yet, doing a theological degree (and doing theology in the process) was also my means of beginning to unravel the confusion in language, and thus practice. For me, this confusion made health care seem like patchwork and the religious concept of salvation seem irrelevant to the work of a Christian as a health professional.

Today the health professions and the church are both becoming more aware of each other. We commonly use terms like "biopsychosocial," "wellness," "wholeness" and "transformation." One hopes that now Christian health professionals, in seeking to avoid being split personalities in their thinking and acting, will receive more support from their professional peers and the church.

To this end, it is my purpose in this chapter to examine the meanings given to the concept of health, and the tendency for both health care and religion to neglect the whole person; the points of departure and interrelationships of aspects of the whole person; the meaning of salvation and the relationship between demonstrating the kingdom of God and healing; and the new practical possibilities for Christian health professionals and their implications for policy, training and management.

THE MEANINGS OF HEALTH

Semantics

In the mind influenced by Western thought, the word health conjures up the vision of a robust physical stature. It commonly implies an absence of physical symptoms and signs as well as normal laboratory and X-ray test results. Rather grudgingly, the medical establishment has given some recognition to mental health as a valid entity. Yet, in order to be included in the medical model, the discipline of psychiatry has had to bend increasingly toward the view of the mind as brain, and of suffering as statistically validated nosology (disease classification). Many health insurance companies and other third-party payers insist on physical evidence regarding diagnosis and treatment; this has increased the danger of abandoning the self in psychiatry.[1] How appropriate is it for us to continue with this tendency toward a one-dimensional materialistic view of health?

Nevertheless, medical research has shown a clear mind-body relationship in disease and health. Interrelationships have been demonstrated between the socioeconomic aspect of the person and the other dimensions of self and living. This is reflected in Engel's call for a biopsychosocial approach to health care.[2] Also, studies are increasingly showing that spirituality shares a mutual relationship with both mind and body.[3]

The biblical world view has long since maintained a unified view of the person. God's action, as well as the healing ministry of Christ and the apostles, relates to the whole person.

Health, therefore, ought to mean *wholeness, or an integration or harmony between body, mind and spirit, between the individual and others, and between the individual, nature and God.* Health in its total sense includes the biopsychosocial perspective of Engel but goes beyond it.

Health also comes to mean not merely the absence of physical or mental disease, but *a maximum quality of life called wellness.* It is not merely a steady state of statistical normality but *a constant becoming.* It is a reaching toward *the maximum integrity and integration (or harmony)* that is possible both within and without the person.

Because health as wholeness does not mean the total absence of pathology, the paraplegic person, for example, can indeed be whole. A properly considered meaning of the term health leads us to a new semantics which calls for the terms wholeness and healing.

Wholeness comes not by "treating" in the narrow sense of the word, which means acting upon an organism. Rather, it comes by *healing*. In healing there is a relationship of the person that is being made whole with the healer, but also with self, God, community and nature. The person being healed is an active participant in terms of expectancy, cooperation and self-help.

Without a doubt, many physicians and other health professionals have been healers in their own right over the years. Yet, it could be said that this has been, by and large, a type of guerrilla warfare.

Because promotion, prevention, cure and rehabilitation lack integration in health care, there is still the need for an open victory on behalf of those now suffering, as well as those who will suffer unnecessarily.

What is the challenge to the Christian health professional? Will we embrace the new semantics and practice, or will most of us remain using the old language?

THE "GREAT DIVIDE"

Dualism and health care

How has the crisis in the meaning of health expressed itself? The dualism of Western thought has compromised medicine's caring for the whole person. It has also undermined the stated mission of spirituality in general, and of the church in particular, to proclaim and enable the true saving of persons. This philosophical and theological split-mindedness has driven the practice of health promotion and care away from spirituality and the Christian faith.[4, 5, 6]

Even where denominations have been involved in health care, there has been an inadequate integration of the spiritual in medical procedures in hospitals or clinics. Local congregations have tended to either abandon their ministry of healing to secular medicine or divorce divine healing from medical and psychological healing.

For both the church and the Western medical model, disease is seen in terms of the individual in isolation. Ignoring disruption of community and social harmony has meant neglecting the resources of the community and the local congregation as healing agents.

As mentioned above, one's wholeness is synonymous with one's health, and any attempt at delivering health care that does not address the needs of the whole person is inadequate. Yet, mental and spiritual health tends to be the stepchild of primary health care worldwide.

Mental health is included in the World Health Organization's 1978 Alma Ata Declaration on primary health care.[7] But there is a widespread lack of systematic integration of mental health services in primary health care systems.[8] The biopsychosocial model is yet to be a part of daily practice. Spiritual concerns that relate to health are not specifically included in the Alma Ata programmatic recommendations. Generally, there is not much attention given to the integration of such care with primary health care.

We often neglect integrating the mental and spiritual with the physical in practice. Despite their practical interrelationships, these aspects of the person have different points of departure at the conceptual level. Thus, they require different methodologies of approach. This will be dealt with later in this chapter.

It is difficult to expect a primary health care professional or lay worker, without adequate philosophical orientation and methodological training, to bring all these disparate-seeming dimensions to bear on the preventive, curative and rehabilitative aspects of community health. This stems from the philosophical dilemma of Western culture.

Health care and the church's mission today are beset by a philosophical and theological dilemma which requires analytical study. An "either-or" stance in Western thought has resulted in extremist and faulty world views, notably the dualism that acknowledges aspects of the individual but denies their interrelationships. This is exemplified by a Cartesian mind-body split[9, 10] and a spirit-matter separation.

Supporting this dualism is materialism, which includes scientific materialism, the capitalist ethic, and Marxism. Materialism sees the person as being determined solely by physical forces.

Western medicine has become largely a commercial exercise in the capitalist countries.[11] This is evidence of the materialistic and mechanistic approach to the person.

Another aspect of the dualism of Western culture and thought is that the individual (autonomous) and communal natures of the person are considered compartmentally. The dualistic view contrasts with the "both-and" or holistic view of human reality whereby various aspects of the person (body, mind, spirit , socioenvironmental) are held together in a dynamic tension known as wholeness.

North and South

Where has the "great divide" in semantics and practice led our world? Deficiencies in views of health, disease and health care and in provision of relevant training and services have led to several related problems in countries both north and south of the equator.[12]

South of the equator and in the ghettoes of the northern countries, consequences include the following:

- Poverty contributes to preventable infectious and nutritional diseases. Poverty limits availability of potable water, food, immunization and family planning.
- Western-influenced one-dimensional spirituality has failed to adequately address justice issues in resource distribution, human rights, peace and community. This has contributed to social oppression, civil war, community violence, racism and inadequate land reform programs.
- Westernized medicine and Christianity have largely ignored non-Western spiritual worldviews that influ-

ence traditional illness behavior and healing practices. This has made many people in the South suspicious of the benefits of Western medicine. Also, it has led to a disrespect that makes it difficult for non-Western people to accept the Christian faith and lifestyle.

In the North and among the upper classes and cities of the South there are the following:

- The crisis of lifestyle is becoming the greatest cause of death.

- The depersonalization and commercialization of health care is making it become less healing and less available.

- The isolation and alienation typical of urban life is contributing to the death of the family and community and hence to the rise of suicide, drug abuse, incest and family violence.

- Secularization has led to normlessness and the lack of values in lifestyle. It has also resulted in a loss of meaning and purpose in life.

In both settings, the neglect, rape and pollution of the environment is producing unnecessary disaster and deaths, as well as toxic and infectious diseases.

WHOLENESS: ASPECTS AND INTERACTIONS

Points of departure

To begin the task of whole-person integration, one needs to understand the points of departure of each aspect.

1. The *physical* aspect of health deals with the person as matter or as a biological organism. Health or disease are seen simply in terms of a preservation or disruption in the adaptive structural, physiological, biochemical or defense systems of the body. Here the laws of natural science apply.

2. The *mental* dimension deals with the individual as a thinking and feeling subject. One understands this subject only in an interpersonal relationship. Problems in childhood socialization or nurture can lead to personality disorders and excessive anxiety or depression, and may contribute to the more complex addictive and sexual disorders.

One's reaction to social reality becomes unhealthy because of faulty conditioning and an internalization of the negative feelings and evaluations of one's parents. Such defects lead to negative concepts of self and others. This results in inner insecurity, emotional distress, and social alienation.

Psychological disorders also relate to the stressors of life. These stressors can relate to the demands made by the developmental stages of life, such as the mid-life crisis. Alternatively, they can take the form of unexpected trauma such as the loss of a job or a loved one.

3. The *spiritual* or religious perspective, according to anthropology, goes beyond the physical and mental. In general, the person as spirit receives integrity in a relationship with a supernatural being that is seen as the creative and sustaining agent of life and being.

The spiritual relates meaning and purpose, ultimate choices, individual and social morality, taboos, communion with the divine, and divine providence and protection. The spiritual person receives paranormal enablement to transcend the limitations of the natural, that is, personality, evil and death.[13] Within the contexts of these elements, the deity preserves the social order and gives humanity stewardship over community as well as over the ordering and distribution of natural resources.[14]

Interactions

Health personnel are challenged to break out of Western-influenced modes of thinking because the mental and spiritual are inextricably bound up with the physical as mutually interacting parts of the whole person. Examples of these interrelationships include the psychological factors of self esteem, personality, social interaction style and life stressors, all of which have an impact upon the physical.[15] These factors can produce syndromes in the following categories:

- Psychophysiological disorders
- Autonomic disorders and fatigue related to anxiety
- Vulnerability to physical illnesses induced by life stresses[16]
- Negative lifestyles and health habits, and a lack of compliance to prescribed treatments—all having deleterious effects on morbidity and mortality.[17]

These interactions relate to most diseases seen by the practitioner of physical medicine. Beyond these, psychological reactions can cause unconsciously simulated disabilities in the form of hysterical conversion reactions (somatoform disorders). Simply put, the ways people think, feel, relate and manage their lifestyle can maim and even kill!

One can have psychological reactions to physical disorders. These affect one's ability to define reality. They include:

- Mental retardation due to congenital or acquired brain damage
- Delirium, dementia and related psychoses (with delusions and hallucinations) due to physiological and structural brain changes
- Genetically-induced psychoses partly related to disturbances at the biochemical level. These include the so-called functional psychoses such as schizophrenia and manic-depressive psychoses (bipolar affective disorders).
- A negative reaction to being ill, to the patient role, traumatic treatment procedures and to being in the hospital.

Further, the spiritual dimension has an impacts the psychological and physical. This is well illustrated in the writing of Tournier.[18, 19] It occurs in several ways, including the following:

- At the physical level, spiritual alienation or despair can precipitate or worsen disease or remove the will to live. Whether it be despair in God or the fear of the medicine man's hex, spiritual crises can kill!

  Conversely, miraculous or divine healing and renewed hope can directly speed up or transcend the normal healing processes.

- A person's spiritual commitment toward responsibility and a divinely enabled preservation of a healthy environment and lifestyle can have a positive impact on physical health.

- In interaction with psychological and spiritual rebellion, temptation and alienation bring about guilt, existential anxiety and despair. A person becomes vulnerable to the stress of natural, moral and supernatural evil, broken relationships, and worsening of personality disorders.

  Conversely, divine forgiveness, reconciliation, deliverance, restoration and personality renewal bring healing of the spirit. This influences the mind and, in turn, promotes the healing of psychosomatic, stress-related and lifestyle disorders, as well as hysterical conversion-type physical incapacity.

- Spiritual ill health and healing affect social harmony and justice, which in turn affect psychological well-being and the provision of resources for preventive, curative and physical health.

- Moreover, through the stress of physical, psychological and socioeconomic suffering, one can become vulnera-

ble to spiritual maladies such as loss of faith, hopeless-
ness, and rebellion.

Psychological problems can lead to sick religion. Here, for
example, a crippling perception of a vengeful or overindulgent
God or a world full only of demonic spirits can exist as a projection
of childhood conflicts or as a form of psychotic delusions.

Space does not allow exploring the many interrelationships
between the dimensions of the whole person. The reader may wish
to extend the analysis to include the socioeconomic aspect.

What is most crucial is to recognize that mutual relationships can set up vicious cycles among various dimensions within
the person. Thus, insecure individuals may subject their bodies to
stress due to overwork and overeating; the resulting cardiac disease
may lead to further stress and insecurity. Negative emotional reactions to physical illnesses (called somatopsychic disorders) can, in
turn, affect one's response to treatment as well as retard the very
will to live. Spiritual despair and loss of faith can retard the healing
of the very physical or emotional illness to which one is reacting.

THE MEANING OF SALVATION

The great divide at the level of practice between health care and
Christianity relates to semantic confusion not only with regard to
health, but also in relation to the word salvation.

Being true to the Bible, not culture

Once Western thought committed the sin of dualism in philosophy
and worldview, both health and salvation immediately lost their
real meaning. So Christian health professionals seem condemned to
live dual lives. At work, they do secular tasks only. Away from
work, they become free to witness to the kingdom of God and
enable the spiritual growth of others. At best, many Christian
health professionals may live out their faith by seeking to give
high-quality, ethical service. We may witness to colleagues, have

fellowship with one another, give free service to the poor or even serve as short-term or long-term missionaries. We may even go so far as slipping tracts to patients or inviting them to church. Yet, despite various forms of witnessing and sharing, our service can still be compartmentalized and fail to be truly whole-person or integrated. We often tend to be *health professionals who happen to be Christians rather than whole-person health care givers*—integrating the spiritual into our diagnosis, patient education, cure, prevention, promotion and rehabilitation.

How has our view of salvation failed us?

Unfortunately, in Western Christianity, with its contracted and dualistic worldview, the concepts of sin and salvation have come to be spiritualized and moralized. Thus, salvation has been portrayed as merely a forensic or law-court concept. Sin has to do with law, rebellion, moral disobedience, guilt and punishment. Salvation from sin, therefore, involves nothing more than repentance, forgiveness, Christ taking on our punishment, moral transformation and striving toward moral perfection.

Once Christians are morally reformed, they are left to continue in their physical, emotional and socioeconomic suffering. The role of God, in this view, is only to comfort and give strength until death and the Resurrection. Any healing in the various dimensions is to be carried out by separate professionals and their teams. The body is left to the doctor; the mind, to the psychologist; the soul to the church; and the socioeconomic to the social scientists and politicians. It is no wonder that as history and current public life shows that the person divided is the person exploited by the dividers.

The biblical view of salvation is quite different from that conveyed in popular language and practice within most churches. The salvation of the Scriptures is transformational rather than simply forensic or juridical. In the Bible, to be saved means to be totally transformed. Inasmuch as healing is total transformation, then *salvation and healing are one and the same.*

In an ultimate sense, our relationship with God is the foundation upon which all other harmony becomes possible, both within and without. Too often we forget that the purpose of the Cross is also to destroy sickness and suffering.

What does the Bible say?

We will address the biblical view of wholeness as what is normative or desired by God, the human being's problem of alienation leading to disintegration and God's action of reconciliation leading to healing.

1. **Biblical wholeness** In the Scriptures, the person is seen as a whole being. Wholeness or health involves harmony between body, mind, spirit—between the individual, the community and the ecosystem—as well as between the individual and God (1 Thessalonians 5:23-26). The person is created in God's image (Genesis 1:27), with responsibility and to live in a relationship with God and fellow persons.

2. **Alienation and disintegration** Alienation or separation from God (sin), occurs through doubt or being self-willed. This separation leaves the individual and his or her relationships to others and the environment unprotected. This makes the person vulnerable to disease (or disintegration) and death (Genesis 3:19).

   In other words, we become vulnerable to a disintegration of self and relationships which leads to disease of the body, mind and spirit, families and communities. The person's alienation from God leads to the problem of condemnation and spiritual guilt. Moral temptation, sins and daily guilt also disrupt one's harmony of body, mind and spirit as well as one's harmony with others. Furthermore, the Devil's direct activity is a disintegrating force.

3. **God's reconciliation and healing** How does God save or meet the most basic problem of the human being? Alienation and its consequences of disintegration are met by Christ's double work on the cross:

forgiving, redeeming and reconciling on one hand; healing (re-integration) on the other.

In Isaiah 53:4-5 (KJV), the prophet tells us, "With his stripes we are healed." Guilt is met by forgiveness as well as the healing of its consequences, as in the case of the paralytic (Mark 2:5-12). The Psalmist speaks of God's double work of forgiveness and healing when he says: "Praise the Lord, my soul and do not forget how kind he is. He forgives all my sins and heals all my diseases" (Ps. 103:2-3).

Implications

Two implications stand out:

- The forgiveness, redemption and reconciliation of the cross bring salvation.
- Salvation also includes healing (or integration).

Thus, through submission to God and through prayer, diseases of the body, mind and spirit can receive God's miraculous healing or health-giving harmony. Disrupted relationships can also experience the healing touch of God. Persons can become inspired and empowered to make the natural resources of medicine as well as social justice available to each other.

Salvation, healing and stewardship

Paul Tournier and the late Bob Lambourne, both physicians and theologians, have stressed the constant association and interchangeability of the terms salvation and healing in the Bible. Indeed, the same association occurs in practice among contemporary Christian professionals and congregations.[19, 20] Anderson has pointed to historical and contemporary examples of the church's mental health ministry. Griffith, a psychiatric researcher, has demonstrated therapeutic effects of church rituals.[21, 22]

As a practical outworking of their own salvation or healing, congregation members are called and sent by God to be a healing community through missions and evangelism. This involves ministering, burden-bearing and reconciling (James 5:14-16, Galatians 6:2, II Corinthians 5:18-19).

The church has significant resources of skilled, trained and gifted manpower, both professional and lay. This calls for stewardship. Each member is called to be a priest to take responsibility for all persons in the body of Christ and in the community at large (1 Peter 2:9).

Evangelism demonstrates the kingdom of God

Having understood more about health as wholeness and salvation as whole-person healing, what are the implications for the Christian health professional's understanding of evangelism?

To receive salvation is to come under the kingdom, or reign of God. Here, there is no separation of sacred and secular or church and state. The sacred and the church serve to heal and not to condemn or coerce (John 3:16-17).

Healing demonstrates the kingdom of God that is proclaimed in evangelism. As the disciples were sent to heal as part of proclaiming the kingdom of God, so are we in the church. Preceding the challenge to heal is the charge to preach the kingdom of God.

In Luke 9:11, the healings of Christ are preceded by his proclamation of the kingdom. "But the crowds learned about it and followed him. He welcomed them and spoke to them about the kingdom of God, and healed those who needed healing."

Too often, the concept of the kingdom of God as projected by the church in today's world lacks relevance. We do not sufficiently show the world how the kingdom affects the person's existence in ways that can be empirically observed or experienced. Empiricism is the basis on which health care professionals work. Should we not encourage our peers, clients and communities to put the same faith in a God who acts and transforms us, as we put in medication, surgery or preventive medical and psychological measures?

Healing is both a sign and manifestation of the kingdom power of God working through Jesus to bring his new order into existence. In this order, "He has put his all enemies under his feet" (1 Cor. 15:25).

Healing is a natural part of the proclamation of the kingdom. Here the medium is the message. Thus, the ultimate goal of healing as a sign is to point persons to the kingdom so that they may know Christ the King and become his subjects. Thus, *healing is central to evangelism* and is not meant to be a secular exercise per se.

Under the liberating reign of God, Christ's healing shows that we are freed from the oppressive reign of sin, Satan and suffering. If we are laborers seeking to extend God's kingdom and if we are to be truly vehicles of the kingdom in deeds as well as words, then healing is to be a part of our ministry.

Where God reigns there is healing. Christ, therefore, gives the church a challenge to manifest that healing, as we proclaim the Good News of the kingdom being available for whosoever will. We are to proclaim the Good News as we manifest that whole person healing which is its sign.

Within the church itself, there is division in approaches to salvation. The Pentecostals stress the baptism and gift of the Holy Spirit, as well as divine healing. The mainline churches promote social action. The evangelicals stress personal commitment to Christ and faithfulness to Scripture. There tends to be mutual suspicion among these three camps. What if all three could unite their valid concerns around the needs of the whole person?

The reign of God among us and the related salvation of Christ involves our ministry of healing, because the primary concern of the kingdom is the greatest good—the *summum bonum.* Christ, in speaking of his role as the Good Shepherd of the sheep, said, "I am come that they might have life, and that they might have it more abundantly" (John 10:10 KJV). This is what salvation is all about: Whole-person health! Wellness!

How much has health and healing been a part of our proclamation and working out of the kingdom of God in today's world rather that being a one-dimensional secular exercise? How much have we as Christian health care professionals been guilty of diminishing one other's awareness of the scope of the kingdom by separating our evangelism from our efforts at health care delivery?

One theological cornerstone of the church's ministry to integrate proclaiming with healing, then, is that it is a mandate of Christ to be obeyed. This mandate comes from the very will and love of Christ. Thus, Jesus empowers and sends his disciples—ourselves included—both to preach the kingdom and to heal the sick (Luke 9:1-2).

THE CHRISTIAN HEALTH PROFESSIONAL

Implications for services

How can the Christian health professional go beyond being merely a health professional who happens to be a Christian? What practical possibilities exist as to how integrated or whole-person programs of health care could function at local and regional levels? Following are some suggestions for work in the community clinic or hospital.

1. Services could be whole-person in approach in order to reflect the need for integrated healing. Mental health care should be in place. Spiritual health care (which includes the ministry of prayer, confession and absolution, spiritual direction, healing rituals and congregational support) should become an integral part of primary health care and hospital facilities.

Here, both psychological and spiritual care would be integrated with existing medical, and socioeconomic services (including community organization). These would be offered as part of a comprehensive array of promotive, preventive, curative and rehabilitative services. Such programs have been developed in the U.S.A. by Westberg[23] and Bakken,[24] and in Jamaica by Allen.[25] Services would stress the vital whole-person issues of wellness, self-responsibility, and community building through people helping one another.

2. Not only the clinic and hospital but also the home and geographical community should be involved. The local congregations as healing communities could be influenced by Christian health care professionals to function both as participants, recipients, and intersectoral collaborators in primary health care.

Here, contributions could include total or partial sponsorship, contributions in cash or kind, providing volunteers and services and participating in needs assessment, planning and evaluation.

In some instances, congregations have individually sponsored a complete program. This occurs in the Jamaican model called Bethel Baptist Healing Ministry.[25] Another approach would be to have a consortium of local congregations within a community provide different aspects of an integrated program held together by a jointly sponsored coordinating agency. Alternatively, congregations may offer a supportive role to a government or privately sponsored primary health care service.

At times, Christian health professionals from various countries have shared with me that, as persons concerned about health, they feel unsupported or even alienated in the local church. It is vital to keep involved in worshipping and in general church activities while trying to bring about change. One's place is as much in the church as it is in outside health care institutions.

The Holy Spirit has a place for all gifts in the church (1 Cor. 12). As we submit to him in prayer and waiting, he will find a place for our service and prepare the local church for it.

3. Given the constant and dynamic nature of the mutual interactions between physical, spiritual, mental, and socioeconomic aspects, multidisciplinary teamwork and linkages will become necessary. These would be at the following levels in promotive preventive, curative and rehabilitative services:

- Integrated health education and screening
- Cross-referral and feedback
- Continuous joint case consultation
- Joint curative management and rehabilitation under the monitoring of a case manager.

4. Services will be complex if they are multi-disciplinary, comprehensive (promotive, preventive, curative and rehabilitative) and involve a variety of target groups in whole-person primary health care programs (local community, congregation and city or rural region). There is a danger of multiplying staff beyond an affordable level. This problem can be offset by the following:

- Training and employment policies that allow for each staff member to perform more than one role
- Policies that facilitate each staff member to function as a *generic whole-person health care giver*

Every local church or geographical community can provide health care promotion activities using the nonprofessional volunteer to become a healer manifesting the salvation of the kingdom. Here the Christian health professional's task is not only to be a healer but also to be a trainer and a trainer of trainers.

5. Health workers could operate by providing physical, psychological, socioeconomic and spiritual help at front-line promotive, preventive, and basic curative and rehabilitative levels. This model should be able to cope with the needs of most clients if there are adequate channels for back-up consultation and referral.

Harding has discussed the selection, training and roles of lay mental health workers.[26, 27] The Balints[28, 29] and Castelnuovo-Tedesco[30] have provided counseling models for general physicians that are still highly relevant. Brammer[31] has done the same for lay workers. Within the Christian tradition, Tournier writes with excellence on the spiritual role of the health worker. MacNutt[32] provides useful, simple guidelines for a ministry of divine healing.

Some of the above suggestions call for special training programs in psychological and spiritual care as well as in the whole-person approach per se. Such a model, developed by the author, exists for church lay leaders in the Jamaica Baptist Union.

More specialized services and consultation in the psychological and spiritual areas could be provided by professional counselors or psychiatrists and clergy. Where these persons cannot be employed full-time, they could work on a session basis providing either direct client services or evaluation and case consultation. Alternatively, clients could be referred to outside pastoral and mental health services. Here close communication links would be necessary.

6. Integrating the spiritual, with its peculiar points of departure and methodologies, into the other dimensions and contexts calls for constant theological reflection, the study of anthropology, and incorporating insights with the discipline of medical and psychological scientific enquiry.

Health personnel, along with the local congregation, clients and community members, will have to be regularly refining their tools of biblical enquiry and working out their understanding of God, humanity, creation, individual and corporate stewardship, sin, salvation, healing, life in the spirit, the church and eschatology. All these themes need to be made relevant to the realities met in health promotion and care.

Theological reflection is needed in areas such as:

• The role of spirituality and liturgy in healing

• The meaning of wholeness, justice and ministry

• The role and function of the church as a healing community

- Possibilities and methodologies in integrating biblical theology with modern psychological medical, sociological and economic concepts.

Work has been done in many of these areas by Lambourne, a physician and theologian; Allen, the author,[33] and the Christian Medical Commission of the World Council of Churches.[34] Theologians Taylor[35] and Fraser[36] have stressed that for true liberation, theology is best done by the people and at the base.

One does not have to become a pastor to do theology. Some seminaries offer courses for lay people. With a pastor's guidance, one can form a study group of health and community workers. Each Christian health professional can seek to build up a personal library.

Learning some anthropology will provide insights to aid conceptual and practical approaches to the religions of non-Christian peoples. This could specifically relate to how others integrate the spiritual into health care practices. Such enquiry will assist the Christian health professional who works with these populations. This would apply to the major religions (such as Islam, Buddhism and Judaism), to animism, as well as to the religious or magical and occult aspects of traditional medicine. One needs to be informed before one can recognize what is compatible with Christianity and genuine healing. One can learn of dangers as well as advantages.

7. Similarly, at the psychological and spiritual level, health personnel will need not only to develop a theoretical knowledge, but also to seek personal growth in terms of their own self understanding and interpersonal relating and caring skills.

At the Bethel Clinic, staff have undergone their own group counseling and receive training in basic counseling skills. Spiritual growth in personal devotion and staff retreats is also a prerequisite for this area of healing ministry.

8. The church as a healing community and as the advocate of the outcast and enslaved has a particular mission in mental health rehabilitation. This includes:

   - Evolving a ministry of the church in relation to the incapacity and stigma of severe chronic mental illness and the related problem of homelessness. Such work has been carried out by Anderson in the U.S.A.
   - Sponsoring whole-person services in relation to problems that mental health institutions find difficult to treat such as alcoholism, substance abuse and other addictions, homosexual conflicts, family member abuse, and adjusting to living with AIDS.

   These critical ministries will also require significant theological reflection.

9. Socioeconomic aspects will also need attention. If health for all by the year 2000 is to be in any way approximated, priority needs to be accorded to the poor. The priority of the poor is a stated, though neglected, aspect of the church's outreach (Matt 11:2-5). It needs to become a motivating factor in our ministry of healing. Inasmuch as wholeness includes integrating the individual with the human and natural environment, then social and economic justice becomes a critical health issue.

10. New types of clinical procedures and skills will become necessary as the spiritual, psychological and socioeconomic are integrated with health care. These new approaches include:

    - **Spiritual history-taking, diagnosis and treatment** Spiritual ill health involves an alienation from God—the being of ultimate importance and supernatural power. Clients will be helped to see how this contributes to spiritual guilt and a lack of purpose, meaning and moral direction in their lives. They will come to see how neglecting the primacy of the deity means a lack of providence and protection from supernatural, natural and human evil, within and without. Without the power to transcend self, they fail in commitments to others and to the integrity of creation. There is existential despair. General themes will be given specific application as clients grow in understanding both God and self.

- **Whole-person history taking, diagnostic formulations and treatment**   At the Bethel Healing Center, we do a holistic intake interview.[25] We also focus on the precise ways and patterns in which various problems in the respective dimensions interact with one other. We identify patterns such as vicious cycles and linear sequences. Factors such as holistic-mindedness and willingness to seek integration and assume self-responsibility are included.

Implications for policy, training, and management

As the Christian health professional tries to become a healer and to reunify health and salvation, what are the management implications of developing and running an integrated or whole-person health care program?

Given the lack of integration at both the conceptual and practical levels of the physical, psychological, spiritual, and socioeconomic, any attempt to reverse centuries of Western-influenced tradition is to tread on a cultural, political, sociological, economic, and academic minefield. In attempting to integrate different disciplines, one runs the risk of offending people and institutions and becoming politically isolated. Yet was this not the very dilemma of Christ, who could not be contained in any neat human system of reckoning?

Some administrative issues

1. Professionals such as physicians, psychiatrists, social workers and clergy, as well as nonprofessionals and administrators who have held political power in terms of leadership and economic control in their respective institutions, must be prepared to share power and resources in becoming part of a multidisciplinary team. It is as the healer loses power that true healing takes place. Though there were physicians in his time, Christ did not heal with the permission of any religious or medical professional establishment or association. These bodies ought to facilitate and regulate rather than being power brokers.

Without the types of theological enquiry, personal growth, interpersonal caring, skill-development and training in community development previously mentioned, it will become difficult for Christian health workers to effectively integrate the spiritual, psychological and socioeconomic into primary health care and hospital services.

For too long, the politics of the church, mental health and social service establishments have perpetuated the myth that such endeavors are beyond the reach of anyone except clergy and professionals in mental health and social work. Yet these endeavors occur daily in several settings and are largely responsible for much of the viability of those church-based and other whole-person health care services that do exist.

2. Given the many potential obstacles to multidisciplinary cooperation at the various levels, there is need for advocacy and dialogue. This needs to be promoted in relation to the various political, governmental, commercial, professional, religious and other institutions and systems of power and influence.

Advocacy would be in the context of seeking the rights of all to receive health promotion and care for the whole person. Dialogue would aim toward developing joint strategies of enquiry and action.

Such advocacy and dialogue would be at local community, regional and national levels. Here doing theology, receiving basic psychological and community organization training and doing reflection will prepare the ground for more effective communication between the Christian health professional and members of other human service disciplines and systems.

3. The academic and practical training of professional and lay workers in the physical health, mental health, social work and spiritual health disciplines will require a broad interdisciplinary base. This could take place in the form of a whole-person core curriculum. This would require more collaboration between respective training institutions, professional associations and field supervisors.

Such collaboration would demand both longer and more rigorous training and retooling by teachers responsible for interdisciplinary integration.

4. Research needs to be carried out into the nature, experiences and effectiveness of historical and existing models of integrated or whole-person primary health care in various cultures. This would facilitate the promotion of successful examples as well as their refinement and adaptation to local conditions.

5. A whole-person approach to health care takes extra time and personnel. This, together with the fact that spiritual ministering is not usually on a fee-for-service basis, provides difficulties for the funding of medical and psychological practitioners in whole-person services. When I share with my medical colleagues that it takes usually over 20 minutes for the average patient at the Bethel Center, the usual retort is, But how can I manage that in my practice?

All this provides challenges for methods of staffing and the adequate financing of health care services. The volunteer and self-help financial support of the church and local community has been a valuable resource in the case of Bethel and other similar projects. Christian relief and development donor agencies with sound joint participation policies are of immense value.

Ignoring the political, training and management implications discussed will lead to problems. It would frustrate the smooth transition to a type of healing care that has been alien to many Christian health professionals worldwide who have been influenced by Western philosophy, theology and medicine.

CONCLUSIONS

Summary

In asserting that semantics is praxis, I have pointed to the confusion that has abounded in Western-influenced health care systems and within the church about the meanings of the words health and salvation. In reflecting from my own experience, I have suggested that several Christian health professionals have experienced problems of identity. We have tended to be living contradictions or split personalities.

The "great divide" in caring for aspects of the whole person has created a crisis in modern health care. I have suggested a rediscovered understanding of health as wholeness—an approach that is truer to science, human reality and thus the Bible. This calls for us to be healers rather than only health professionals who happen to be Christians.

I have also explored the biblical meaning of salvation as related to God's action for the whole person and all aspects of life. To see transformation to wholeness or abundant life in Christ as the ultimate work of the Cross is to span the great semantic divide and once again recognize healing as salvation.

This recognition calls for us to perceive healing not as a secular exercise, but as the total ministry of evangelism. It points to the kingdom of God as a divine reign with empirical manifestations. Rediscovering health as wholeness and healing as salvation calls for rigor in reasoning and biblical exegesis, as well as for innovativeness in practice.

I have argued that the problems in integrating mental and spiritual health begin at the level of faults in Western culture and philosophy that need to be overcome. These faults deter bringing together disparate-seeming conceptual points of departure and methodologies of the physical, psychological and spiritual.

I have outlined these points of departure. I also have illustrated the dynamic relationships in health and illness between the person as biological object, the person as subject interacting with self, others and the environment, and the person as spirit relating to God as the ultimate meaning and the ground of being.

I have given some practical possibilities for the Christian health professional relating to whole-person services, involving local congregations as healing communities. The services would be largely promotive and preventive, run by well-linked multidisciplinary teams where most people would function as generalist whole-person caregivers. Personnel would need to do theology and to seek personal growth in self-understanding and interpersonal caring skills. Priority recipients of the services should be the stigmatized, people with severe mental health problems, and the poor. Spiritual and whole-person history taking, diagnostic formulations and treatment approaches will be necessary.

I have also outlined policy, training and management issues relating to political implications, the relevance of culture, economic issues and academic aspects.

Final thoughts

How much flexibility exists in medicine and psychology, on the one hand, and in the church, on the other? The church itself is somewhat guilty of Cartesian dualism and tends to be polarized between the material and the spiritual. Yet despite comparatively recent historical influences, the church did not originate in Western culture. It came out of a background of God's dealing with the

Hebrew people, who gained their cultural understanding from his relationship with them.

Many parts of the the body of Christ have been, in fact, faithful to the Lord's mandate to heal the sick as part of preaching the gospel. Indeed, as Jesus did, from time to time in history several churches, denominations, and Christian health professionals have seen the healing of the sick as accompanying and fulfilling the proclamation of the kingdom of God.

Today's Christian health professionals need to be healers. To this end, they will have to also be lay philosophers and theologians. They need to be innovators, enablers for the church, trainers, community builders and advocates.

No longer can wholeness be the stepchild of health care. Health professionals must lead the way if:

- Health care is to truly lead to health for all by the year 2000;
- With God's help, we seek the way of spiritual renewal for all, leading to justice, peace, and the integrity of creation; and
- We want to see the earth "filled with the knowledge of the glory of the Lord, as the waters cover the sea" (Habakkuk 2:14).

Notes

1   Wilson, Mitchell. "DSM-111 and the Transformation of American Psychiatry: A History." *American Journal of Psychiatry* 150:3, 399-410, 1993.

2   Engel, G. L. "The Need for a New Medical Model: A Challenge to Biomedicine." *Science* 196:199-136, 1977.

3   Larson, D. B. and S. S. Larson. *The Forgotten Factor in Physical and Mental Health: What does the Research Show?* Arlington: National Institute for Healthcare Research, 1992.

4   Allen, David F. "Whole-Person Care: The Ethical Responsibility of the Physician." Edited by D.F. Allen, et al. *Whole-Person Medicine* 21-42. Downers Grove: InterVarsity Press, 1980.

5   Kelsey, Morton T. *Healing and Christianity.* 1st Edition. London: SCM Press, 1973.

6   Anderson, Robert G. "The Role of the Church in the Community Care of the Chronically Mentally Disabled: Reclaiming an Historic Ministry." *Pastoral Psychology* 28:38-52, 1979.

7   World Health Organization. *Alma-Ata 1978 Primary Health Care.* Geneva: WHO, 1978.

8   World Health Organization. *The WHO Medium-Term Mental Health Program 1975-1982,* Geneva: Who, 1978.

9   Dubos, René. *Man Adapting.* 1st Edition. New Haven: Yale University Press, 1965.

10   Lewis, John. *History of Philosophy.* 1st Ed. London: The English Universities Press, 1969.

11   Starr, Paul. *The Social Transformation of American Medicine: The Rise of a Sovereign Profession and the Making of a Vast Industry.* New York: Basic Books, 1982.

12   Christian Medical Commission, World Council of Churches. *Healing and Wholeness: The Churches' Role in Health.* Geneva: World Council of Churches, 1990.

13   Hoebel, E. Adamson. *Anthropology: The Study of Man.* 3rd Ed. New York: McGraw-Hill Book Co., 1966.

14   Nottingham, Elizabeth K. *Religion and Society.* 12th Ed. New York: Random House, 1964.

15   Eastwood, M. R. "Epidemiological Studies in Psychosomatic Medicine." In Z. J. Lipowski, et al. *Psycho-Somatic Medicine* 411-420. New York: Oxford University Press, 1977.

16   Rahe, Richard H. "Epidemiological Studies of Life Change and Illness." In Z. J. Lipowski, et al. *Psycho-Somatic Medicine* 421-434. New York: Oxford University Press, 1977.

17   Milsum, John H. "Lifestyle Changes of the Whole Person: Stimulation Through Health Hazard Appraisal." In Davidson, Park O. and Sheena M. Davidson, editors. *Behavioral Medicine: Changing Health Lifestyles* 116-150. New York: Brunner/Mazel, 1978.

18   Peaston, Monroe. *Personal Living.* 1st Ed. New York, London: Harper & Row, 1972.

19   Tournier, Paul. *A Doctor's Casebook in the Light of the Bible.* London: SM Press, 1973.

20   Lambourne, R.A. *Community Church and Healing.* London: Darton, Longman & Todd, 1973.

21   Griffith, Ezra E.H., et al. "Possession, Prayer and Testimony." *Psychiatry* 43:120-128, 1980.

22   Griffith, Ezra E.H., et al. "An Analysis of the Therapeutic Elements in a Black Church Service." *Hospital and Community Psychiatry* 35: 464-496, 1984.

23   Tubesing, Donald A. *Wholistic Health.* New York: Human Sciences Press, 1979.

24   Bakken, Kenneth L. *The Call to Wholeness.* New York: Crossroad Publishing, 1985.

25   Allen, E. Anthony. "A Whole-Person Health Ministry: The Bethel Baptist Experience, Kingston, Jamaica." *Contact* No. 113. Christian Medical Commission, World Council of Churches, Geneva, 1990.

26   Giel, R. and Hardin, T.W. "Psychiatric Priorities in Developing Countries." *British Journal of Psychiatry* 128:513-522, 1976.

27   Harding, T. W. "Mental Health and Primary Health care—The Role of the Village Healthworker." Unpublished manuscript, Brazzaville, 1979.

28   Balint, Enid and Norell, J. S., eds. *Six Minutes for the Patient: Interactions in General Practice Consultation.* 1st ed. London: Tavistock, 1973.

29   Balint, Michael and Enid. *Psychotherapeutic Techniques in Medicine.* 1st ed. London: Tavistock, 1961.

30   Castelnuovo-Tedesco, Pietro. *The Twenty-Minute Hour.* 1st ed. London: J. and A. Churchill, 1965.

31   Brammer, Lawrence M. *The Helping Relationship.* 3rd ed. Englewood Cliffs: Prentice-Hall, 1985.

32   MacNutt, Francis. *Healing,* 3rd ed. Indiana: Ave Maria Press, 1974.

33   Allen, E. Anthony. "The Church's Ministry of Healing: The Challenges to Commitment" in *Health, Healing and Transformation.* MARC Publications, World Vision International. Monrovia, 1991.

34   Christian Medical Commission, World Council of Churches. "In Search of Wholeness." *Contact.* Special Series 2, Geneva, 1979.

35   Taylor, Michael H. People at Work." In Amirtham, Samuel and Pobee. John S., ed. *Theology by the People.* Geneva: World Council of Churches, 1986.

36   Fraser, Ian M. "Theology at the Base." In Amirtham, Samuel and Pobee, John S., ed. *Theology by the People.* Geneva: World Council of Churches, 1986.

2

The laws of health and wholeness

Paul Brand

There is an infallible antidote to the mindset of
the self-sufficient doctor: *a sense of wonder*.

When we as Christian physicians speak of holistic medicine or holistic health, we are clearly accepting the principle that real health and healing involve the body, the mind and the spirit. However, when we, as specialists in some field such as dermatology or urology, are consulted by a patient who complains of a problem in our own field of specialization, we turn at once to the familiar patterns of thought which lead us to identify a physical problem with a physical solution. We may have difficulty in defining the way in which the mind and spirit have to be dealt with in the sick people who come to us.

If we are psychiatrists, we may be familiar with the laws that affect the mind and we should always be ready to refer a patient to an internist or a surgeon if we feel that there is a physical problem as well. We may call in a chaplain or pastor if we suspect that spiritual issues are involved. Pastors know spiritual laws but sometimes feel nervous and even inferior talking with medical doctors about patients who are already under treatment because of symptoms that seem to be physical in nature and responsive to physical laws. It may be even more difficult at the interface between psychiatry and Christian faith.

The problem arises from our training. We are all trained in our own narrow specialization, and get used to thinking in terms of the laws that govern aspects of health and healing that are responsive to those laws. If we are Christian physicians, we need to accept disciplines of thought which take into account the basic laws of wholeness of body, mind, and spirit together. It is always good to speak to our patients in a way that helps them to realize the extra dimensions of their life and health that may be beyond the immediate problem for which they have come to us.

We do not need to enter into much detail in the areas that are not of our primary concern. We do need to understand enough to indicate to our patient that these other areas exist, and are important to real health. We must consider the laws that govern each aspect of the whole person in a way that recognizes that neither can be considered alone. We are not three persons but one. We are a trinity. In somewhat the same way, we recognize that we worship one God, a God who is manifested sometimes as a very human Jesus, sometimes as the all powerful Creator and Judge, and perhaps most often as the intimate and indwelling Spirit, yet he is still one. So in our personal trinity, the way we use our physical hand may be a reflection of a mental plan which may be part of a spiritual purpose.

So in this chapter I will look at the laws that govern the body, the mind and the spirit, keeping in mind the intimate interaction between them all.

Physical or natural law

Natural law is largely a matter of chemistry and physics. It is mediated by enzymes and by osmosis, by heat and cold, mass and volume, the laws of thermodynamics. These are all very physical and tangible things which can be subjected to chemical and physical analysis. Their effects can be calculated and predicted. Doctors during their training spend many years studying and trying to understand physical law. They may come to feel that they are expert at manipulating it and controlling it and have no need to turn their thoughts to any other possible aspect of life.

This is a dangerous state of mind. Not only is it likely to give the physician an unmerited sense of his own omnipotence, but it is dangerous because it is untrue and is likely to result in a haughty and harmful approach to patients whose complex needs can never be met by manipulations of chemistry and physics alone.

In my own experience there is an infallible antidote to the mind set of this self-sufficient doctor. It is a sense of wonder.

The education of a doctor has been planned on a utilitarian basis. We study chemical reactions because we need to alter them or control them. We have no other reason to learn about them and therefore we tend to accept all of the existing patterns of life-sustaining chemistry, simply as the raw material on which we are to work. When patients recover after we have introduced some new factor into their physiology, then we take credit for the whole of the health to which our patients return.

I have found in my own experience that it is better to take the opposite approach. We need to recognize and wonder at the incredible fact that we are alive, that we can think, that we can sustain our life and propagate our species, most of the time without any help or interference from any expert.

I like to make a habit of thinking in depth about the whole range of amazing physical laws that have come into being and sustain health without any help from us. One day I will think about the clotting of the blood. Another day I think about the cough reflex, without which we would all drown at an early age, or about the transparency of my cornea. I think about the mechanisms in my inner ear for balance, or how nerves transmit sensations and control my muscles. I ponder the sarcomeres, the muscle elements that produce all my movement and activity; the chemistry by which slack muscles will suddenly contract, for precise action, and then relax within a tenth of a second at an impulse from my brain.

In each case, my object is not to check on whether I know what happens at the physical and chemical level, but whether I can fathom how such a pattern of chemical reaction could possibly come together or evolve as part of a total human being, starting with the raw materials that are available in the environment. I try to think how I could have done it myself or caused it to come into being if I had available to me all the resources of modern scientific laboratories.

For example, I think about the clotting of the blood and I know how frustrated we feel with the problem of hemophilia, the congenital defect in which children are born with a small defect in their genes, so their blood never clots. These children bleed to death any time they have an accidental wound or have a tooth removed unless we are able to interfere and save their lives.

We may feel proud that medical science is now keeping such children alive so that they grow up into adult life. But how do we do it? With all our resources we have not been able to give them the ability to clot their own blood. All that we can do is to arrange for normal blood to be transfused into them at regular intervals so that they may have a supply of clotting factors donated by large numbers of normal healthy individuals.

Then again, we complain about the fact that in old age, blood sometimes clots inside blood vessels. We get thrombosis formation in the heart, giving heart attacks or in the brain causing a stroke, or in the arteries of the legs so that muscles cannot contract strongly without pain because of the diminution of their blood supply. We recognize these thrombi as a defect, and we sometimes operate and ream out the arteries or put in grafts of artificial blood vessels to bypass vessels that have clotted. We have discovered that much of this thrombosis is due to improper eating habits and collections of cholesterol, but have we ever stopped to wonder at the original design of the system that allows blood to flow freely, round and round the body, squeezing through the tiniest microscopic capillaries, remaining fresh and unclotted for 60, 70, 80 years, and yet clotting immediately if there is a wound which would allow blood to be lost. We may have a rough idea of how it is done. We know about blood platelets that allow a chemical clotting factor to circulate continuously in the blood without clotting the blood until it is stimulated to clot by spilling outside the blood vessel. Incredible!

I remember in World War II when many British planes were being shot down in flames, someone offered a prize to any chemist or physicist or engineer who could design a system whereby petrol in the fuel tanks of fighter and bomber planes would behave like blood. It would flow freely from the tank and pipes to the engine, but if a bullet penetrated the wall of the tank and petrol began to spill out, then it would immediately clot and block the bullet hole, allowing the plane to continue flying.

Compared to the problem of clotting blood, this was a very simple proposition and many of the best scientific brains in Britain thought about it. Somebody came up with a three-layered wall for the tank: a layer of chemical jelly sandwiched between two layers of metal. If the inner metal layer were ruptured, the petrol would react with a chemical factor in the middle layer producing an extension of the jelly-like clot which would seal the leak. It never succeeded. The clot sometimes failed to block the holes. At other times the jelly clot propagated into the tank and solidified some remaining petrol, blocking the outlet to the engines!

I mention this because engineers and scientists failed, even on a short-term basis, to do what every normal baby human comes equipped to do on a long-term basis, clotting scores of wounds for many decades, and yet leaving the complex and tortuous vascular system free flowing for year after year.

An Australian molecular biologist, Michael Denton, has written a book called *Evolution: A Theory in Crisis.* Denton does not believe in God, but one of his chapters is entitled "The Puzzle of Perfection." He points out that wherever one looks in the body, in whatever system or organ, one finds an extraordinary level of perfection. Every system, developing independently, fits in perfectly with every other system and has its own built-in method of restoring its function following injury or stress. This perfection has not led Denton to believe in God. But it has made him recognize that any explanation of human development based on chance and the "survival of the fittest" has to be abandoned or drastically rethought. To us who have experienced the wonder of interaction with the Holy Spirit of God, the idea of his authorship of creation fits in perfectly with our own observation and wonder at what we find in the human body.

Even for us Christian physicians, I think it is a necessary discipline that we foster that sense of wonder and appreciation of the human body. I find that to some Christians, the idea that God had to work out the details of all these wonderful systems of chemistry and physics somehow detracts from their concept of his omnipotence. They like to think of God waving a wand or speaking a word and everything happens without anything that would correspond to what we would call careful planning. To me, the idea of God having to sit down and think out how to make blood clot at once when it spills yet never clot inside the system does not detract from my concept of his greatness, but enhances it.

If the wonders of creation just happened, in response to spoken words, it means that inanimate matter had to understand and interpret God's spoken language. Amino acids and enzymes had to have enough intelligence to know what God expected of them. For me, the wonderful interactions throughout the human body are living evidence of design. However quickly or apparently effortlessly that design was accomplished, every detail of it had to be planned. The supreme intelligence it took to solve all the puzzles of perfection is that aspect of the Godhead that stirs my imagination and stimulates me to worship. The fact that on top of all of that, creation bears evidence of the concern and love of the Creator, adds a greater dimension to the sovereignty of God. That God should then deign to desire fellowship with his creation and be willing to come into human flesh and experience both the wonder and the limitations of that human flesh is just the crown of his wonder. It is the aspect that I can reach out and touch.

In my interaction with patients, it has become a basic part of my philosophy in almost every single case to draw the patient's attention to the wonder of his or her own body. They may appreciate my help and intervention if they like and if their experience warrants it, but it is basic to the restoration to their health that they should share the wonder of who they are and of the real forces that work for health in their body. My medicines or my surgery probably makes a difference, but real healing is accomplished by the systems of defense and healing that have been built into their own physiology. As a surgeon I make a wound. I may remove something or rearrange something that has gone wrong, but it is their own wonderful fibroblasts which knit the wound together and that build the new tissue strong enough to undergo stresses and strains for the remainder of their lives.

A sense of wonder in patients helps them to heal better, and to respect their bodies in the years ahead. Ultimately it may form the basic platform from which they may build an understanding and a faith that leads them to Jesus Christ.

I find that my obvious appreciation of patients' own cells and chemistry is well-accepted by them, as a compliment. They also sense that I look upon all the wonder of natural law in health as a tribute to the Creator. I find that the recognition of the wonders of creation in respect to our physical bodies is the most acceptable way to witness about my faith. It may be the best way to introduce a subject which may be raised again when our patients become aware of their spiritual need.

Moral law

In the original design of the human race, the purpose and plan of God was for an intimate relationship between the spirit, the mind and the body. The spirit was to be in fellowship with the Spirit of God. The mind was to be an instrument for the spirit and the body was to be responsive to the mind. This perfect triangle of mutual influence, one part with the other, was broken at the Fall when men and women rebelled against God and decided to go their own way.

There is a sense in which the body and the mind may seem complete in themselves. The mind initiates behavior and the body carries it out. Christians often think of the body as being the source of fleshly lust and evil desires. Even the apostle Paul in Romans 7 seems to be saying that he himself would like to do good, but he finds a law in his flesh that is at war against the law of his mind. I personally feel that Paul is not really saying that he himself was living a defeated life. He is describing the plight of one who has not accepted the Lordship of Christ and the power of the Spirit. He finishes Romans 7 with a cry, "Who will deliver me from this body of death? I thank my God through Jesus Christ my Lord!" Paul had been delivered! He then goes on to say,

> And if the Spirit of him who raised Jesus from the dead is
> living in in you, he who raised Christ from the dead will
> also give life to your mortal bodies through his Spirit,
> who lives in you (Romans 8:11).

Paul points out that the body and the mind together are incomplete without the spirit and are subject to the frustration expressed in chapter 7.

When God saw the human race after the Fall, he expressed anger and frustration:

> The Lord saw how great man's wickedness on the earth
> had become, and that every inclination of the thoughts of
> his heart was only evil all the time. The Lord was grieved
> that he had made man on the earth (Genesis 6:5-6a).

It is worth noting that God did not say that it was man's flesh that had been the cause of sin and evil, but that "every thought" had been evil. The mind planned the evil. The body simply did what the mind told it to do. St. Augustine said it best when he wrote, "Corruptible flesh made not the soul to sin. The sinning soul made the flesh corruptible."

Having already developed natural law to make it possible for the body to be healthy, God now created a moral law to teach people how to control their minds and their thoughts in such a way that behavior would be affected and people could be healthy, even though sin was still a barrier to the indwelling Spirit of God.

This moral code we call the Ten Commandments. It is interesting to me that, other than the first three commandments which relate to man's relationship to God, all the rest basically form a code of behavior, and thus of health. When I, as a physician, read them in the context of health, I find that individually and as a whole they are laws of health functioning through the mind rather than directly through the body.

When I was with the United States Public Health Service, I used to attend some of the annual review meetings in which all the major health trends in the United States were discussed at length with reports from the Centers for Disease Control. I was very impressed with the striking difference between health problems in the United States today as compared with the health problems that were at the top of our agenda at similar meetings I used to attend in India organized by the Indian Council of Medical Research.

In those days in India, most of the major health problems were due to attacks on the human body from outside: attacks by bacteria, viruses, parasites; through mosquitoes, polluted water. We discussed malaria, typhoid, dysentery, hookworm, filariasis, tuberculosis. In the United States, most of those diseases were not mentioned or were relatively minor problems. They had been overcome by hygiene and sanitary engineering, as well as by antibiotics.

The diseases that took most of our time in the United States Public Health Service were those which related to the way people chose to behave. Alcoholism and drug addition accounted for a rising mortality, partly by their direct effect on the human body, but also because of the behavior of people who were out of control because they were drunk or high on drugs, or as a result of violent crime and road accidents. Then there were the diseases associated with stress and ambition, resulting in hypertension and heart disease, and diseases associated with sexual promiscuity. Sexually transmitted diseases have been growing to epidemic proportions, culminating now in the rising incidence of AIDS.

These are all due to the way people choose to live. It brings God's moral law up to date if we go through the Ten Commandments, looking at them in reference to health and disease. We find that the fifth and seventh commandments promote family solidarity: respect for parents and faithfulness in marriage. If people lived by these principles, how quickly the epidemics of sexually transmitted diseases and AIDS would disappear! Likewise, obeying the sixth and eighth commandments and respecting human life and property would mean that most violent crime would disappear, together with attendant injuries and death.

Respect for truth is next, followed by the injunction against the sin of covetousness, the craving for a lot of things that we do not have. It seems to me that the major thrust of advertising today is to make people desire what they do not have, and I see no comparable thrust to help people be content with what they have and to enjoy the basic pleasures of simplicity. This is the healthy way to live. It removes stress; it lowers our level of ambition. Hypertension and heart disease would become much less common. People would have less craving for wealth, and would have time to spend with each other and with their families, because they don't need to earn high salaries.

Of course, it would play havoc with the economy but I wonder whether that would be a bad thing. All of us, including Christians, have become so used to identifying by the bottom line the worth of everything we do, that it seems almost unthinkable that a decrease in the GNP might really be a very good thing and a contribution ultimately to real happiness.

Simplicity of lifestyle is a great contribution toward health. Statistics in Britain during the years of World War II showed a striking improvement in levels of health, and reduction in levels of disease in every year of the strictest rationing of food.

There is no doubt that the Ten Commandments or the moral law would be a wonderful contribution toward health if it were obeyed. Half the agenda of the annual meeting of the United States Public Health Service would disappear if all Americans obeyed the moral law of the Ten Commandments. The problem is that we fail. Even setting aside the spiritual and eternal results of that failure, the immediate result of disobedience of the moral law is a severe impact on health.

Spiritual law

The most obvious contribution of the spiritual law to health is that the Spirit of God, dwelling within us, helps us to keep the moral law. In other words, the Spirit affects health through his effect on the mind. The body works better and all of natural law works better if there is harmony or homeostasis between the spirit, the mind and the body. If there is a unified direction and a loss of conflict between the mind and spirit, then the body is healthier.

In saying this, I do not want to deny what is commonly thought of as "spiritual healing." There's no doubt that Jesus Christ sometimes healed people directly by the power of the Spirit. There's no doubt that it was prevalent in the early church and that from time to time miracles of spiritual healing have been demonstrated today in which organic bodily ailments have responded, apparently directly, to the impact of faith and prayer. However, I believe that we should regard these things as "signs" reserved for special purposes.

In my experience, spiritual healing and holistic health arise from the process of the living power of the Holy Spirit working through the will and the behavior of human beings and leading them into a healthy and godly way of living. The healing process is usually, but not always, unremarkable. Some people are affected by sickness caused or exacerbated by the way they have lived and where the mind is full of conflict and guilt. When such people are led to faith in the Lord Jesus Christ and the Holy Spirit enters and takes control of their bodies and minds, there may indeed be a spectacular change. Inner peace supplants conflict. Homeostasis infiltrates all the systems of the body.

Whatever disease happens to be in control of the body at that moment is rapidly overcome by the organized defenses of the body, operating by natural law under the control of a redeemed mind and the indwelling Spirit of God. The actual biochemical steps of the healing, the actual role of the lymphocytes and macrophage, still are obedient to the natural law that was designed by God to keep the body healthy. Yet the source of change from sickness to health has been spiritual. The center of control of the body has come under the lordship of the Spirit of God through faith in Jesus Christ.

One more aspect of spiritual law needs to be addressed. Although moral law, if obeyed, is a source of health, it is often seen as something restrictive or oppressive. Properly understood, it is not so. But the effort involved in keeping within the law is something that goes against the grain of the natural man.

When the natural man accepts the lordship of Christ and comes under the influence of the Spirit, it would seem that he is under still further restraint. Not only does the moral law remain as a requirement for health, but now, in addition, he is under the lordship of the Holy Spirit and thus less of his life is under his own control.

Yet, Jesus Christ himself has the audacity to assert that such obedience and servitude is the pathway to true freedom! He said,

> If you hold to my teaching, you are really my disciples.
> Then you will know the truth, and the truth will set you
> free (John 8:31-32).

Note that Jesus had just explained,

> I do nothing on my own but speak just what the Father
> has taught me. The one who sent me is with me; he has
> not left me alone, for I always do what pleases him (John
> 8:28-29).

If Jesus admits that he himself did nothing on his own, how dare he then say that if we choose to do likewise, the resulting servitude will bring us freedom? The apostle Paul says the same thing when he exclaims,

> Through Jesus Christ the law of the Spirit of life set me
> free from the law of sin and death (Romans 8:2).

We can never understand the real nature of freedom until we recognize that the most severe loss of freedom that humans can experience is not by oppressive law from without, but by helpless subjection to evil desires from within. Simple physical examples abound. The person who, by discipline, escapes from the habit of smoking, suddenly realizes that he is free to run up stairs without getting out of breath. He realizes that food tastes much better. People who have undertaken the discipline of training for a race recognize the joy of running, the freedom to speed over the ground without their weight dragging them back while they gasp for breath.

Discipline brings the joy of freedom. Any time we master a new skill it gives us freedom to do things we previously could not do.

The wonderful thing about the law of the Spirit is that it is not an external imposition of an alien will but is implanted into the very fibers of our being. It is woven into the fabric of the neurons in our brains. It makes sense when it lets us know who we are and whom we serve. It brings the excitement of knowing that we are part of something much greater than we ever thought we could be as individuals. It helps us to delight in things that might otherwise have been a burden. We discover a deep longing to do the very things and be the very people that had seemed out of reach.

Final comments

I have spoken of natural law and the wonder of creation. I have spoken of moral law as being the way in which health may be maintained. But when I come to spiritual law I hesitate even to use the word "law." Although the effects of spiritual law are as predictable as laws of chemistry and physics, it much more like freedom than law.

I prefer to look upon spiritual law as a gift rather than a law, as a freedom rather than a requirement. It is the very essence of health itself, not simply a means to that end.

3

Healing: a dimension of ecclesial-missionary action

Christoffer Grundmann

"The body is the pivot of salvation" – Tertullian

The topic of healing is neither new nor irrelevant for the Christian church. The biblical findings are unambiguous in principle. Both the ancient and the modern church have grappled repeatedly with the phenomenon.

General context

The only thing new about the topic is the timeliness that it has regained. Forty years ago, healing captured the attention of the churches. Big evangelical healing revivals were held by William Branham, Tommy Hicks, Thomas L. Osborne and Hermann Zaiss.

Why do the Euro-Fire conferences led by Reinhard Bonnke of Christ for All Nations, the Vineyard Ministries, or the interde-nominational charismatic congregational renewal movement still command such an astounding amount of public attention even today? Are healings proof of the Spirit and God's power? Are they signs of a particularly Spirit-filled age, and should they be inter-preted as an expression of the work of the Holy Spirit, or even be demanded as a dimension of ecclesial-missionary action?

As the early Christian church took shape, it was confronted (especially in Asia Minor) with the popular Hellenistic healing cult of Asclepios. This confrontation clearly left its mark on New Testament texts such as the Lukan and Johannine writings, particularly the Acts of the Apostles, the Gospel of John and Revelation. Asclepios was considered to be the absolute savior (i.e., healer), whom the Christian confession opposed with Jesus Christ as the one who is indeed the Savior of the world (John 4:42; 1 John 4:14) and who, unlike Asclepios, was even able to bring the dead back to life (John 11).

Of interest to us here is an argument made by North African theologian Origen of Alexandria (185-254). He was writing within the framework of this controversy in his early third century treatise "Against Celsus" with regard to the judging of healing gifts. In a way that may surprise us, he declares:

> Were I to . . . admit, that a demon, Asclepios by name, has the power to heal physical illness, then I could remark to those who are astounded . . . by this healing, that this power to heal the sick is neither good nor evil, that it is a thing which is bestowed not only upon the righteous, but upon the godless as well . . . Nothing divine is revealed in the power to heal the sick in and of itself (III, 25).

So said Origen more than 1700 years ago. He does not deny that miraculous healings occur, but he does deny that they have the character of a divine, let alone a Christian, proof of authority. What does he say in the end, other than that healing is not a specifically Christian issue?

This statement deserves our wholehearted assent. From time immemorial, the experience of sickness and the experience of healing have gone hand in hand, and evidence of efforts to maintain health and heal illness to prevent an untimely death can be found in all cultures everywhere. In some cultures such efforts fostered regular systems of healing and led to the development of complete bodies of medical science, e.g., the Ayurveda system in India, the Unnani system within Islam, or the Hippocratic medicine of Classical Greece. In most cultures, however, such efforts never progressed beyond modest beginnings.

Anyone wanting to address the problem of healing must first deal with the general human, indeed, the general creatural phenomenon of sickness and healing in their various respective relationships to healing arts, which are really just typically human. To discuss healing adequately, one must address these basic existential realities of life as a human being and their varying interpretation in the diverse cultures. One must not disregard the answers given by the different cultures in various established systems of healing. This goes beyond the scope of this article. But it may help us to more appropriately understand the biblical witnesses of the Old Testament and New Testament, i.e., in this case, to come to the reality. After all, it would have been odd if an existential problem of this type had not influenced the writings of ancient Judaism and the message of Christianity.

But it is impossible to found an exclusively Christian claim to healing on the fact that there are various reports of healing in the New Testament. This would not only abridge the biblical understanding of healing, but distort the Christian message as well. Healing must, of course, be described from a Christian point of view against this background, but it cannot be monopolized by Christians. Herein lies one of the special difficulties of describing healing as a dimension of ecclesial-missionary activity.

Current trends in healing

Today there is a confusing multitude of healing movements of every kind, not only in Europe, but also and above all, overseas. The movements draw their followers from all strata of society: intellectuals and illiterates, unemployed visionaries and highly paid experts, Christians, Muslims, Hindus, and Buddhists, those with ties to natural religion or dedicated atheists and irreligious persons of every kind.

Take, for example, the syncretist cults of Brazil such as Condomblé and Umbanda and the "Modern Religions" in Japan (e.g., Sekai Kyusei Kyo, Mahikari and Soka Gakkai) in which healings play a dominant role. We also know, however, of spirit-healers in the Philippines and miracle-working gurus in India who have often been a last resort for many desperate Europeans and Americans in the throes of illness. The New Age movement has made healing

55

one of its key words; the twentieth anniversary of the "Frankfurter Ring" on Pentecost 1989 was held under the motto "healing ways." Training in esoteric astrology includes a seminar on the subject of the "The Medium Coeli and the Law of Healing"; a Mother Earth Center teaches mind-body healing and mail-order stores sell "precious stones with healing powers."

Growing criticism of high-tech medicine based on natural science has harnessed interest in so-called alternative, gentle, or holistic medicine. Popular remedies and therapies such as acupuncture and herbal medicine, which were once thoughtlessly disparaged, have gained new respectability; shamanistic and Indian healing rites are also meeting with current interest. In the stimulated search for entirely different kinds of healing, however, people often forget that dealing with illness conscientiously from a medical point of view is an essential part of holistic treatment.

Of course, trends have had an effect upon the Christian church as well; after all, Christians are children of their times just like other people. Seeing the topic of healing surface again need not amaze us and is not necessarily a sign of special spiritual presence and spiritual empowerment.

Thus the spectrum of healing as practiced within the Christian church ranges from the "healing churches" in Africa, of which there are well over 6000 according to recent estimates, to the Pentecostal churches of Asia with their swelling membership, or the healing service of the Shepherds in the Lutheran Church of Madagascar. We have already referred to the charismatic movement. Many people may be familiar with the Churches' Council for Health and Healing in England and Wales, as well as with the practice of holding individual intervention and blessing services in some congregations and with the "biblical ministry to the sick." For all of these groups, as for the Chrischona movement as well, healings by the laying on of hands and through prayer are nothing extraordinary or even unusual.

Both within and without Christianity, we are currently confronted with healing phenomena all over the world. Within and without Christianity, there is a flood of mostly dubious literature about this topic. In fact, there is so much literature on the subject that it is impossible to keep track of it all. So there is every reason to speak of an honest-to-goodness healing boom at the close of our ever so enlightened and advanced twentieth century. The reasons for this are difficult to make out, for they vary widely.

Where highly industrialized, wealthy and secular nations are concerned, one of the reasons for the healing boom may well be a response to the technical reality of the performance-oriented society, a reality which can now be manipulated by critical-rational means. Overseas, these developments are probably due to the lack of the capital required to establish and maintain an extensive, efficient health care system. This has little to do with a genuine rediscovery of healing powers, let alone with a particularly "spirit-filled" period in history. What has been born of need, namely the recourse to old, native healing institutions and medicines, merely leads to additional offerings in our culture group in addition to the already established, extensive and effective medical system. The much-praised "alternative" methods of healing are an expression of the overabundance of a prosperous society which can afford alternatives in this area as well.

The widespread interest in healing today is often marked by a fascination with the esoteric, which is a reaction to the cool rationality and economic profitability needed to master the highly technological present. People are searching for private areas in which nothing has to be explained or justified precisely because things can no longer be explained, as the events of healing are apparently beyond explanation. Every attempt to make the "miraculous" event accessible to reason runs the risk of being looked down upon as sacrilege.

The current interest in healing is not without its problems. It could be an expression of the *sacrificium intellectus* (sacrifice of the intellect), which leads to flight from societal responsibility. Thus we must ask ourselves why this topic is so important and why it seems so up-to-date to us. Perhaps missionary societies and institutions are also no longer able to bear the global misery which becomes more and more apparent each day. Perhaps the well-meant effort to

57

heal is reactionary behavior, supported by the argument that it is precisely the disastrous (i.e., unhealthy) condition of the world and the people in it that makes healing a topic for church and mission. Reactionary behavior is understandable, but this does not make it Christian.

The factual justification for these serious injunctions becomes immediately obvious if one considers the fact that healing is available to modern human beings in a measure which was never before possible. How did this happen? Quite simply: through the sensible application of medicine based on natural science; through rational pharmacy and psychotherapeutic methods in the hospitals and private practices; through a public health system which we scarcely take conscious notice of any more, through mobile emergency medical services. But thanks as well to good sanitary facilities and effective medications, today we are better able than ever not only to treat illness in cities and villages, in the schools, homes and families, but even to prevent it. In conjunction with the insurance systems, we have almost perfectly systematized healing for all members of society. But the routineness and the almost totally smooth functioning of this complex health care system make it easy for us to forget that, in fact, this is also genuine healing.

Healing is, thank God, no more an extraordinary topic than it is a specifically Christian topic today. We should not merely acknowledge this; we should expressly emphasize this with regard to our topic for two reasons. First, how would it be possible to speak of healing as a dimension of ecclesial-missionary activity and at the same time disregard the determined efforts of doctors, nurses and therapists in the existing caritative and diaconal institutions both at home and overseas? Here, in the hospitals and the institutions operated by the Diaconal Works, Caritas and the Medical Mission, healing has taken shape over the years as a dimension of ecclesial-missionary action.

Second, the spontaneous disappointment at having to permit the healings that have become common in the medical institutions today to count fully as such is a critical filter for showing what interests are actually guiding our questions. For the greater our dissatisfaction with the answers given up until now, the greater is our secret interest in the extraordinary, the irrational and thus exclusively in a single, small aspect: so-called miracle cures. It is good to be aware of this, because it can throw some light upon a specialized formulation of the question.

An urgent challenge for the church

The topic of healing as a dimension of ecclesial-missionary action has to do with more than just the problem of how the universal human phenomenon of healing (which, moreover, can be manipulated today to an extent never before possible) can be interpreted in a Christian sense and adapted to be seen as a legitimate dimension of our action.

For the Christian church, the inner necessity to do this arises from the biblical commission to heal (Matt. 10:8, Luke 10:9). The outer necessity arises from the confrontation with the spirit of the times and through the apparent presence of charismatic persons. The churches and missionary societies would do well not to address these challenges in order to justify themselves or defame one another.

Christianity has a timely opportunity in connection with the phenomenon of healing to provide orientation and formulate Christ's message credibly in view of the spirit of the times as the living, up-to-date Word of God. This huge opportunity is all too often squandered, as shown by the behavior of some officially accountable church and mission administrations.

In 1986, for example, the Catholic bishops of Rwanda warned their congregations in regard to the healing meetings of one Eugenia Mukakalisa from Coko:

> Be extremely careful and cautious when faced with people who claim to have supernatural powers of perception or be charged with a divine mission, because Christ cannot approve of such irregularities (EPS, Geneva, 1986, 06.33).

The case of the former Archbishop of Lusaka, Zambia, Emanuel Milingo, is more widely known. After Milingo became aware of his healing powers, he used these in his pastoral ministry in the form of healing services and blessings and met with unexpected popularity. In 1982, however, he was called to Rome for interrogation in connection with other questions and has been employed there as a legate in the section for refugees, migrant workers and tourism ever since. Closely affiliated with the charismatic congregational renewal movement, he holds monthly healing and blessing services outside church precincts. Europeans flock by the thousand to these services.

Matters look much the same on the Protestant side. Take for example the African Independent Churches. They emerged because the old European mother churches and missions failed to satisfy young African Christianity's passionate longing for healing (i.e., restoration of an undistorted relationship with their own cultural roots). The most famous and probably the largest of these is the Kimbanguist Church in Zaire. These churches have not yet joined together to form large church associations and are thus "independent" (individual, self-supporting, single congregations of the first generation). However, a healing church was founded not long ago in Hamburg, Germany, not spontaneously, but because a group of people broke away from the established church.

Behind the official and theological difficulties of this kind in recognizing healing gifts—and we assume for now, that these are genuine *charismata* or spiritual gifts and not a demonstration of spiritually embellished individualism or a sublime issue of power—lies the issue of *the binding nature of revelation*. The healing phenomenon suddenly appears as an additional source of revelation alongside the Word of God, which is, after all, supposed to be preserved and protected from corruption and distortion by the institution of the church and its theology. Moreover, this new source of revelation appears to have a compelling persuasive power for the masses because of its simple, personal immediacy and conspicuous concreteness and appears to need no further explanation.

There are good reasons that the healing churches, with their emphasis on the physical experience of the efficacious presence of God, place hardly any value on pure doctrine or even formal theology. However, because their independence calls the sole authority of the officials of the institutional church and its agencies into question, conflicts and the often seemingly helpless official church reactions to such healings (which are, after all, mostly reported by lay people) are practically preprogrammed. In this case, the church and missionary administrations have to deal with the classic, virtually unmanageable conflict between institution and *charisma* and appear to be able to make their peace with the presence of places of healing and grace such as Lourdes more easily than with individual charismatic persons.

After all, one of the trademarks of a genuine spiritual gift is that it pays no heed to institutions or ecclesiastical regulations. Genuine gifts of the Spirit cannot be regimented, but they can be integrated, as the encounter in Mark 9: 38ff shows:

> John: "Teacher, we saw a man driving out demons in your name, and we told him to stop because he was not one of us."
>
> Jesus: "Do not stop him. No one who does a miracle in my name can in the next moment say anything bad about me."

We assume similar events happened in the church at Corinth as well, according to 1 Corinthians 12. This way of integrating the healing *charisma* in the congregation is the real challenge.

But the topic that occupies us here is, at heart, neither an issue of recapturing a *charisma* that once so obviously and naturally belonged to the spiritual gifts of the Christian community (1 Cor. 12), nor a mere reaction to the spirit of the times just in order to be up-to-date, nor a justification of diaconal works, caritas, and medical missions.

Healing as a dimension of ecclesial-missionary action has at heart to do with the credibility of Christian proclamation as a whole. This is the real stumbling block, which nowadays can unfortunately no longer be cleared out of the way with a reference to the New Testament mandate to heal; then what meaning does the appeal to old, even religious authorities have in this age of total secular individualism? No, this no longer has to do with trivial matters; rather, it concerns the whole of Christian theology and the church. The entire church faces a significant challenge today in this regard.

Healing: A perspective for Christian theology and mission

We have seen that healing, as a phenomenon common to all living people, cannot be monopolized by Christians. Thus it must, if it is to be claimed as a dimension of ecclesial-missionary action, be described and interpreted from a Christian standpoint. What would such a description and interpretation look like?

The theological starting point for such considerations is the first article of faith, in particular the doctrine of Creation and the Fall. Healing, after all, assumes the presence of sickness, thus responding in a life-affirming manner to an acute threat to life. It is possible because there is apparently a life-sustaining power which can be understood in the Judeo-Christian tradition as God's sustaining creative action, as *creatio continua* (continuous creation).

But the common phenomena of sickness and healing demand exacting interpretation, one that has to do with epistemology and only seems to be a matter of choice. It makes a big difference, for example, whether a goiter is diagnosed as "witch's sickness" or as an iodine deficiency. The diagnosis determines the therapy; witch's sickness and iodine deficiency are treated differently. What applies to diagnosing illness holds true for understanding healing as well. In this case, however, it concerns the consequences for the individual's future way of life.

It is important to recognize the agent of this healing power. Is it the "body's capacity to heal itself," "mental energy" or "nature" that caused healing to occur, or the expressed will of a personal God who sustains this acutely endangered life? The first set of interpretations explains healing in a diffuse way or represses it by means of reason. Healing, especially if it happens very dramatically, becomes an impressive experience of an individual who, thanks to "nature," the charisma of a healer, or even merely the wonders of modern medicine, was lucky enough to escape illness.

Healing, never an anonymous event, always takes place in a concrete and incarnate manner. It is a personal event focusing on the human individual. It is experienced by the person in concrete social and historical relationships. Healing becomes a genuinely personal experience only when it can be understood as a call to a personally lived response.

So healing can well be understood as an authentic personal event. This rests on the revelation of the living God, the God who created and sustains the world, in the person of Jesus Christ to whom we bear witness in the second article of faith. Where healing is concerned, even limited recovery of vitality implies a commission to live a new kind of life, to live in such a way that the true source of all life has more effect than before; in secular terms, to remain safe from further harm. In this regard there are many good suggestions and advice on how to live one's life, in which the entire spectrum of the various methods of healing and world views is reflected in all its breadth.

In this connection, an odd phenomenon enters the picture: congregation building. Healing, observation shows, builds congregations. Even the secular healing movements build congregations or communities; take homeopathy, herbal medicine, anthroposophic medicine, chiropractic, holistic medicine or even academic medicine, for example. A war of faith is raging between the various camps which is every bit as fierce in its anathemas or condemnations as the one waged during the Reformation. But this war is prosecuted with more refined methods. Why all this doggedness?

This question pushes a little deeper toward the heart of healing. It makes us aware that Christian theology cannot grapple with this phenomenon adequately without remembering the third article of faith and its doctrine of the Holy Spirit, of the church, and of the last things.

Healing—and this holds true for every kind of healing and is merely particularly obvious in the classic borderline cases of the so-called miracle or faith healings—is an observable physical empirical reality which can, however, be objectivized only to a limited extent. Healing is "attested," whether (to present two extremes) by the person affected on the basis of new health or by the attending physician on the basis of the laboratory values. One is *declared to be healthy* and still *feels ill*; another *feels healthy* but is *declared to be ill*.

The reason that subjective feeling and objective diagnosis can diverge from one another so much is that understandable explanations and comprehensible interpretations are by no means compelling. Because the final authority lies with the person affected, the healing movements have a confessional character, and thus an inherent community-building element. Only a clear pneumatology, in particular the careful *discernment of the spirits* can keep one from treating the problems exclusively as power issues and in turn pronouncing condemnation or declaring heresy.

The demand for a discernment of the spirits must be made emphatically, because many of the much-praised methods do not live up to what they promise. They often have exactly the opposite effect; they destroy life, including both the lives of individual human beings and those of entire communities and larger groups. This is why, when an illness occurs in an animistic culture, the search for the cause triggers terrible fear within a potential circle of persons, because each one might suddenly be found guilty of causing the illness. And what about those times when our medicine is left to its own devices and human birth and death are treated merely as technical processes? In those cases, discerning the spirits means nothing other than maintaining the necessary critical objectivity when faced with the claims and the reality of healing activities, whether they call themselves alternative, holistic, homeopathic, or academic.

This casts an entirely new light on the old Christian command to heal, the critical potential of which suddenly becomes apparent. The delegation of the healing commission by the churches and missions to their medical experts has obviously not taken care of the mandate once and for all. On the contrary: because the commission says "go and heal," it leads without fail to a substantial critique of the established forms of medicine and their highly specialized professionalization. Healing is the mandate, not biotechnology; we are called to sustain life, not to prevent or destroy it.

But the critical potential of the healing commission also has another thrust: the church and mission themselves. Here the commission becomes the appropriate yardstick for the credibility of the message of the church and mission, it becomes a court for them or serves to liberate them. It preserves them from false spiritualization by binding them to the concrete-incarnate side of life, for the command to heal is the unfolding in incarnate reality of the commands to preach the gospel in all the world and baptize. But precisely that forces us, if we are honest, to admit with embarrassment how little word and deed, proclamation and life correspond in mission and churches in a credible way.

In view of this realization, healing as a dimension of ecclesial-missionary activity cannot be an additional description of our reality, but instead merely describes an actual commission, the commission to truly embody the gospel. Concrete embodiment is needed. To quote a lovely phrase of Tertullian (ca. 160-220 A.D.), from his treatise "The Resurrection of the Flesh,"

> The body is the pivot of salvation, *caro cardo salutis*
> (c. 8, 6).

Would not *authentic incarnateness* be a fascinating model of ecclesial-missionary activity? In this model, would not the church have to do the same as its Lord, the eternal Logos, the Word of God that truly became flesh, became human? Would not authentic incarnateness entail both for church and mission the rediscovery and reshaping of received forms of liturgy and sacraments, the service of worship, and missionary work? Is this not a stimulating vision of what church and mission could be? Would not this entail genuine incarnateness for both of these?

I think so. But despite all my enthusiasm about this and all my fascination with true incarnateness of this kind, we dare not forget that healing is not something we can dispense at will, neither by the laying on of hands and prayer, nor through magic spells and high-tech medicine. Healing is expected and hoped for in the case of illness, while the experts (one hopes) do their very best to make healing possible. But in the end they all, medicine man and heart surgeon alike, depend upon the life of the ill body and the distorted social framework to once again find their way to healthy organization. But precisely this decisive element is not at our disposal.

Even Christianity does not dispose over the healing of sick, diseased people and its sick structure as a demonstrative sign of healing and salvation. It cannot control the revelation of God, which is only—and always—given anew. We can only bear witness to this revelation and, when it is granted, gratefully recognize it as such. Thus, we must truly allow God to be God. This is our duty.

Thus, healing as a dimension of ecclesial-missionary activity is subject to a certain reservation that results from the nature of healing itself and keeps churches and congregations from degenerating into healing sects. Only a clear eschatology (the doctrine of the last things, the *eschaton*) makes it possible to bear the tension between the "already" and the "not yet"—dynamic tension between, on the one hand, already-granted but always temporary healings that are always in need of renewal, and on the other, eternal healing or salvation. But also, only a clear eschatology frees the church, the mission and the healing arts from paralyzing resignation. Only a clear eschatology makes possible true objectivity about what can be done here and now to sustain acutely endangered life. *Caro cardo salutis!*

The challenges presented by modern healing movements force us to do nothing less than spell out our theological repertoire again, take a fresh look at the commission to proclaim the gospel, and rethink the concrete shape of our ministry under the sign of genuine incarnateness.

Summary

In conclusion, let us summarize the above thoughts, which are perhaps confusing in their diversity, in a brief series of theses:

1. Healing in and of itself is not a specifically Christian topic or issue.

2. Today, healing is available to an extent previously unknown in human history thanks to medicine, pharmacology and therapy founded on the principles of natural science.

3 The internal necessity of describing healing as Christian results from the commission to heal (Matt. 10:8; Luke 9:2; 10:9); the external necessity results from the contemporary situation.

4. Healing as a dimension of ecclesial-missionary action has to do with the credibility of the Christian proclamation as a whole with regard to its concrete, incarnate reality.

5. The manifold phenomenon of healing can only be completely understood and theologically interpreted if the Christian doctrine of the Trinity is fully taken into account.

6. Today, as centuries ago, healing as a dimension of ecclesial-missionary action takes place primarily, although not exclusively, in caritative-diaconal institutions and therapeutic and nursing activity.

7. The New Testament commission to heal can only be understood fully if the implicit medical-, theological-, ecclesial- and missionary-critical potential is apprehended and actualized.

4

A Christian response to
ethical issues in health care

John Wilkinson

> God created man healthy in all aspects of his
> being—body, mind and spirit. Health care must
> therefore cover the whole of a person's being; it
> must be holistic.

The title of this chapter names three important subjects. We
begin by looking at each of them in turn.

A Christian response

A Christian response means the response made by committed
Christians to a human situation either as individuals or as a community. God created man in his own image (Genesis 1:26) and so
gave him dignity and worth. This means that anything connected
with the welfare of men and women must be the concern of Christians.

When man disobeyed God and fell into sin, God in his great
love sent his Son to die on the cross so that men and women might
be forgiven and restored to fellowship with their Creator. Men and
women are thus not only the creation of God but also those for
whom Christ died. This means that God is concerned for their life,
health and welfare and that Christians should be also.

Finally, Jesus himself told us what he expected the Christian
response to be when he was asked which was the greatest commandment in the Law. He said there were two. The first was to love

69

God with our whole being, the second to love our neighbor as ourselves (Matthew 22:35-40). When he was asked who was our neighbor, he told the story of the Good Samaritan who provided emergency health care to a wounded stranger out of compassion for him in his injured state (Luke 10:25-37).

Christians, therefore, have a responsibility to respond to the problems of human life and health because of God's acts of creation and redemption and because of Christ's command to love their neighbor as themselves.

Ethical issues

Ethical issues are the questions of right and wrong human conduct that arise in human relationships. In daily life we are frequently faced with making decisions in situations in which we have a choice between two or more options. Problems arise because we feel an obligation to do the right thing before God and before our fellow human beings, yet because of our sinful nature we often do the wrong rather than the right thing, as the apostle Paul found in his experience (Romans 7:15-20).

Health care

Like life, health is the gift of God. It is therefore our responsibility to care for it. When God created man, he created him healthy, for he was made in the image of God and there is no ill-health in God. Man was created healthy in all aspects of his being—body, mind and spirit. Health care must therefore cover the whole of a person's being; it must be holistic. Health care cannot be limited to medical care, which usually means giving medicines or doing surgery. It must include the maintaining of a healthy body, mind and spirit, and preventing disease and disability where possible. Health care must aim to produce well-being of the body, peace and serenity of mind, and wholeness and holiness of spirit (1 Thessalonians 5:23). Forgiveness of sin is just as important for health as taking of medicine or exercise.

Important ethical issues arise for health care in three periods of life:

- Ethical issues in life at its beginning.
- Ethical issues in the course of life.
- Ethical issues in life at its close.

Life at its beginning

Marriage and sex

For the Christian, sex means marriage, and marriage means the union of one man and one woman, or monogamy. This means no sex before or outside marriage, and love and faithfulness within marriage. The Christian response to the ethical issue here is quite simple: sex without marriage—called adultery or fornication in the Bible—is a wrong choice.

Pregnancy spacing

Having too-frequent pregnancies often means ill health for the mother. Having too many children may mean that the parents cannot find enough money to clothe, feed and educate all their children properly. It is therefore a responsible (that is, an ethically right) decision to space pregnancies and limit the number of children when it is done to preserve the health of the mother and in order to bring up the children adequately.

There are a number of ways to prevent the conception of a child. It is for the husband and wife to agree on what is acceptable to them. A wrong choice is for these methods of contraception to be used by unmarried people or by married people outside their marriage.

Assisted pregnancy

Some married couples are unable to have children because one or other of them is sterile or infertile. In some cases their marriage is childless because God is calling them to some special type of service. Where this is not so, there are now several methods by which the wife can be assisted to become pregnant. Some of these methods use the sperm of the husband to increase the chance of fertilization of the wife's ova. There can be no objection to those methods, which are called artificial fertilization by husband (AIH) or in vitro fertilization (IVF). However, other methods use sperm from another man or ova from another woman, introducing a third party into the marriage. This is contrary to the Christian ideal of marriage.

Abortion

By abortion we mean terminating a pregnancy before the child is able to survive by itself. Abortion may occur naturally when the child in the womb is so abnormal that it will not survive if it is born. In such cases, the body itself will get rid of the abnormal pregnancy by spontaneous abortion or a miscarriage. (A miscarriage does not always mean that the child is abnormal; it occurs from other causes.)

Abortion may also be induced by medical or surgical methods. This type of induced abortion may produce ethical problems. In some Western countries, the view that induced abortion should be available to women on demand has gained ground in recent years. This is not a Christian view, for it means that abortion may be induced for purely selfish reasons.

Some Christians believe that abortion should not be permitted under any circumstances. Other Christians believe that it may be permitted where the pregnancy is seriously endangering the life or health of the mother; where the baby is known to be seriously defective or deformed, or where the pregnancy is the result of rape.

In the course of life

Research

Research is systematic study and investigation that seeks to increase our knowledge of ourselves and the situation in which we live. It is carried on by observation and experiment, which may be simple or complex in nature. It is by research that modern health care has developed, and for this we must be grateful.

There are various types of research. First, there is the study of the normal structure and function of the body and the effects of disease. Second, there is the use of new and untried clinical procedures in the diagnosis and treatment of disease. Finally, there is the trial of new medicines for the prevention and treatment of disease.

In each type of research there are ethical limitations to the methods used. These methods must not humiliate the subject or treat him as less than a person. They must not put the subject's life at risk or cause him unnecessary suffering or harm. They must not interfere with the provision of normal health care appropriate to the subject's condition. The methods must be approved by a competent group of professional people and administered by clinically competent health care staff.

One area in which ethical issues may arise in an acute form is that of genetic research. There need be no ethical problem for Christians where this is undertaken in order to understand the genetic basis of disease and to treat particular diseases by gene therapy, which is a procedure by which abnormal genes are replaced by normal ones. However, where research is conducted for eugenic reasons in order to produce a race of supermen, or for the possible production of abnormal human beings for purely experimental purposes, then acute ethical problems arise. These problems in turn raise the issue of how far it is permissible for man to manipulate the genetic basis of normal human life and development that God has laid down. A Christian response to this issue would be that such activity is not permissible unless it is for the prevention or removal of disease or the alleviation of suffering.

Consent

Because God has made human beings responsible for their own life and health, no one may do anything to them without their consent or agreement. This means that in providing health care for people, we should not do anything to them without explaining it to them in words and ideas that they can understand, and then asking them for their agreement. This is called informed consent. Such consent is necessary for the normal procedures of health care as well as the conduct of research. Sometimes, of course, a person's consent is implied by their seeking health care, but as far as possible the health care professional should try to obtain informed consent.

There may be situations in which it is not possible to obtain personal consent of any kind because the person cannot understand the situation or is unconscious. In these cases the consent should be sought from others, from parents in the case of young children or from relatives in the case of mentally handicapped or unconscious adults.

In acute emergency situations, it may not be possible to obtain consent from the person involved or from any other competent person. In such situations it is justifiable to proceed with any necessary treatment without consent, especially if such treatment is necessary to save life or prevent permanent disability.

Confidentiality

A common ethical issue in health care is that of confidentiality. By this we mean the need to keep secret any personal information we may obtain in the practice of health care that should not be told to other persons. There are, however, situations in which the rule of confidentiality may have to be broken in the interest of the patient or for the protection of society.

Resource allocation

Resources are the means by which we can provide health care. They include people, buildings, equipment and money. These are the things which we can see. Resources also include things that we cannot see such as beliefs, motives and attitudes. Thus the Christian faith is an important resource in health care, for it provides the basis of love and compassion, of trustworthiness and concern, without which health care cannot be fully effective.

The ethical issue in the allocation of resources arises because although health care needs and demands of people are unlimited, the resources to meet these needs and demands are limited. It is here that the Christian response to a situation of scarce and limited resources must seek a fair share of these resources for all according to their needs and in relation to the needs of others.

At the close of life

Prolonging life

There are various methods of prolonging the physical life of a person. The first is by special or intensive care of a person who, because of a serious disease or injury, is in danger of dying. For this purpose hospitals may set up intensive care units.

If there are only a few beds in these units, an ethical problem may arise if there are more seriously ill patients than beds. On what grounds do we choose to admit some patients to these beds and refuse to admit others?

Another method of prolonging life is by resuscitating persons who have just died. A number of ethical issues arise here:

- Should we try to resuscitate everyone who dies?

- If we cannot do this, how should we decide who should be resuscitated?

- If we do decide that a person who has collapsed should be resuscitated, what means should we use, ordinary or extraordinary? Extraordinary means include those which may be uncertain or risky in their effect, experimental in nature or very expensive. In most cases, ordinary methods of resuscitation should be sufficient.

A modern method of prolonging life is by the transfer of body tissues or organs from one person to another in order to improve the condition of the person who receives them. The first example of such a transfer was blood transfusion, a procedure that has prolonged many lives.

A technique that has been introduced more recently is transplanting an organ from a living person, or from someone who has just died, into the body of a living person to replace an organ that is seriously deformed or damaged by disease. From a Christian and technical point of view, organ transplantation is a permissible form of treatment, but it is expensive and resources may not be available to perform it or to pay for it. The ethical issue then becomes the proper allocation of resources that could be used to benefit many more people than the few who would benefit from organ transplants.

Ending life

An important ethical issue at the end of life is that of euthanasia, "a pleasant death." Advocates say that health care should include producing a painless and pleasant death for everyone when they come to die. However, euthanasia frequently means the deliberate killing of such people, and this can never be a Christian response.

A common argument for active euthanasia, which is another name for killing a person whose life is said to have become unbearable due to physical disease, is that compassion demands that a person's suffering should be ended. However, compassion can never be an acceptable motive for killing a person. The Christian response to such a situation is that suffering should be prevented or alleviated by effective and relevant pain and symptom control and not by the physical destruction of the body.

There is an important difference between ending life and allowing life to end in as comfortable and dignified a way as possible. Once it is clear that a person has begun the process of dying, then the Christian response is to provide all that is necessary for that person to die in physical comfort, human dignity and spiritual peace.

The test of a Christian response

When we are faced with an ethical issue, how we are to know what a Christian response is? We can ask ourselves four questions to test such a response:

- *What does our conscience tell us?*   God has implanted in the hearts of everyone certain laws of human nature. These are the laws that require us to do good to all, to deal justly with them and show mercy and magnanimity to them. These laws are made known to us through our conscience. It is inadvisable for us to act against our conscience, though we should not depend on it alone.

- *What does the Bible teach us?*   Is there a general principle, a specific command or a similar incident given in the Bible from which we may derive guidance for the solution of our ethical problem?

- *What have other Christians done?*   When Christians faced this problem in the past, what did they do to solve it? Are other Christians facing the same problem today? If so, how are they solving it?

- *What does the Holy Spirit tell us?*   What is the Holy Spirit guiding us to do as we seek his guidance in prayer and his inward assurance in our hearts?

The greater the amount of agreement we obtain between the answers to these four questions, the more certain we can be that our response is a Christian response.

Further reading

1   A careful reading of I Corinthians will show how the apostle Paul faced the ethical issues he found in the Christian church at Corinth. See especially chapters five to ten.

2   The subjects mentioned in this chapter are dealt with in greater detail and with full references in the author's book *Christian Ethics in Health Care: A Source Book for Christian Doctors, Nurses and Other Health Care Professionals* (Handsel Press, Edinburgh, 1988).

5

Healing of the spirit

Eric R. Ram

Often we Christian health care professionals are
so busy healing that we fail to help people meet
the Healer.

Introduction

Science has concentrated on healing the bodies of men and women
and, with the development of modern psychology, doctors have
come to recognize that sickness of the mind can also be treated.
And yet the spiritual dimension of man is difficult for medicine to
deal with, since precise measurement of the invisible aspects of
spiritual sickness or health is impossible. Spiritual illness may be
expressed in feelings of emptiness, loneliness, violence, greed, or
general meaninglessness of life. These may be indicators of broken
relationships with man and with God.

It is not always easy to distinguish between spiritual and
psychological problems, yet psychologists frequently recognize that
they are dealing with more than mental illness. The spiritual
dimension may have to be experienced before it has much meaning, even though it is usually the missing ingredient in the search
for wholeness.

Exploring the spiritual dimension demands a special relationship between doctor and patient. Both are, to some extent, sick
and in need of healing; the idea that one is well and the other is sick
is only illusory. Therefore, the process requires empathy between
them.

79

An increasing volume of medical literature is recognizing the close relationship between the body, the mind and spirit, and is reporting exciting results. Dr. Bernie Siegel, an oncologist and surgeon at Yale University, reports that after he became discouraged at the high surgical failure rate that was usual among cancer patients, he began listening to them. Over a period of years, he found that patients, given an opportunity to talk about their feelings and broken relationships, often discovered for themselves that they were in effect committing suicide. Then most patients either found another way to deal with problems and experienced complete resolution of their cancer, or they reaffirmed their desire for life to end and soon died.[1]

The basis for the Christian belief in the spirituality of man is the Bible. We read again and again that nothing in the created world is unrelated to God. Whether it be matter, body or spirit, it is still of his creation. The book of Genesis tells us that spirit comes directly from God; the word *spirit* means *the vitality of the flesh*. Man himself becomes a spirit. When he dies he is a "dead spirit."

Non-Christians, too, have recognized the essential unity of creation. One of the guiding principles of Mahatma Gandhi's *satyragraha* (nonviolent resistance) was his conviction that man is an indivisible whole. He affirmed that man's actions cannot be neatly compartmentalized.[2] Albert Einstein's theory of relativity maintains that the universe is one single whole. If any one part of the universe is affected, the rest of the universe is also affected.

What difference does all this make for the practice of medicine? It calls for recognition that each person is a part of God's creation, unique in one sense and yet shaped by the community of which he is a part, so that individual and community can never be separated.

Since all are of God's creation, all belong together. A refugee woman crying her heart out in loneliness and frustration represents all the unresolved tensions of our world, just like the boy with his needle on some Harlem rooftop, or the man in the Sudan quivering for want of chloroquine. No one can be fully healthy living in a sick society.

Early practitioners of healing arts understood man as a whole being whose body, spirit and mind were not separate. For them, all symptoms of disease affected the whole person. A deep change occurred in the 19th century when medicine allied itself with the natural sciences. Subsequent advances in science and technology have led to rapid perfecting of diagnostic, therapeutic and rehabilitative skills. Modern medicine is able to transplant organs, replace joints and prolong life. In the process, however, the close relationship between doctor and patient has given way to depersonalized, sophisticated technology.

Health and spirituality

We used to believe that more doctors and more hospitals would result in better health. As we look at today's world, we see that although health care is necessary, most disease stems from such basic factors as poverty, poor housing, lack of safe drinking water, malnutrition, illiteracy, loneliness or isolation. Modern health problems point to the need to recognize the unity of mind, body and spirit, and the essential unity of the universe.

Just as man is a product of his total environment, disease is a product of the whole man. We desperately need a new approach to health and healing in order to deal with it.

Health is based on harmony with one's self, with one's neighbors, with nature and with God. It depends on one's physical, mental, spiritual, economic, political and social well-being. We have learned that there is an inseparable unity of body, mind and spirit, and that disturbance in harmonious relations of these factors can cause ill health.

So health cannot be considered to be something physical, but total. In the Twenty-third Psalm, Yahweh restores my *nephesh*, which means not only spiritual refreshment, but also physical recovery and social rehabilitation. The word for health in Hebrew is *shalom*; the same word also means peace, welfare, well-being and harmony. Health is total. It is personal well-being. It is social harmony and justice. It is walking humbly with God. *Shalom* is the work of righteousness (right relationships), as the prophet Isaiah says (Is. 32:16).

Despite the wonders of modern medicine, we see that certain fundamental diseases of today's society have not been cured because the best medicines of the best institutions are not capable of listening, caring, touching and loving. These are human attributes. Only humans can provide them.

It is this dimension of human care that is so important in healing. Dr. Paul Tournier called it the third dimension of medicine.[3] Loving and caring involves one's entire being, the sharing of one's self with others. It requires humility, a continuous learning about the other person while respecting his human dignity.

Loss of self-worth and human dignity, along with a certain abdication of the personality, have become major causes of unhappiness throughout the world. Those who are able to face up to these challenges and move beyond them have the spiritual flame of faith, hope, love and zeal, a flame which burns brightly within them in the face of adversity, despite all odds.

Within every person is a latent energy, normally dormant. This energy has to be activated and then developed slowly and gradually. When this inner flame reaches its efflorescence, a person possesses extraordinary strength and power.

Otherwise ordinary people who develop spiritual and human values and hold them as a source of strength against the onslaught of their enemies become leaders in their own communities. Not only are they examples of health themselves. Such people are also able to free others to search for a harmonious balance of mind, body and spirit and to become leaders themselves.

Take for example St. Peter, Mahatma Gandhi, Martin Luther King and Mother Teresa. All were ordinary people at the beginning of their lives. Each of them had failures and serious problems. Peter betrayed his responsibility three times and ran away. Gandhi was an average, ordinary child in an ordinary family who grew up to be called Mahatma, or great spirit. Every person has the energy and potential. The potential must be enhanced; the energy must be released.

These great persons all cultivated attributes of spirituality that gave them strength when they needed it. They exemplify the idea of health as a balance of the physical, mental and spiritual. They hold the flame of faith in their hearts and pass it on to others.

Concepts of soul and spirit

Accepting the existence of spirit is by no means unique to Christianity. I have selected some examples from various regions and eras to see how people in different cultures have viewed soul and spirit.

Vedic concept of health, soul and spirit

Ayurvedic Medicine ("science of life") is an Indian system rooted in antiquity.[4] Written in Sanskrit, most people today cannot read it. Exact meanings are difficult to render due to the lack of equivalent English words. However, here is a rough outline that may give an appreciation of the concept (see box, next page, for some key ideas).

Life (*ayu*) is defined as unity of body (*sarira*), mind (*satva*), spirit (*atma*) and senses (*indriya*). Health is a state of dynamic equilibrium between the universe and man, who is the microcosm of the universe. The disturbance in this balance causes ill health.

All the matter of the universe is made up of five elements, collectively known as *pancha mahabhuta* (five basic elements). These are *aksha* (word) identified by *shabda* (sound); *vayu* by touch, *agni* by color, *jala* by taste and *pruthvi* by odor.

When spirit joins the five basic elements, matter assumes life and becomes *purusa*, a living soul. Thus, even though the human body (*sharir*) is made of the basic elements, it attains life only when spirit, senses and mind join it.

To be healthy, a person needs to maintain an equilibrium of digestive enzymes (*dosha*) and metabolic enzymes (*agni*), proper functioning of body fluids and of tissues (*dhatu*) and metabolic by-products and excretions (*mala*), and possess happiness of spirit, mind, senses and body. This means complete psychosomatic equilibrium that brings about happiness to spirit and mind. It is more than absence of disease.

The Vedic concept recognizes soul as a living being (*jiva*); mind (*manas*) or breath of life (*asu*) are unique dimensions of a human being. On the other hand, *Paramatman* connotes the universal soul who is *Vishvakarman* (maker of everything) and *Prajapati* (lord of all living beings). "Living being" is one's biological and functional personality, that aspect of one's being that distinguishes one individual from another and that suffers or enjoys existence in mortal and post-mortal life according to the acts one performs while in this world.

Mind is that subtle or immortal structure of one's being by which one knows that one is related in various ways to other divine and human beings. It is that incorporeal and cognizant division of the human being in which awareness resides and from which the sense of being alive derives.

Some Ayurvedic Ideas

- Life is unity of body, mind, spirit and the senses.

- A soul is a living being, a biological and functional personality. Mind, incorporeal but cognizant, is the seat of awareness. The breath of life is the vital force that animates the human being's essence.

- A person is an ever-changing combination of five building blocks that, in turn, are comprised of effervescent elements.

- The universal soul is maker of everything and lord of all living beings. The body is a temple for the divine self, which is to be worshipped.

- Health is more than the absence of disease. It is a dynamic equilibrium between the universe and the person. Disturbing this balance causes ill health.

- To be healthy, a person needs an equilibrium of enzymes, proper function of body fluids, tissues and metabolic substances, and happiness of spirit, mind, senses and body.

"Breath of life" is the vital force that brings life to inert matter, creates sentience and that in general serves to animate the human being's essence (*Prakruti*). One's self is comprised of immutable physical matter and immutable non-manifest spirit which is deathless.

Maitreya Upanishad (2:2) says, "The body is said to be a temple." The self within it is none other than the Universal or Divine Self. Having discarded all the residual effects of ignorance, one should worship him with the words, "I am He."

A person, then, is an ever-changing combination of five *skandhas* (building blocks): *rupa* (physical body), *vedana* (physical sensation), *samjna* (sense of perception), *samskara* (habitual tendencies) and *vijnana* (consciousness). These fine aggregates fall together in various configurations to form what is experienced as a person, much in the same way that a chariot is built of various parts (*Milindapantra* 2.1.1). But just as the chariot as an entity disappears when constituent elements are pulled apart, so does the Universal Self disappear with the dissolution of the five building blocks. These, in turn, are comprised of *dharmas* (effervescent elements), which are like bubbles on the surface of a stream: they form different shapes as they flow in and out of contact with each other. The different configurations determine the nature of individuality.

Chinese view

In ancient China, the thinking was that each person has two souls, both composed of very subtle matter. The *hun* (air soul) comes from the upper air and is received back into it at death. The *p'o* (earth soul) is generated by the earth below and sinks back at the end to mingle with it. Of the two, the air soul receives ancestor worship. This two-part system corresponds to the *yin-yang* equilibrium, the air soul being the *yang* aspect in which the spiritual dominates, and the earth soul being the *yin* aspect in which the domestic dominates. In later tradition, the thinking was that the air soul gives rise to the seminal and mental essences, while the earth soul is responsible for the existence of the flesh and bones of the body.

Greek and Hellenistic concepts

Pre-Socratic philosophers like Empedocles and Diogenes identify two qualities of the soul: movement and knowledge. For Empedocles, the soul knows all natural things, and natural things have four constituent parts—earth, air, fire and water. The soul is a combination of the four elements, together with the principle of love and strife.

For Diogenes, the soul has an air-like nature that guides and controls the living being and has the attributes of sentience and intelligence. Air is the element most capable of originating movement, because it was the finest in grain. In this characteristic lay the soul's own power of knowing and originating movement. The internal air in the body plays an important role in how the sense organs function.

The present Western idea of the soul includes eschatological and psychological attributes. The presence of the Greek word *psuché* (soul) in psychiatry and psychology suggests that the Greeks viewed soul in the modern way. However, earlier and later uses of *psuché* differ in meaning.

Early uses of *psuché* include the soul of the living as well as that of the dead. This implies life after death.

In the late Archaic age (800–500 BCE), *psuché* becomes the center of consciousness or inner life. This is the necessary precondition for the Socratic view that a man's most important task is to take care of his *psuché*. This view of soul is taken up by Plato; throughout his work, concern about the *psuché* remains axiomatic. Plato even included intellectual functions in the *psuché*.

Aristotle, on the other hand, almost completely disregarded *psuché*. But care for the soul and cure of the soul remained important topics for the philosophical schools of the time.

The ancient Greeks, like many other peoples, consider the soul of the dead to be a continuation of the free soul of the living. In the Homeric epic (7th and 8th century BCE), it is always *psuché* that leaves for the underworld. The dead in the afterlife are called *psuchai*. The body-soul—*thumos, menos,* and *nous*—end their activity at the moment of death. Their connection with the body is the cause of their disappearance.

Homer's *Iliad* and *Odyssey* speak of two types of soul. On one hand, there is the free soul, or *psuché*, an unencumbered soul representing the individual personality. This soul is inactive when the body is active; it is located in an unspecified part of the body. Its presence is the precondition for the continuation of life, but it has no connection with the physical or psychological aspects of the body. *Psuché* manifests itself when it leaves the body, never to return again. On the other hand, there are a number of body-souls, which endow the body with life and consciousness.

The most frequently occurring form of body-soul in Homer's epics is *thumos*: the soul that urges people on and is the seat of emotions. There is also *menos*, which is a more momentary impulse directed at specific activities. At one time, *menos* seems to have meant mind or disposition, similar to the Vedic concept of *manas* (which has all the functions of the Homeric *thumos)*. The Greek word *thumos* is akin to the Sanskrit word in Vedic, *dhumah*, which connotes smoky or ethereal, and the Latin word *fumus*.

Nous is the mind or act of mind, a thought or a purpose. In addition, a number of other body organs like the heart, liver and lungs, have both physical and psychological attributes. For Homer, the soul of the living does not yet constitute unity. That concept comes toward the end of Archaic age.

The ancient Greeks believe minimally in the life hereafter and do not worship ancestors. The gods of the Hellenistic period are effective in this life. It was with the advent of Christianity that the Greeks develop a new interest in the soul and life hereafter.

The Hebrew view

For the Hebrew thinker, man does not have a body or have a soul; he is a soul-body unity. Flesh and spirit, however, are opposed as evil and good aspects of man. Recognition of this may have opened the way to a later accommodation to the Greek soul-body dualism. In Hebrew thought, the soul is sometimes seen as a sort of liquid in the jar of the body; it can be both depleted and replenished. In Genesis 2:7 (KJV) God breathed his Spirit into the very dust out of which he made man, and "man became a living soul." This imagery haunts Hebrew thought. The New Testament writers inherit the model it fostered.

In the Bible the role of breath rests on several concepts. The Hebrew word *ruah* means breath, wind or Spirit. *Ruah* is also the spirit in man that gives him life; the spirit is created and preserved by God. It is understood to be God's Spirit—the *ruah elohi* in Genesis 1:2 that is breathed into a man at the time of creation.

The term *neshamah,* although used considerably less than *ruah,* carries many of the same meanings. The breath of God is wind (hot, cold, life-creating or -destroying). The breath of man is breathed into him by God. Breath is found in every living thing (Gen. 1:30).

The concept of breath figures prominently in many religious views and people's quest for understanding life.

- Egyptian   *Ka*
- Hebrew   *nefesh* and *ruah*
- Greek   *psuché* and *pneuma*
- Latin   *anima* and *spiritus*
- Sanskrit   *Prana*
- Chinese   *Ch'i*
- Polynesian   *mana*
- Iroquoian   *orenda*

Breath is associated with vitality and energy, with views of soul, and with questions regarding the mortal and immortal aspect of life.

The individual soul of man is usually designated in Hebrew by *nefesh.* This is the inner being, the life force that makes flesh alive. Since the living are distinguished from the dead by breath, *nefesh* indicates the individual, the person or self that goes to *shéol* after death. As the life force in individual beings, *nefesh* is present in both animals and humans. The relation between *neshama* as breath and *nefesh* as person is seen in Genesis 2:7:

And the Lord God formed man of the dust of the ground,
and breathed into his nostrils the breath (*neshama*) of life;
and man became a living soul (*nefesh*).

This belief in the body and soul is continued from the biblical period into Jewish philosophy.

Like *ruah, pneuma* in the New Testament denotes spirit, and it refers both to the Holy Spirit and the spirit of an individual person, as well as to the evil spirits or demons that are responsible for mental illnesses. Although it has the same psychosomatic implication as *ruah,* its ties to the notion of breath are less obvious.

The New Testament term *psuché,* on the other hand, although it continues to carry the old Greek sense of life force, corresponds more to the Hebrew notion of breath of life than it does to its use in Plato or the pre-Socratic thinkers. Like *nefesh, psuché* is the individual soul, the "I" that feels, loves, and desires, and that lives only because it has been infused with breath. Nevertheless, under Greek influence, the *nefesh*–become–*psuché* concept gradually becomes opposed to the mortal body and designates the immortal principle in man.

Tertullian emphasizes the union of body and soul and said that "soul is born of the breath of God, immortal, corporeal, and representable," although it was only Adam's soul that was created by God, and all others come into being by an act of generation.[5]

Christian concept

The human spirit is evidently the part in which and upon which the Holy Spirit works, and through which he controls the person. The human spirit has no function except in connection with the Divine Spirit. Without the Divine Spirit, it is like having ears in a world without world. The real agent in substituting holiness for sin in man is God, not man. Whenever God is represented as a diffused presence, he is represented as working through the Spirit. According to Paul, Spirit is to God what the spirit is in man (1 Cor. 2:10; but in God this is objectified, represented as a distinct personality (Rom 8:27, Gal. 3:5, John 14:26, 16:13).

The soul is not a separate entity apart from the body but forms a unit with it and animates the flesh. Frequently the word for life is *nephesh,* and there is a close connection between *nephesh* (life) and blood (Lev. 17:14). In Job 13:14, flesh and life are parallel.

The soul is the seat of emotions (Ps. 86:4; Jer. 6:16) of love and hatred (Gen. 34:3) and of religious affection. It is lifted up to God (Ps. 25:1, 86:4). It hopes in God (Ps.33:20, 130:5-6); glories in God (Ps. 34:2; 35:9) and rests in God (Ps 63:1,5-8).

Hebrew *nephesh,* usually translated as "soul," refers to the breath, as does the term *neshamah,* which became the most common word for the soul in post-biblical Hebrew thought. *Nafash* and *nasham* mean to breathe. These two words are found together in Genesis 2:7, which narrates how the first human Adam (clay) received the breath of life from God and became a living soul (*nephesh hayyah*). Another meaning of *nephesh* is life.

The word *ruah,* which is often rendered as spirit, refers to powers or actions outside the body and often has the meaning of wind. *Ruah* is the mysterious vitality in the material body, which is considered a divine gift. *Ruah* sometimes denotes forces external to the body that operate in or through the body or the mental faculties.

The English words "soul" and "spirit" are attempts to represent two sets of ideas found in the Bible. "Soul" is continuous with Hebrew *nephesh* and the Greek *psuché.* "Spirit" is continuous with the Hebrew *ruah* and Greek *pneuma.*

The one set of ideas, however, cannot be entirely dissociated from the other. For example, when we think of the ideas of wind, breath, or spirit, we would probably associate any one of them to *pneuma* rather than *psuché.*

With the translation of *nephesh* as *psuché* in the Septuagint (the Greek version of the Bible that the New Testament writers used), the ground is laid for a coalescence of the ideas suggested by the terms *psuché* and *pneuma.* Both words focus on the traditional Semitic preoccupation with the idea of life.

What matters to the spiritual man is not the life we measure in days or years (*bios*) but the spiritual energy, the inner life of man, his *zoé,* which has the capacity to become everlasting. It is to this that the soul is to be resurrected. Resurrection then entails an ongo-ing, everlasting state that Christ has made possible even for us sin-ful men and women. Thus our struggle in this life is not so much against flesh but against the spiritual army of evil agencies (Eph. 6:12).

By extension, then, the soul, as the part of a person, becomes indistinguishable from the spiritual dimension of that per-son's being.

Confession, forgiveness and faith

We Christians in the Protestant tradition somehow seem to have lost the value of confession, but it is a very significant factor in one's healing and inner renewal. For the Roman Catholics, penance or confession is seen as a sacrament of reconciliation. The Orthodox always see the Eucharist as the therapeutic event of forgiveness of sins and granting of peace. Jesus said,

> And when you stand praying, if you hold anything
> against anyone, forgive him, so that your father in heaven
> may forgive you your sins (Mark 11:25).

Confession and forgiveness open our lives to the grace and mercy of God. Then we are set free from the burdens of fear, guilt and anguish and receive healing and inner renewal.

Whenever we offer acceptance, love, forgiveness, or a quiet word of hope, we offer health. When we share each other's burdens and joys, we become channels of healing. No matter how timid or tired, selfish or crazy, young or old we may be, we all have some-thing important to offer one another. Each of us is endowed by God with that gift of healing.

Carl Gustav Jung says,

> The best we can do is to give the inner doctor, who
> dwells in each patient, a chance to become operative.[6]

How do we do that? By having faith. Through faith, we open ourselves to the saving and healing power that comes from God and touches the innermost being, as if a doctor were dwelling there.

Several times Jesus spoke explicitly of the connection between his healing power and the faith of the individuals he healed or the faith of the person's friends. Whether it was a blind man's plea for his sight, or a bleeding woman's anguish to find a cure, or a paralytic person's cry for help, he replied, "Go; your faith has healed you" (Matt 9:29; Mark 2:5; Mark 5:34). Faith has the power to fill us with trust in God's healing forgiveness and free us from guilt and anguish.

Compassion and healing

Compassion, the recurring theme of Christ's own acts of healing, is more than pity or sympathy. The word is derived from the Latin words *pati* and *cum* which together mean "to suffer with." Compassion transcends social work, health work, philanthropy and all governmental and nongovernmental programs. It is the capacity to feel and suffer with persons in need, to experience something of their predicaments, fears, anxieties and temptations, the loss of freedom and dignity, the utter vulnerability, the assault on the whole person and the alienation that poverty and illness produce and portend.

Compassion is more than a feeling. It flows over in a willingness to help, to sacrifice, to go out of one's way as the Good Samaritan did. As Henri Nouwen wrote in *The Wounded Healer*,

> None of us can help anyone without entering fully into the painful situation the other person is in, without taking the risk of becoming hurt or getting wounded in the process.[7]

Compassion entails understanding in depth the suffering experienced by another. When we have suffered ourselves, we are usually better able to understand suffering in others. An Indian proverb says, "Illness tells you who you are," Or, as the Spanish writer Miguel de Unamuno puts it,

> Suffering is the substance of life and the root of personality, for only suffering makes us persons.[8]

In addition, compassion helps us realize that our brothers and sisters in need are not alien to us. They are very much fellow travelers on this planet. I have found that they, in fact, are vital to our own spiritual renewal and growth.

For the health professional, compassion is the quality that separates a mere career from Christian vocation. The compassionate health professional recognizes that illness transcends biological aberrations in our body's systems. It fractures our image of ourselves, upsets harmony and balance, and begins to destroy us. We also see someone's illness as a sign that he has fallen away from God's order.

Love, hope and healing

Paul, in his letter to the Galatians, lists several qualities known as the fruit of the Spirit (Galatians 5:22-23). Dr. Paul Brand, a globally known medical missionary and surgeon, calls this a polyvalent vaccine for the prevention of almost every disease that has a behavioral basis.[9] Imagine how much healthier we all would be if people everywhere were willing to be filled with the Spirit and brought forth the fruit of the Spirit: love, joy, peace, patience, gentleness, goodness, faithfulness, humility, self-control.

From this own experience, Dr. Bernie Siegel says that love, joy and peace of mind have physiological consequences, just as depression and despair do.[10] The contribution of lifestyle and emotions to the health of the individual was a concept easily accepted centuries ago. Today, people want scientific proof. Feelings have to be shown to create chemical alterations in our bodies in order for us to accept them as physiological. Fortunately, we now have the scientific know-how to document those changes.[11]

We have learned over the years that body, mind and spirit are one unit and that what happens to one affects the other. Body and mind seem bound by nerves and messenger molecules allowing them to communicate.

Psychologists have shown that the effects of love on the body can be measured. For example, an unloved infant will have retarded bone growth and may even die early. A stroked infant, on the other hand, grows faster. People who meditate regularly and confide their traumatic experiences to diaries rather than repressing them are shown to have an enhanced immune function.

Love and peace of mind do protect us and allow us to overcome the problems life brings our way. Anything that offers hope has the potential to heal, including thoughts, suggestions symbols, and placebos. Some experiments have shown that the administration of placebos leads to an increased production in the brain of endorphins, which are pain killers.

Scientists are searching for other chemicals which are produced in our brain as a response to various feelings and which may become the basis of many therapies in the future. Norman Cousins says that the will to live is most important, enabling the body to make the most of placebos. Placebos play the role of emissary between the will to live and the body.

Nero Asistent is one of the few known long-term AIDS survivors. She has managed to reverse test results from HIV positive to HIV negative. Asked to summarize her successful efforts, she says, "When you live in your heart, magic happens."[12] Though the precise mechanisms of the healing response remain elusive, many factors work together to create body-mind-spirit communication and unity and bring body functions under the control of mind and spirit.

We have known for some time that both environment and genes play a significant role in a person's vulnerability to certain diseases. But the emotional environment we create within our bodies—through compassion, love, hope and peace—activate mechanisms of healing. Everyone has the ability to create such an environment within the body to facilitate healing.

God has placed within us a never-ending desire to love and be loved. He has also given us a never-ending supply of people to love. As Christian health professionals, we need to love ourselves and others; in the process, we experience healing just as much as those who are sick.

Compassion, hope, love and peace enable the healing process to mend and reconstruct a person, to make one whole again. We must assist in the healing of the hurt spirit as well as the attack on the body. Compassionate care also means that we help a person suffering from a terminal disease to die in dignity. Further, compassionate care is not limited only to an individual person but extends to the entire community.

Healing of the spirit

It is becoming apparent that the present view of health, illness, life and death, based on the seventeenth-century model, is limited. It must give way to a holistic model where spirit plays as important a role as does the body and mind.

As a matter of fact, many health care professionals are beginning to accept the holistic concept and its health implications for the whole person. However, one of the problems they face is recognizing that there is a relationship between sickness, sin and spirit, body and mind, just as there is a relationship between health, salvation and spirit, body and mind. "Sin is integrally related to sickness, both to personal sins and physical sins," says Rev. Dr. William Watty, former dean of the School of Theology in Kingston, Jamaica.[13]

A sense of guilt, a false accusation or the pronouncement of a curse can induce physical illness because relationships are fractured, disturbed and unhealthy. The restoration of relationships will manifest in physical recovery. Yahweh restored the fortunes of Job when he prayed for his friends (Job 42:10).

More and more people are sharing their life stories, and the evidence is mounting that there is a natural connection between much of our illness and our spiritual and mental health. Paul Tournier realized this as a physician, so he went on to study psychology and theology so he could heal his patients at various levels as whole persons.

The church has long known the power of Christ to forgive sins and many heal illnesses which may be physical or mental in nature. The story of the paralytic man lowered by his friends through the roof is an apt example of how sin and paralysis were interconnected. Through this healing Jesus was also able to show to the unbelieving Pharisees that he has the power to forgive sins (Mark 2:1-5).

Sickness of our spirit is caused by our personal sin (often contributing to mental illness and sometimes to physical sickness). When there is an inner or spiritual healing, we experience:

- Healing of spiritual wounds, signifying inner peace and joy that no psychiatrist or doctor can possibly give.
- A sense of heightened belief in God and knowledge of his love. Our most basic need is to know we are loved.
- A healthy relationship with others and a sense of participation in the community.
- The end of spiritual turbulence or inner vacuum within us. We are filled with love and hope.

In order for the spiritual healing process to begin to take place within us, we need to repent. This may mean we must forgive ourselves and those who have hurt us. We need to empty ourselves of anything that prides our spirit and poisons our soul. When the poisons of hurt and resentment are drained, they must be replaced by love.

Then there is a need for reconciliation. This plays an important role in activating new hope and confidence within a person, a life force which has a powerful influence in healing. For when hope is lost, the will to live slips away.

The foremost healing of the spirit is brought about by Christ through forgiveness of our sins. If sins like resentment and bitterness are manifested in a physical illness, no healing is likely to take place unless one deals with resentment first. This also shows how intimately forgiveness of sins is connected with physical or psychological healing. Unfortunately, often one does not recognize resentment or bitterness as sins in themselves. According to the Gospel of Luke (6:36-38), forgiveness and healing is a two-way process. If I forgive, I will be forgiven; if I am willing to heal others, I will be healed.

Francis MacNutt says that our physical sickness, far from being a redemptive blessing, is often a sign that we are not redeemed, not whole spiritually, and that forgiveness of sin is required. Our spiritual and physical sickness are so interrelated that we need God's help to tease out and untangle the complexity of the problem.[14]

Especially in the West, most sicknesses are rooted in isolation and lack of belonging. When people become like lost sheep without a shepherd, they lose hope. They develop all manner of manifestations and cry out for help. Yes, they need healing. But more than that, they need the Healer. Often the church and we Christian health care professionals are so busy healing that we fail to help people meet the Healer.

Most people have no difficulty accepting the fact that God can heal people. But they do not always know that he wants to heal them not only in body and mind but also in spirit. Health and healing are a part of their inheritance. Jesus referred to it as the children's bread (Matt 7:9). Every child deserves bread from his father.

This bread is the body of Christ which was broken for us (Matt 26:26). As Christians, when we partake in the Holy Sacrament we are already ascending to a higher level of spirituality and experience spiritual healing, the sense of being one with the Spirit.

Notes

1	Siegle, *Love Medicine and Miracles*
2	Erickson, *Ganghi's Truth*
3	Tournier, *The Whole Person in a Broken World*
4	Kuvalayananda, *Pranayama*. This is the source for much of the material presented here on Ayurvedic medicine.
5	MacGregor and Geddes, "Christian Concept of Soul"
6	Jung, *The Structure and Dynamics of Psyche*
7	Nouwen, *The Wounded Healer*
8	In McNeill, et al., *A Reflection on the Christian Life*
9.	Brand, "Health, Wholeness and Salvation." See also chapter two, above.
10	Siegel, *Love, Peace and Healing*

11   Siegel, *Love, Medicine and Miracles*
12   in Badgley, *Healing AIDS Naturally*
13   Wattey, "Man and Healing—A Biblical and Theological View"
14   MacNutt, *The Healing*

References

Allen, E. Anthony, Luscombe, K.L., Myers, B.L. and Ram, Eric R. *Health, Healing and Transformation,* MARC/World Vision International, Monrovia, California, U.S.A., 1991.

Badgley, Laurence E. *Healing AIDS Naturally.* Foster City, Calif.: Human Energy Press, 1987.

Bakken, Kenneth. *The Call to Wholeness.* New York: Cross Road Publishing Company, 1985.

Brand, Paul. "Health, Wholeness and Salvation," in Shalom News, No. II, Nov. 1990. Health and healing track of Lausanne II Congress. Monrovia, Calif.: World Vision International.

Erickson, Erik H. *Gandhi's Truth.* New York: Norton & Company, 1969.

Frankl, Victor. *Man's Search for Meaning.* New York: Touchstone, 1984.

Iyenger, B.K.S. "Hathayoga," in *Light on Yoga (Yoga Dipika), New* York, 1966.

Jung, Carl G. *The Structure and Dynamics of Psyche,* second edition. Princeton: Princeton University Press, 1968.

Jung, Carl G. *Modern Man in Search of a Soul.* New York: Harcourt Brace Jovanovich, 1955.

Swami Kuvalayavanda, *Pranayama.* Bombay, 1966.

Kurup, P.N.V. *Handbook of Domestic Medicine and Common Ayurvedic Remedies.* Central Council for Research in Indian Medicine and Homeopathy. New Delhi, 1978.

Locke, S. And D. Calligan. *The Healer Within: The New Medicine of Mind and Body.* New York: New American Library, 1987.

MacGregor and Geddes. "Christian Concept of Soul," in *The Encyclopedia of Religion,* Vol. 13. New York: MacMillan Publishing Company, 1987.

MacNutt, Francis. *The Healing.* New York: Doubleday, 1990.

McGilvray, James C. *The Quest for Health and Wholeness,* German Institute for Medical Mission, Tubingen, 1981.

McNeill, Donald P., Douglas A. Morrison and Henri Nouwen. *Compassion: A Reflection on the Christian Life.* New York: Doubleday, 1982.

Nouwen, Henri. *The Wounded Healer: Ministry in Contemporary Society.* New York: Doubleday, 1979

Olyle, Irving. *The Healing Mind.* New York: Pocket Books, 1975.

Ram, Eric R. "Health Begins with Good Relationships." *Together,* 26, World Vision International, Monrovia, California, U.S.A, April-June 1990.

Siegel, Bernie. *Love, Medicine and Miracles.* New York: Harper and Row, 1988.

Siegel, Bernie. *Love, Peace and Healing.* New York: Harper and Row, 1989.

Tournier, Paul. *The Whole Person in a Broken World.* New York: Harper and Row, 1964.

Watty, William. "Man and Healing—A Biblical and Theological View," presented at Christian Medical Commission's Caribbean Regional Conference on the Churches' Role in Health and Wholeness. Geneva, 1979.

Part two

Making Health a Reality

6
Health for One Million

Lawrence Mar Ephraem

> The world has poverty of health amid abundant
> health resources. Millions die for lack of com-
> mon preventive medicines. The challenge is to
> ensure that the most people possible have at
> least basic health care.

Midnight, November 13, 1992. A knock at my presbytery door.
"Father, Father, open the door. We are all in water. Water is
coming up. Up every second."

An unusually severe cyclone lashed the southernmost districts of South India. Kanyakumari District experienced havoc. It
caused the worst flood havoc in the people's memory.

In Kanyakumari District of Tamil Nadu, a program called
Health for One Million (HOM) had been operating for a few years.
As soon as the catastrophe struck, the HOM volunteers and local
women leaders spontaneously came forward for relief activities
such as arranging for food distribution and medical care. In spite of
the calamity, no child or woman had to starve. Elsewhere, the
storm caused heavy damage to property and furniture and loss of
life elsewhere. Only one person died in the HOM program area—
while saving others.

The village volunteers of HOM, hearing of possible floods,
warned everyone through an established network of woman-to-
woman communication and put people in safe places.

Within a couple of months, more than 2000 temporary and
semi-permanent houses were constructed. Flood victims were reha-

bilitated; the people's cooperative work was supported by food for work and materials made available by voluntary agencies. All this was made possible by the Health for One Million (HOM) program.

Backdrop

HOM took its inspiration from Christian concern for the social dimension of health care. Christ went about healing people and making them whole. He sent his disciples to the ends of the earth with his mission of salvation and healing.

Moved by this call of Christ, sponsors of HOM gave thought to how all people could be made whole as Christ wanted and how health care could be extended to all, especially the unreached poor. This goal was reaffirmed in the light of Alma Ata declaration of 1978—Health for All by the Year 2000. The intention is to create a situation everywhere that enables people to lead productive and useful lives.

Inception

Health today is accepted as a basic human right and a worldwide social goal. Still, the world at large—developing countries in particular—continues to experience poverty of health in the midst of an abundance of health resources. Millions of poor people die despite easily available preventive medicines. This unconscionable situation prompted health planners to turn to alternative strategies of health care and health delivery systems. Health for One Million is one such attempt to make minimum, essential, and basic health facilities available to the maximum number of people.

HOM is best understood as a program on the move rather than a one-time project. It is a concept that assumes concrete shape as it progresses. The seed was sown at the National Convention of the Catholic Hospital Association of India in the year 1973, which had its theme Health for the Millions. This motto was further pursued by the Voluntary Health Association of India (VHAI). The Health for One Million program tries to make this slogan a reality.

Health for One Million has two main aspects: concept—HOM program; and activities—HOM projects.

Concept

Health for One Million (HOM) is a community-based program of health and development. People from some 200 families promote the program at micro levels, under a macro plan that covers one million people.

Community-based

As a community-based program, HOM is family-centered and focused on women. The first effort is to motivate mothers and women to get involved in their personal and family health as well as the development of their community. When the mother benefits, the whole family benefits. Women are not just beneficiaries or objects of health and development promotion. They are subjects and effective agents of activities and social change.

HOM promotes health and development. Health and development are so interrelated that one promotes the other, and both promote well-being.

Micro level

At the micro level, HOM consists of 20 basic groups of ten families each, covering 200 families with about 1000 people. This is an integral unit of HOM.

Up to this level, HOM operates completely on volunteerism. The 20 mother leaders representing the 20 groups serve without remuneration at least two hours every month in promoting and building up HOM. They attend two fortnightly training programs and communicate what they learn to others in their group. A woman must do this voluntary work to be a HOM mother leader and be eligible for other positions. The program cultivates the spirit of volunteerism by motivating local people.

Without some degree of volunteerism, even the Alma Ata declaration, Health for All, will remain mere rhetoric. After ten years of experimentation, the declaration had to be expanded to add All for Health. If all are involved in health for all, who will pay, and to whom?

Macro plan

HOM's aim is to form 1000 units of 1000 people each to reach one million people.

HOM is organized to help people become healthier and more developed. Concerted, joint efforts are necessary. Several HOM units will have to come together to plan small and big health and development projects. This will call for resources and finances beyond the capacity of a single HOM unit. Holding to the basic principle of using volunteers to the maximum, HOM units will go in for necessary financial resources raised by the people, pool their own resources, and secure government grants and bank loans.

Remuneration for additional time and efforts of volunteers and others will be in the form of incentives rather than wages or salaries. Once the project is over, all financial benefits and responsibilities on that basis would cease; voluntary efforts and the minimum HOM activities would continue. The HOM program is the tree and the projects are its fruits.

Objectives

The main objective of the HOM program is to evolve:

- A self-sustained system
- Of continuous education
- On health and development
- Reaching the mothers of families (especially the poor)

Structure

The self-sustained system of HOM is supported by the following organizational structure:

- Mothers of ten neighboring families voluntarily formed a *group*. They made one of them their leader. The group is the basic cell of HOM, and the leader is called *mother leader*.
- Twenty such groups and mother leaders make one integral *unit* of HOM; the one chosen to represent them is called a *volunteer*.

- When five such units and volunteers are formed, it becomes a *center*; the leader is called a *promoter*.

- When twenty such centers and promoters come into being, it is a *zone*; the leader is called an *organizer*.

- Ten such zones and organizers are supervised by a *coordinator*.

Continuous education

Promotion of continuous education takes place as follows:

- The 20 mother leaders meet once in two weeks under the volunteer, learn the principles of health care and development and discuss how to implement them in each group. This is called the HOM unit meeting.

- What the mother leaders learn at this meeting they communicate within a fortnight in an informal way to the other nine mothers of their groups.

- The volunteers meet monthly with the promoter to learn more about health and development topics and discuss how to effectively motivate the mother leaders. This is called the HOM center meeting.

- The promoters meet at the zone under the organizer once a month to learn more and plan activities at the zonal level. This is called the HOM zonal meeting.

- The organizers meet under the coordinator once a month to learn and to plan the whole HOM program. This takes place in both the Tamil-speaking area and the Malayalam-speaking area.

- Special training courses are conducted as necessary.

Monthly bulletins
To ensure that correct and appropriate information on health and development is imparted, a set of HOM notes is prepared by experts, printed every month and made available.

Bundles of notes are distributed at the organizers' meeting by the coordinator. These notes are passed down to various levels by the organizers, promoters, volunteers and mother leaders. The mother leaders distribute the notes to the families of their groups. Classes and discussions at various levels are based on the topic of the notes. The notes keep up the quality of HOM education content.

To ensure that the contents of the notes and other information from the coordinator reach the mothers of families at the grass-roots level and to check the impact on the community, an HOM bulletin circulates from the coordinator to the volunteer and back in the following way:

Stacks of copies of the bulletin from the coordinator travel through the organizational layers, breaking up into smaller bundles until single copies reach the volunteers at the individual units.

The content of the bulletin is introduced and explained by the volunteer at the meeting of the 20 mother leaders.

Each mother leader contacts the nine other mothers in her group before the next fortnightly meeting when decisions are taken that reflect the views of the unit's 200 families. The blank spaces in the bulletin are then filled out.

The paper starts its return journey to the coordinator, incorporating any comments of volunteers, promoters and organizers. The coordinator culls useful information and statistical data, assesses the work of the unit and sends the paper back to the center, where it is kept for some time as reference. It takes one month for a bulletin to complete its circular course.

Guiding principles

Several guiding principles emerged as the HOM program grew:

- Health *care* is more important than disease *cure*.
- Health can be maintained only in the context of *total human development*.
- Development means self-growth. Community development means community growing from within. *Self-help* and *self-sustained programs* are the most effective.

- Outside assistance is helpful mainly in bringing people together. The role of the outside helpers should be to work *with* rather than *for* people. They help mainly by coordinating efforts and encouraging local leadership.

- Community *decision* is more meaningful than community *participation* alone.

- *Local resources*—personnel, financing, government facilities, social structures—are used to the fullest, without regard to religious affiliation, caste distinction or political bias.

- Principles of *appropriate technology* are followed to the greatest extent possible.

- *Formal* as well as *informal educational methods* are adopted to educate people on health and development.

Evolution of HOM

The formative phase

HOM took shape as an organized program in 1976. The first span of five years was the formative phase. During this period, village-level volunteers were identified, motivated and trained. Some of them were further trained as promoters, a few as organizers. These organizational leaders emerged out of a natural selection from the community on the basis of personal ability and commitment to voluntary work.

In 1980 a convention of health volunteers was held in Trivandrum. It was reported that 1057 village-level volunteers had been identified.

The second phase

The following twenty years (1981 to 2000) is the second phase. This period is divided into four quarters of five years each:

1981 to 1985   1986 to 1990   1991 to 1995   1996 to 2000.

The focus of the second phase is to implement various activities of health and development promotion following the

HOM approach—utilizing the HOM organizational setup of volunteers, promoters, organizers and the fortnightly and monthly meetings, as well as the HOM notes and monthly bulletins.

Ten community-based activities

Four activities are proposed by UNICEF for the benefit of children under five years and mothers through their GOBI program (G=Growth monitoring; O=Oral rehydration; B=Breast-feeding; I=Immunization). These were the first activities included in the second phase of the HOM program.

To GOBI were added the three F's (F1=Female education, F2=Food complement, F3=Family planning, natural). HOM, on its own, added three more items: RED (R=Rehabilitation of disabled, E=Environment care and D=Development and income generation).

To conclude this presentation of HOM, a list of the ten community-based activities is followed by a brief report on each one.

G   Growth monitoring of children under five years

O   Oral rehydration of children suffering from diarrhea

B   Breast-feeding encouraged among mothers

I   Immunization against preventable diseases; control of communicable diseases

F1   Female education leading to leadership

F2   Food complement and nutrition

F3   Family planning, natural

R   Rehabilitation of the disabled

E   Environment and ecology care

D   Development and income generation

GROWTH MONITORING

PROJECT AIM: To see that every child under five years enjoys normal weight for age

METHODS: Checking and recording once a month the weight-for-age of every child under five years of age

Assessing the health status of the children (Normal, 1st degree malnutrition, 2nd degree, 3rd degree or less)

Providing supplementary food to severely malnourished children

Health education of mothers through fortnightly classes and HOM notes

Promotion of kitchen gardens

ACHIEVEMENTS in a typical unit of 200 families:

	1978	1985	1990
Children in			
3rd degree malnutrition	2.75%	0	0
2nd degree malnutrition	22.25%	10%	6.75%
1st degree malnutrition	42.42%	24%	11%
Normal	32.58%	66%	82.3%

This activity has been conducted in 255 HOM units covering a total population of 222,746 in 46,800 families.

ORAL REHYDRATION

PROJECT AIM: No child under five years of age getting diarrhea should go without ORT treatment

Every mother should know how to prepare ORT fluid

METHODS: Instruction and demonstration through fortnightly classes; circulation of HOM notes

ACHIEVEMENTS in one typical HOM unit of 200 families:

	1980	1985	1990
Average no. of under-fives in a unit	50	50	50
.... who got diarrhea	41/50	25/50	24/50
.... who got ORT	12/41	20/25	22/24
Percentage	21.5%	86%	91.2%
Mothers learning to prepare ORT fluid	20/50	40/50	50/50

ORT is implemented in 255 HOM units. a population of 22,746 people in 46,800 families, among 3,527 children out of 3,868 children who had diarrhea.

BREAST-FEEDING

PROJECT AIM: Encourage all mothers to breast-feed infants as long as possible. Particularly, teach mothers the importance of the first milk (colostrum) to the child.

METHODS: Instruction through fortnightly classes and HOM notes.

ACHIEVEMENTS:

In 1990 this project was implemented in 255 HOM units covering a population of 220,891 in 50,945 families.

	1985	1990
Children born	3,491	2,845
Breast fed for over 6 months	2,807	2,674
Percentage	80%	94%

IMMUNIZATION

PROJECT AIM: Immunize all children under five years against the communicable diseases (polio, DPT, BCG, measles).

Leprosy-control integrated with other activities.

METHODS: Fortnightly education classes; HOM notes; monthly clinics

ACHIEVEMENTS:

Immunization. By year end 1987, in a child population of 13,570 from 33,882 families 11,474 children have been fully immunized (85% of the children under five).

Integrated leprosy control. Integrated leprosy care is given in 51 HOM units. Here, 110,241 population has been covered 87,300 population has been examined. 488 leprosy patients were identified. Out of them, 1226 were lepromatous, 798 were non-lepromatous, 82 were NL. After treatment: a total of 49 patients have been released from control.

FEMALE EDUCATION

PROJECT AIM: Educating women on health and development items

Educating women to leadership

METHODS: Fortnightly classes; HOM notes; nonformal (women to women) communication; seminars and conventions.

ACHIEVEMENTS in one unit	1980	1985	1990
Mother leaders in a unit	20	20	20
Average attendance in fortnightly classes/meetings	12/20	15/20	18/20

Total no. of HOM units (registered)—6444

HOM units satisfactorily running (i.e., with regular meetings)—4000

HOM units running very well (i.e., with mother leaders attendance of 15/20 or more)—250

FOOD COMPLEMENT AND NUTRITION

PROJECT AIM: All under-five malnourished children to get enough food

All anemic women of childbearing age to get enough food

METHODS: Nutrition education through HOM notes & fortnightly classes; medical check through weekly clinics; distribution of supplementary food; encouragement of kitchen gardens

ACHIEVEMENTS:

Under-five children. In 1990 the nutrition project was implemented. In 255 HOM units covering 46,800 families with 222,746 people in these units, there were 10,602 children under five. Improvement in nutritional status has been as follows:

	1978	1985	1990
Children in 3rd degree malnutrition	2.75%	0	0
Children in 2nd degree malnutrition	22.25%	5%	2%
Children in 1st degree malnutrition	42.42%	24%	16%
Children in normal nutritional status	32.58%	71%	82%
	100%	100%	100%
Infant Morality Rate (Kerala)	47/1000		22/1000

Nutrition. 150 anemic women of childbearing age are provided with supplementary food on request. 20,800 out of 46,895 families maintain kitchen gardens.

FAMILY PLANNING, NATURAL

PROJECT AIM: Making information available on nonchemical alternatives in birth control to all women of child-bearing age.

METHODS: Fortnightly meetings/classes; special classes/seminars

ACHIEVEMENTS:

Natural family planning programs were implemented in 144 HOM units with 29,026 families. Here 12,142 couples have learned the methods of natural family planning and 6,502 couples follow N.F.P. The methods learned and followed are:

Symptom thermal method, identifying days of fertility and infertility by changes in basal body temperature in combination with other signs.

Cervical mucus method, where days of fertility are identified by self-observation of cervical mucus during menstrual cycle.

REHABILITATION OF THE DISABLED

PROJECT AIM: Early detection of signs of disability so remedial steps may be taken; prevention of disability to the maximum

METHODS: Community awareness programs; intensive surveys; HOM notes & fortnightly classes; medical clinic

ACHIEVEMENTS:

Community-based management of disabled children is being implemented in 120 HOM units covering 23,789 families with 87,407 people.

Here are 127 children with fits, 737 children with difficulty in speech/hearing, 68 children with difficulty in learning, 147 children with difficulty in seeing, 36 children with strange behavioral problems, 546 children with difficulty in movement, 187 children with multiple disabilities.

Out of all the children, 406 had severe disability, 825 had moderate disabilities, 617 had minimal disability.

ENVIRONMENT CARE

PROJECT AIM: Community-based care of ecology and environment.

METHODS: Educate people through fortnightly classes and HOM notes on soil conservation & water harvesting; make people build bunds and pits to sink rain water on their own property

ACHIEVEMENTS: 8,000 families have been motivated. 52 hectares of land brought under soil conservation activities.

DEVELOPMENT AND INCOME GENERATION

PROJECT AIM: Organize income-generation activities in families.

METHODS: Encouraging people through HOM notes and classes to undertake income-generation activities; utilizing bank loans, pooling small savings and utilizing HOM revolving funds.

ACHIEVEMENTS:

Through goat rearing, poultry keeping, bee-keeping, rabbit rearing, sea shell works, vegetable cultivation, small business, the per capita income increased by RS 7.76 between 1980 and 1985.

People below the poverty line came down from 80 percent in 1980 to 66 percent in 1985.

114

7

Pastoral of the Child

Zilda Arns Neumann

> By the grace of God, millions of lives are being
> changed by the love, dedication, blood and
> sweat of women and men organized in small
> communities, teaching and learning, living out
> the union of faith and life.

M ummy, is there any bread in heaven?" This question came
from a 4-year-old boy, one day before his death. Anselmo
was starving and in a feverish delirium when he asked his mother,
Joana Matias, this question. They lived in Pirambu, a slum in
Fortaleza, northeast Brazil.

The president of the National Conference of the Bishops of
Brazil, Dom Luciano Mendes de Almeida, remarked on this sad
account. He said,

> The question is like a prayer and reinforces our certainty
> that Anselmo is now with the Lord our Father, away
> from the injustices and cruelties of this life. However,
> before God, we are all bid to seek solutions to the needy
> child's situation.

Poverty and Brazil's families

Anselmo is only one of the 300,000 children under 5 years of age
who die each year in Brazil principally of starvation or diseases
derived from malnutrition. Today, in Brazil, 32 million people are

destitute and struggle with starvation. Nine million families live in miserable conditions.

Brazil is, however, a country of great potential. It has pro-duced, in the last seven years, around 59 million tons of grain—rice, beans, wheat, corn and soybeans. This number makes it evident that the starvation problem is not a matter of lack of food, but of lack of income because of the progressive concentration of income and land in the hands of a minority. In Brazil *a lot* have *very little* and *very few* have *a lot*. The same is true of most countries in Latin America.

Poverty has increased during the last ten years. This is largely due to the constant pressure of Brazil's external debt—in September 1992, US$104.5 billion.

But worst of all, some 2.7 million children under 2 years old are undernourished. This is the stage of childhood development in which the damage caused by malnutrition is the most serious and sometimes irreversible.

Brazil's impoverishment, added to poor schooling and unemployment, causes constant migration of those seeking better opportunities of work and living conditions. Due to being exposed to so many difficulties, this great fraction of the population is easy prey for criminals and all sorts of questionable practices. The groups mostly exposed to violence are children, adolescents and women—who also carry the heavy burden when families fall apart due to financial problems.

Family dissolution is an ever-growing problem, whether due to the husband's need to leave the family to seek employment in other regions, the wife's obligation to work outside the home during the week, or even daily financial pressures that make for a violent environment in which to grow up. This is likely the main cause of an ever-growing number of under-age children who work, mainly to help their mothers with family support.

Reversing this harsh reality depends on structural changes. Priority must be given to health and education actions so that the country's leaders may make better decisions, working with families within a context of community organization.

Seeds, bread, fish

It was due to this situation and in response to Christ's summons that the CNBB (National Conference of the Bishops of Brazil) conceived *Pastoral de Criança*—Pastoral of the Child. The seeds were rooted during a meeting between Dom Paulo Evaristo Arns, Cardinal Archbishop of São Paulo (my brother) and James Grant, the Executive Director of UNICEF, in May 1982. After CNBB's decision to start this program for pastoral care of children, I was charged with organizing and assessing the process together with Dom Geraldo Majella Agnelo, then Archbishop of Londrina, Brazil, and presently Secretary of Congregation for the Divine Cult and Discipline of the Sacraments of the Vatican.

In September 1983, when working out the first draft of a church-based strategy to save thousands of children's lives and promote their development, I felt sure within myself that I was sailing my boat in the right direction. After all, most of the problems related to health and basic education were easily preventable. They would not require a large amount of material or financial resources. They would need motivated people trained to undertake the cause.

Because of my professional experience, I decided to work with communities at the family level. Working with women is the best way to begin. Fathers and children enter the program because they recognize the work the wife and mother is doing.

On the other hand, people of the public services found it difficult to deal with the families; they would hardly ever enter into family guidance, where great transformations may take place. They were organized as a system that should have attracted the population. But the poorest families lacked courage, what I would call breath and oxygen, and succumbed on the way.

From the beginning of the Pastoral of the Child, the methodology was inspired by the Gospel as with the sharing of bread and fish (John 6:1-14). After elevation to heaven, science could also be shared. After a final evaluation of this effort, some baskets of knowledge and kindness would still be left over.

The words of Jesus the Good Pastor have always taught us to give priority to children and families at high risk, starving people, unemployed people, prostitutes, drug users, people living in miserable areas whether slum, rural area or a suburb of a big city.

Church, family, community

The church is always and everywhere close to the families. Its people can arrive at the right time to clarify and enlighten decisions on child care and other health issues.

As I see it, the church can best help families in communities through trained pastoral agents who live in the same community. These agents work with neighborhood families in an ecumenical process that respects popular culture, practices a new kind of evangelism and values lay ministry.

This is doubtlessly the easiest way to attack the root problems of disease, education, faith, violence and marginalization. At the same time, the process promotes Christian values and relationships.

Besides involving the families, it is also important to involve the community. From 1988 to the present, Pastoral of the Child has almost tripled; the number of organized communities increased from 6,000 to some 16,000.

In visiting dioceses and communities, I have seen the joy of many bishops who believe that the Pastoral of the Child is the great presence of the church on the side of the poor. I have also seen the dedication of so many religious orders—127 in 1991—who release their sisters for this work, which is so important to the church in Brazil.

Gifts, workers, results

St. Paul, according to Romans 12:4-8, taught us that people should be stimulated by the gifts they are given so that everything might work in the best way possible. He further advises us not to isolate ourselves; when one is sad, another encourages.

Thus, in the Pastoral of the Child:

- Some weigh children; others teach about alternative food, homemade serum or medicinal plants.

- Some look after pregnant women, breast-feeding or vaccination; others speak on the radio or on T.V.
- Some make puppets and perform in the theater; others teach mothers to develop their capacity to love through breast-feeding, caressing, talking, singing and praying.
- Some listen to complaints and send them to God; others promote income generation and teach teenagers and adults how to read and write and many other things.

As of early 1993, Pastoral of the Child is present in all 27 Brazilian states, 93 percent of the archdioceses, dioceses or prelates and 38 percent of the parishes. More than 53,000 leaders and agents work in nearly 16,000 organized communities. Over 1.1 million families are followed up, door-to-door, including more than 84,000 pregnant women and over 1.63 million children under 6 years old. Among these and other actions, Pastoral of the Child also produces a weekly 15-minute radio program that is broadcast by 583 stations throughout the country.

All this work costs Pastoral of the Child, annually, less than a hospital of average size. We spend much less to prevent diseases and violence than is spent to cure diseases and to assist marginalized children. In 1988, we assisted a little more than 300,000 families per quarter; five years later we have tripled that number.

The organized way of making the communities agents of their own transformation, stimulated by the church, has enabled us to fulfill objectives that, taken together, mean significant results in preventing marginalization:

- Reducing infant mortality
- Educating women to become agents of transformation of their families and the community
- Improving health and nutrition
- Spreading scientific knowledge regarding the health of

- Preventing children from being driven to the streets

119

- Developing cultural values and Christian attitudes among families

Workers who love Brazil's children

The program's ten years have been marked by a history of love through more than 53,000 people—leaders and agents of the Pastoral of the Child promoting human potential according to God's program. They have chosen the best part as their priority; that is, to work so as to *be*, without which it is no good to *have*. They incarnate faith and life every day. But it is not us, it is Christ who acts in us; it is he who saves, through our lives.

Our success, by the grace of God, has come from these partners working—almost always anonymously—in favor of children all over Brazil, driven by the strength of making faith the center of life. Many times, in the midst of a thunderstorm, they stand up on the boat and ask, "Where are you, Lord?" And they see the Lord walking on the water, and all becomes calm (cf. Mt. 14: 22-23).

The secret of these ten years was to develop, within the drama of life, the living of love—which leads us to make the changes needed so that all children might have life, and plenty of it.

Encouraging signs

We already see many signs of change. A study carried out by the University of Pelotas showed that the rate of children with low birth weight in assisted communities 9.6 percent against 18.8 percent in communities not assisted. Also 50 percent of mothers in rural areas assisted by the Pastoral know how to interpret the growth assessment chart, against 1 percent of mothers not assisted. In urban areas this difference is 57 percent against 28 percent.

Also documented has been a decrease in the mortality rate of children under 1 year old in assisted communities. In these communities, the rate of 53 deaths per thousand births in 1989 went down to 32 deaths per thousand births in 1992.

In October 1991, a law was passed on the rights of children and adolescents. Governmental and non-governmental organizations are working together to implement policies about children.

Meanwhile, local health councils are increasing their ability to enforce a law on a unified system of health.

Today, the Pastoral of the Child has matured in size, in activity and in achievements in favor of children. The program has achieved credibility inside and outside Brazil, in the scientific community, among governmental and non-governmental organizations.

But most importantly, we have credibility and a sense of shared mission with families and communities. We will continue to work together so that never again will we have to hear a single child repeat Anselmo's question: "Mummy, is there any bread in heaven?"

8

Loitokitok Child Survival

Alemu Mammo

> We need to work for integration of transformation
> and empowerment. Sustainability is a synthesis of
> the combined process.

Projects that deal with immunization against childhood diseases, oral rehydration therapy, focused nutritional problems and reduction of high-risk births are inexpensive yet effective ways to improve infant and child health. This is a proven approach, given appropriate community entry, project planning and design.

On average, successful global immunization coverage and treatment of diarrheal diseases with oral rehydration therapy has increased. However, in spite of the impressive results, the task of ensured child survival has to continue. A large number of children are still dying from preventable diarrheal diseases, immunizable diseases, malaria, pneumonia and, more recently, of HIV and AIDS. Many governments are spending huge amounts of money for curative treatment of these diseases, which are preventable.

Background

In 1984-85, Loitokitok Division of Kajiado District, Kenya, like the rest of East Africa, was affected by a severe drought and famine. Consequently, at the invitation of the community, World Vision (WV) provided relief assistance and further assisted 300 families to settle in Namelok, which later became the pilot site and headquarters of the Loitokitok Child Survival and Development Project

(LCSP). From such an experience, WV was able to implement community development activities including preventive and promotive health and food security in the area.

However, the most significant activity was building the Namelok dispensary, using funds jointly raised by the local community and World Vision. The dispensary became a base for both static and mobile clinical activities, since it provided essential "cold-chain" facilities for vaccines (to ensure cold system storage). Furthermore, it provided curative, preventive and promotive health care as it attracted the population from surrounding areas.

The project area lies in Southwest Kenya, about 260 kilometers south of Nairobi. Although the area is in the foothills of Mt. Kilimanjaro, it has an average of 540 mm of rainfall per year and supports some scanty and fragile Saharan-type vegetation.

The current population in Loitokitok Division is estimated at 84,000, of which 22 percent are women of child-bearing age (ages 15 to 45). Another 21 percent are children below five years of age. The population density of 12 people per square kilometer is one of the lowest in the country.

In 1986-87 the major diseases reported by patients at local health facilities in the Division were acute respiratory infections, 27.1 percent; malaria, 26.1 percent; diarrhea, 8.1 percent, and skin diseases, 7.1 percent. Only 35 percent of the population had access to clean water; only 15 percent had latrines. Out of 49 percent of the children under five weighed in the District, 25 percent were reported as severely malnourished (below 60 percent of weight-for-

Some abbreviations

PEP	Participatory Evaluation Process
PHC	Primary Health Care
WV	World Vision
USAID	United States Agency for International Development
LLLs	Listening Looking and Learning survey
BLS	Baseline Survey
LCSP	Loitokitok Child Survival Project
IC	Immunization Coverage

age of median standards).

The immunization coverage rate for children under five was less than 30 percent. Fewer than 10 percent of the mothers had accepted modern family planning practice.

Community entry

At the request of community leaders, WV Kenya, with assistance from the United States Agency for International Development (USAID) and World Vision in the U.S.A., began a child survival project among the Maasai people of Loitokitok Division. The action recognized the importance of curative and preventive care, as well as promoting community-based development services to isolated communities

World Vision staff initiated a series of visits to the community for a Listening, Looking and Learning survey (LLLs) to meet community members, to look at what they have, learn about their situation, listen to their problems and their plans on how to solve the problems. World Vision staff further learned what human and material resources existed within the community.

An LLLs team is comprised of an anthropologist, an epidemiologist, a community development practitioner and various members of the community. The team members were careful to observe local social norms and presented themselves in an informal manner with a locally acceptable dress code. Whenever team members were offered a seat, they made certain the elderly community members were seated first. The team members usually did not carry pens and paper, or if they did, they did not attempt to take notes while community members shared their experiences.

At the end of the day, the team members gathered together at their residence and asked themselves, What went wrong? Why? Who was responsible? How would they avoid similar mistakes the following day?

As a group, the team had made a commitment not to present themselves as experts but to be ready to learn from the community members. In practice this commitment was not difficult to keep, since the team was genuinely interested in learning from the community; the mentality of "we know it for them" was not visible among the team members.

As a result of the LLLs exercise, participatory evaluation process (PEP) and an actual baseline survey (BLS), the team discovered that the community's prioritization of concerns was considerably different from the list in the initial child survival proposal.

The LLLs strengthened World Vision's relationship with the community and gave WV some exciting insights into the endemic situation of the community. Furthermore, the LLLs team discovered that the Maasai had their own history, culture, sense of ownership, integrity and direction.

Community organization

As a result of a careful community entry process, World Vision staff began discussions with the community regarding the project prospectus. WV realized that without the community's active participation, ownership and leadership, the project could not succeed.

World Vision further recognized that the community has its own organization and distinctive history, which has existed for centuries. The development process and community organization are an integral part of the Maasai just as they are of other communities in Africa.

WV also saw that leadership already existed in the community. The community was found to have a strong sense of self-awareness. This awareness needed to be acknowledged and then built upon. What the community needed was genuine non-manipulative facilitation in order for appropriate development to take place at their pace and within their context.

Resources may be limited and technology may be underdeveloped, but *human dignity*, *culture* and *process of development* were visible and ripe among the Maasai.

Immunization

Immunization intervention was used as an initial community entry process. The immunization exercise was limited to the pilot community—Namelok, about 4,500 people of whom 1,500 were children under five years of age.

In less than one year, WV raised full immunization coverage for the pilot area from a baseline of less than 20 percent to more than 90 percent. This estimate may seem unrealistic, but for those of us who have gone through the exercise, it is not surprising. Furthermore, the midterm evaluation of the first phase revealed that the immunization coverage for the whole Division had risen from less than 20 percent to 87 percent in two years.

The parents already had a basic knowledge of health and disease. They understood what killed their children. Measles had been identified as a number-one killer during LLLs and the preparatory baseline survey.

When we originally set our course to work in this rural community—where there are no good roads, where there is a low literacy rate (less than 20 percent) and where the people are pastoralist—we had our doubts as to whether we could achieve our goal of immunizing more than 80 percent of the target population within four years. However, with a careful community entry process and community participation it was possible to attain our initial goal.

At the outset, an LLLs (Look, Listen, Learn Survey), a baseline survey and a Participatory Evaluation Process (PEP) were conducted to identify the basic needs in the community. (The results of these surveys and techniques are available in the World Vision Kenya Office).

The pilot site is an isolated area, 15 kilometers from the main feeder road. The main purpose of the pilot phase was to provide information on the characteristics of the area's population, provide information on aspects pertaining to disease patterns, identify the groups most at risk within the community, and most importantly, to gain direct experience with a community-based approach to development. Valuable information was gained in the pilot phase. For example, we learned about the number of households effectively covered by health workers (i.e., intensity and extent of coverage and cost per beneficiary). We also got basic information necessary for setting the direction of a suitable training program that could be adapted by Community Health Workers (CHWs), Traditional Birth Attendants (TBAs), Community Motivators (CMs) and other voluntary and professional health workers.

The first phase of the child survival and development project was extended for an additional three years to consolidate gains made during the first phase and to strengthen elements of sustainability.

Integrated interventions

After the final evaluation, the specific objectives of the project were revised. The following are the revised objectives and the interventions implemented:

- Train 500 Community Health Workers (CHWs) and 500 Traditional Birth Attendants (TBAs).

- Provide malaria prophylaxis to 70 percent of children 0-2 years of age.

- Immunize 99 percent of infants 0-11 months of age.

- Promote literacy within the community through parallel child sponsorship and development projects.

- Create awareness and behavioral change for the prevention and control of HIV-AIDS and sexually transmitted diseases in at least 80 percent of the community through *barazas* (community meetings), schools, churches, tourist lodges and in-group ranch participation.

- Implement environmental conservation practices through afforestation, agroforestry, soil conservation measures and spring protection, with at least 50 percent of the community participating.

- Initiate and promote income-generation for women's groups, with at least ten women's groups participating.

Accomplishments at final evaluation

The following tables highlight the major achievements of the Loitokitok Child Survival and Development project. The figures represent percentages.

Table 1(a)

Variable	Baseline	Final	Projection
BCG	39	95.5	90
DPT3	32	85.4	90
OPV3	22	84.7	90
Measles	28	78.5	89

Table 1(b)

Variable	Baseline	Final	Projection
Prevalence of diarrhea	54	33	15
Mothers using ORS	24	71	87
Malnutrition among 0-5	25	2.3	2
Using modern contraceptive	5	9.8	15
Birth spacing*	74	91	91
Trained CHWs	15	157	250
Trained TBAs	5	106	128

* The reason for a higher percentage of birth spacing in the Maasai community is prolonged breast feeling. It has been documented that, in a society where there has been undernutrition, prolonged breast feeding will result in approximately 40 percent birth control. Most Maasai women breast feed an average of 24 to 36 months; their dietary habits are not remarkable.

Note: There has not been a recent formal baseline survey conducted in the area. These results are projections based on medical records gathered by WV monitoring staff who have qualitatively evaluated the findings, other NGOs, and MOH observations and previous pre-project baseline survey, mid-term and final survey of first phase of the child survival project.

Community participation

At the project initiation, WV was concerned that the Maasai, who are traditionally pastoralist, might not be willing to participate in the health and development activities in their community. However, after careful planning, a strategic community entry process applying the mechanisms of LLLs, PEP and actual baseline surveys, systematic community dialogue, and relationship building, the community's active involvement became indisputably evident.

The community contributed almost 10 acres of land for the office, staff houses, dispensary, guest house and demonstration garden. WV had facilitated an irrigation scheme to encourage the Maasai community to be self-reliant in food security and in a short time the people picked up the idea. They formed a committee to oversee the distribution from the irrigation scheme, which heightened their excitement and promoted a change of attitude about agriculture and kitchen gardens. Currently Maasai people in the area have introduced onions, beans, tomatoes, and maize for income generation and to provide food for their families.

WV has witnessed real transformation: the Maasai have adjusted their lifestyle voluntarily to a changing environment without compromising their human dignity and self-worth. Through the project, WV has been able to integrate the spiritual and the physical. Advances in both areas have taken place concurrently and harmoniously.

There are more children in school today than at the time of the baseline survey. There are also more schools.

Participation demands increased ownership, influence and contributions; it further demands increased community empowerment. Through the committee, women's groups, CHWs and TBAs, grass-roots participation was strengthened and a process of empowerment has taken place.

The community may lack modern technology, a high level of education and abundant material resources, but it is wealthy in culture, interpersonal relationships and self-awareness. World Vision has found that effective influence can emerge only after:

- Genuine respect and a relationship based on appropriate process and pace (the community's pace).

To empower the community, change agents must be willing to relinquish their own power gained through:

- Technology, training, organizational prestige and individual expertise (Philippians 2: 7-8).

Mothers and fathers in Loitokitok are in the process of empowerment. It is they who have to decide to get their children immunized, manage scarce water resources, maintain their health center, manage their development and remain involved and informed. It is a process based on the right approach and understanding that makes the difference. With that process in place and with World Vision's commitment to stay in the area, the results will be transformational and sustainable.

A holistic ministry of this sort is dependent upon the volition of the participants. Yet, it is not necessarily independence alone, but interdependence, based on genuine relationship, true commitment and unconditional service that brings success. *Once a community has decided to serve its own needy members, transformation has been translated into action.* This process is being evidenced in Loitokitok.

Sustainability

Sustainability, as applied to health and development, involves structured processes to maximize the level of positive benefits that will be provided to as many people in the project area as possible, for as long of a period of time as possible. The challenge is organized around the two root words of "sustainability," *sustain* and *ability*.

If project benefits are to be continued or sustained, project staff through project design and implementation must demonstrate the ability to build into the community a sense of ownership of the project's activities, to encourage, empower, and support the community. The community must learn how development is tied to the necessity of offering their own resources and assuming responsibility for their own lot in life.

On the other hand, sustainability is a process of transformation. A clear process is fundamental to sustainability. *A plan that has a clear view of the end at the inception and maintains consistency can enhance transformation and sustainability.* The essence of a good development process is developing the people with sustained human dignity and self worth, resulting in a change of habits based on appropriate knowledge, attitude and practice (KAP).

A benchmark by which to measure this general definition would be to achieve a continuation of at least 50 to 80 percent of the benefits generated by the project to at least 50 percent of the community for at least five years after project support ends. These relatively arbitrary, quantifiable targets must remain flexible. They depend on the degree of support that is generated for the project from within the local community and local government and other non-government organizations (NGOs).

The local community leaders and project staff have developed and implemented a formal action plan for sustainability. All have acknowledged that sustainability is a process that seeks to maximize the effectiveness of health and development activities. The process has been designed and managed with open participation of the community, other sectors and NGOs in the area.

The village and the project staff have been involved in the development and implementation of the sustainability action plan. The village motivators and village-based community health workers have been essential players in this challenging endeavor. They have been providing the essential liaison for encouraging, enabling and empowering village leaders and village members to understand and own development initiatives. Participation from Kenya's Ministry of Health has also been essential, as was the participation from other NGOs and government ministries. The village motivators have been spending significant amounts of time in the community practicing "going back to the basics" of community development and involvement.

Sustainability strategies occupied a good part of the project from the inception of project design through each stage of implementation. Request for an extension indicated interest in consolidation of the process of sustainability within the local community and the government context.

Sustainability attitudes and techniques continue to permeate the project activities. All village motivation activities and training address dimensions of sustainability. Formal, written plans of action on how best to sustain each project component in each village are being streamlined.

A large portion of the second-phase project budget has been allocated to the support and strengthening of sustainability activities i.e., additional training for village motivators, renovating of local dispensaries, ongoing dialogue with local community and operation research to learn about the culture and habits of the community.

Sustainability benefits of the project

- The mothers, in particular, have gained from the knowledge, attitude and practice (KAP) program. The community in general has gained from training introduced by the child survival project. Their changed attitude about diseases and health will remain with them beyond the project's life span. For instance, the young girls who had witnessed their sisters and brothers being immunized against six killer diseases will be taking their children for immunizations with minimal facilitation.

- The KAP concerning oral rehydration, prolonged breast feeding, use of ante-natal and post-natal care, the kitchen garden, use of irrigation schemes for small-scale farming, improved housing, and the enrollment of more children into local schools are a few indicators that the community is convinced and will be carrying on sustainable activities on their own. If WV pulls out, their KAP remains with them.

- The community volunteers (CHWs, TBAs, development committee) remain in the community and, with the community's encouragement, they will continue their volunteer work at least at a reduced level.
- The churches in the area remain in the community. They will also carry on some of the development activities as indigenous organizations in the country.
- The dispensaries (small health centers) and health centers renovated by WV remain in the community to provide primary health care services.
- The enrollment of children in school and the expansion of schools continues as the awareness of parents increases as a result of their children's educational progress.

Significant in the case of the Loitokitok Child Survival project is the integration of spiritual and physical (health and development). The project has taken the first four to seven years to increase primary health care service utilization (oral rehydration, immunization coverage, control of diarrheal diseases and basic curative services).

The existing staff houses, guest house, project offices, and solar lighting system continue to be part of the sustainability process. The guest house and staff houses, while meeting the housing needs of project staff outsiders, also provide local income from rental charges. These will eventually become self-sustaining.

Lessons learned

We have learned two important lessons from our experience with the Loitokitok Child Survival and Development project:

- We need to work for integration of transformation and empowerment.
- Sustainability is a synthesis of the combined process.

References

"Loitokitok Child Survival and Development Project Initial Proposal." WV Kenya, 1986.

"Loitokitok Child Survival and Development Project Mid-term Evaluation," 1989.

"Loitokitok Child Survival and Development Second Phase Extension Proposal," 1991.

"Loitokitok Child Survival and Development Project Fund Evaluation," 1991.

Mammo, A., M. O'Leary, et al. "The 1992 Evaluation on the Area-Based Program." UNICEF, Kenya, July 1992.

"Human Development Report 1993." United Nations Development Programme, Oxford University Press, 1993.

"World Development Report, Investing in Health, World Development Indicators." World Bank, Oxford University Press, 1993.

"Child Survival—A Fifth Report to Congress on the USAID Program." USAID, Washington, D.C.

9

Water sustains life and health

Joe W. de Graft Johnson Riverson

Some 80 percent of the world's disease and
illness is due to contaminated water.

Water is a basic feature of human existence. About sixty percent of human body weight is water. Water is necessary for digestion—the process through which food is broken down and then absorbed into our bodies. Most of the chemicals called enzymes, which help to break down food into small particles, work best when food is mixed with water. Water is also necessary for respiration—the process through which oxygen is taken in and carbon dioxide is expelled from the body.

A person can live for many days without food, but without water to drink he will die after a few days; without enough water for personal hygiene he will fall ill. He needs water to grow food. Beyond this, he needs water to enjoy such amenities as swimming or flower and vegetable gardening. Water is so essential that people would travel long distances in search of it, and where only little water exists, all efforts are made to find more sources of it.

The daily water requirement of the average adult is between 1.8 and 3 liters per day. This is the minimum amount needed to sustain bodily processes. In addition, much larger quantities are used for domestic and washing purposes, for agriculture and in industry.

Health consequences of inadequate water supply

The water supply of most rural people in the Third World is polluted and unsafe for drinking. People may pollute rivers by washing clothes along the banks or wading to cross in the absence of bridges. Human and livestock excreta may litter river banks. Children may bathe or relieve themselves in the river. Pollution of wells may be attributed to shallowness of the wells, human and animal excreta, contaminated buckets, and lack of covers, care and maintenance.

Water-related diseases
Water and health are closely related. The World Health Organization estimates that 80 percent of the world's disease and illness is due to contaminated water. Owing to heavy pollution of rural water supplies, water-related diseases are prevalent among rural communities in many Third-World countries. Contamination of drinking water supplies can cause intestinal and parasite infection like diarrheal disease, dysentery, typhoid and cholera. Water can provide an environment in which disease carriers can flourish, for example, the larvae of mosquitoes, which cause malaria; larvae of black flies, which cause onchocerciasis (river blindness); and tsetse flies, which cause trypanosomiasis (sleeping sickness); water fleas or cyclops, which are the intermediate hosts for guinea worm infection; and the snail hosts of schistosomiasis (bilharzia).

Lack of water results in poor standards of personal hygiene. Poor hygiene leads to the transmission of infection by unwashed hands and crockery; it is responsible for eye complaints like trachoma and skin diseases like scabies and yaws.

Also associated with poor sanitation are infections due to intestinal worms such as roundworm, hookworm, threadworm and whipworm. Feces containing eggs of worms are deposited on the ground. Some worm eggs hatch into larvae that develop in damp soil; for example, the larvae of hookworm penetrate the skin of children and infect them. The eggs of roundworm, threadworm or whipworm in the soil may infect children through contaminated fingers, food or water.

Improving water supplies and sanitation

Several recommendations and strategies came out of the UN International Drinking Water and Sanitation Decade (1980-1990). Many governments, international agencies, nongovernmental organizations (NGOs) and private voluntary organizations (PVOs) made efforts to help improve access to safe water supplies and adequate latrines for millions of people, especially those living in the rural areas of the Third World.

It is well known that many rural water supply projects in the Third World, especially those that concentrate on boreholes and hand pumps, have not been too successful. There has been inadequate and ineffective community participation and hygiene education in most communities regarding these facilities. This has resulted in poor or nonexistent programs of village-level operation, maintenance and cost recovery. Promoters of water supply and sanitation projects need to involve communities in the planning, implementation, maintenance, monitoring and evaluation of their water supply and sanitation projects. However, the techniques and skills for achieving effective community participation must be learned.

World Vision's Africa water program

In 1986, a special Africa Water Program matching grant from USAID-Washington enabled World Vision International to meet critical water development needs of World Vision-assisted rural communities in Ethiopia, Ghana, Kenya, Malawi and Senegal.

In October 1987 a workshop was held in Nairobi, Kenya, for managers of World Vision water projects to develop a common understanding of the Africa Water Program's purpose, the roles and responsibilities of its members and the complexities of large scale water supply and sanitation projects. Recommendations included developing health education components as well as community participation to enhance long-term sustainability.

The Ghana Rural Water Project

Ghana has some 16 million people (as of 1993). Approximately 51 percent of them do not have access to potable water. Only 15 percent of people living in communities of fewer than 500 inhabitants have access to clean drinking water; however, some 70 percent of those living in communities of between 500 and 5,000 and 93 percent of those living in communities of more than 5,000 inhabitants enjoy such access.

The sanitation situation is also poor. Only 50 percent of the urban and 15 percent of the rural population have adequate sanitation facilities. The national average is 27 percent.

Most urban communities have either pipe-borne water and water treatment plants or package-treatment plants that draw from surface water resources. Most rural communities get their water from ponds, springs, rivers and streams. During the rainy season, rivers overflow their banks and water abounds. But in the dry season, water sources dry up. Rural people endure long and arduous searches for water, sometimes travelling 18 kilometers or more.

In 1985, some Ghanaian scientific consultants conducted a study on behalf of World Vision Ghana. Many villages supported by World Vision had high incidences of guinea worm disease, schistosomiasis (bilharzia) and diarrheal diseases due to polluted sources of water.

A large-scale water and sanitation program, the Ghana Rural Water Project, began in October 1985. Funding came from USAID and World Vision support offices. It was conceived as a comprehensive water development project, including not only the construction of potable water sources, but major hygiene, sanitation and health education components. A series of workshops equipped World Vision technical and operations staff to organize, train and facilitate communities to plan, implement, and sustain their own water supply and sanitation projects. The aim was to eliminate or drastically reduce water-related diseases and diseases due to poor sanitation, from World Vision-assisted rural communities.

By September 1990 World Vision Ghana had acquired vehicles and capital assets for drilling wells and installed 455 boreholes and hand pumps in scattered communities throughout Ghana. Whole communities received education on water, hygiene and sanitation; two representatives in each community learned basic pump maintenance to ensure sustainable operation and maintenance of the facilities. The result was a significant reduction of guinea worm and diarrheal diseases; people returning to villages they had abandoned due to scarcity of water; improved personal and environmental cleanliness; increased women's involvement in development activities; and an enhanced self-help spirit in the communities.

However, an evaluation in November 1989 indicated the need to concentrate efforts in specific demarcated districts, rather than scattering development projects over large areas. More emphasis was needed in health, hygiene and sanitation education, and community participation was to be intensified, especially community cash contribution for maintenance of pumps.

The second phase of the project began in October 1990. World Vision Ghana staff held extensive dialogue with key officials in the regional and district administrations in the proposed project areas. Local district assemblies provided a list of poor rural communities badly in need of potable water and other basic amenities.

The design of this five-year project incorporated the recommendations of the November 1989 evaluation. It is a combined water and sanitation project funded by a US$5.0 million grant from the Conrad N. Hilton Foundation and US$3.2 million in matching funds from World Vision United States. The project entails drilling 500 successful boreholes fitted with hand pumps, building 800 latrines and training 1,000 community volunteers to maintain and repair the pumps. The locations are needy rural communities on the Greater Afram Plains in south-central Ghana. There is also an intensive program of educating community members about health and the importance of clean water, hygiene and sanitation, mobilizing communities and local agencies to participate in the project, and promoting the construction of latrines, laundry and drainage facilities.

The major concerns of this project are guaranteeing sustainable systems in the communities, improving people's knowledge, changing attitudes and behavior with regard to water, sanitation and health, and promoting community participation in their own development. The project is using a collaborative approach to integrated rural development by building an effective network with the government's decentralized administrative systems (district authorities, traditional social structures, community leaders and members) and other nongovernmental development agencies. Through a series of workshops, seminars and dialogues involving all of these stakeholders, and their active involvement in all the stages of the project, water is being used as an entry point to sustainable, integrated, holistic, people-centered development on an area basis. This is known within World Vision International as the area development program (ADP) approach.

Health education and sanitation
A health education and community participation unit is in charge of community education, pre-drilling and post-drilling activities and sanitation education.

For community education, visits are made to the beneficiary districts to interact with them. Data on the development status and needs within the district are collected regarding various development programs that have already taken place or are in progress in the district.

Project start-up workshops bring together identifiable stakeholders and project partners such as heads of decentralized government departments, district assemblymen and women, traditional rulers, community representatives, NGOs and other development agencies in the districts. The key objectives of these workshops are to:

- Share information on the project
- Create an awareness in stakeholders and get them committed to the program

- Identify the existing work of the stakeholders and ensure against duplication of programs
- Identify stakeholders' roles and responsibilities in the water project
- Identify beneficiary communities
- Identify and mobilize resources for the water supply and sanitation program in the district
- Develop an action plan for program implementation

The district administration helps World Vision enter into the communities. Visits are made to community members in their homes to inspect their water receptacles. Essential topics discussed during these visits include the various sources of water available in the community, the interrelationship between sanitation, the environment, personal hygiene, good health and nutrition. Members of the community are urged to help assess the existing health situation after which the community is assisted to identify their needs through the administration and analysis of a simple generic questionnaire. The communities are also educated on good environmental sanitation, such as the proper disposal of refuse, proper maintenance of refuse dumps and also the siting of these dumps.

Where there is an outbreak of diseases such as guinea worm, the communities are educated accordingly. For instance, for the prevention and control of an outbreak of guinea worm disease in one district, house-to-house visitations were made to victims. This was followed by health education to improve their knowledge and enhance control. Members of the communities were taught how to use a special material to filter water, and it was emphasized that water had to be filtered before its use.

Pre-drilling activities include mobilizing village resources such as communal labor, sand, stones and gravel, and a set cash contribution. A local water and sanitation committee becomes responsible for monitoring and sustaining the project on a community basis. The World Vision Ghana team helps community members design an action plan to meet the tasks ahead.

Introduced by the health educator, a hydrogeologist works with community members to select drilling sites. An ideal site is on the periphery of the community and away from latrines and refuse dumps. Women are included in the siting process; the location of wells affects their recreation and leisure. The pump site is where women talk about village matters, get to know each other, and (for young adults) meet their lovers.

Post-drilling activities include mobilizing resources to build a concrete pad; filling the borehole site with stones; introducing the pump installation team to the community; and mobilizing community members to work closely with the team. Before the pump installation team begins its work, women help by cleaning the sites. Community members then build soak-aways (drainage areas) around the pump. The health educator teaches them to operate the hand pumps gently and with care; check for any cracks around the pedestal in the platform and rectify it immediately; do washing at least five meters away from the pump; ensure that receptacles used in fetching water from the pump are clean; and inform volunteer pump mechanics if the pump breaks down. Weekly scrubbing and daily cleaning are emphasized. Women are encouraged to involve themselves in community activities and to care for their homes and keep their environments clean.

Construction of latrine and laundry facilities

The construction of latrines and laundry facilities has been a vital component of the second phase of the Ghana Rural Water Project. Community members attend a one-day workshop on latrine construction. The objectives are to:

- Learn from partner communities about their experiences with rural latrine facilities
- Get community recommendations on latrine planning, design, implementation, operation and maintenance
- Reinforce linkages between potable water supply, sanitation facilities and the hygiene education program
- Facilitate community participation in strategies for future sanitation programs

- Discuss the technical design of the latrines (safety, comfort, and hygiene), the involvement of community members in construction and maintenance, the role of women, and latrine usage and health education needs.

Community members are asked to draw on their community experiences with latrines. Each participating community gives a brief summary of the latrine facilities available, identifies problems, and with the help of the above guidelines, offers possible solutions, identifies resources needed and organization of persons responsible for action. Each group elects a chairman to coordinate the discussion to allow for free interaction and a secretary to record accepted findings.

As a result of these workshops, community members realize that hygienic latrines play a vital role in health promotion. Though pit latrines are the commonly used latrines, much improvement needs to be done to render them more hygienic, providing safety, comfort and privacy for the users.

The selection of a site for latrine construction is a major issue that influences the acceptance and usage of the facility. Care must be taken in selection of the sites so that the water sources are not contaminated. In addition, sociocultural factors that inhibit latrine usage need to be identified and addressed.

The latrines constructed are Ventilated Improved Pit (VIP) latrines. The components of a VIP latrine are a stable pit; a durable pit-cover with a drop-hole; a vent with a fly screen; and a roofed superstructure for privacy.

The K-VIP latrine, designed at the Kumasi University of Science and Technology, is recommended for rural areas of Ghana. The pits are designed to be used alternately and indefinitely. Multiple-room alternating VIP latrines are suitable as institutional or communal latrines. They are, however, rather expensive to construct, so in the Greater Afram Plains area, a number of communities have chosen to improve upon the common pit latrines, making them ventilated and much safer to use. World Vision Ghana has also introduced to the villages the Blair toilet, a cheaper but equally effective single-room VIP latrine designed in Zimbabwe; individual families are encouraged to own their own toilets. All these types of improved latrines are to be found in the Greater Afram Plains area.

After the construction of the community latrines, members of the community are motivated, trained and assisted in constructing laundry and personal washing facilities adjacent to the pump. The aim is to improve personal hygiene and to ease the burden on women by relieving them of the need to carry large amounts of water away from the well. The World Health Organization (WHO) recommends a daily ration of 20 liters of water per person for all uses. To the water carrier of a typical family of eight, this represents a burden of 350 pounds every day!

Women and children play an important role in the maintenance of the latrines, since they are mostly responsible for cleaning them.

Pump maintenance

A long-lasting solution to the acute water problems that hit our rural folk does not come by drilling boreholes and fitting pumps to them, if the pumps cannot be properly maintained.

A maximum number of 4 volunteers (including women) from each community are trained. The aim of training local personnel for this exercise is to ensure sustainability and proper maintenance of the pumps.

After the pump maintenance course, trained volunteers can pull out a broken hand pump to assess any fault. For the meantime, they travel to Accra to purchase the required parts for replacement. The volunteers have access to tools from the common site nearest them to perform necessary repairs. In the long term, government-assisted district service centers will likely be involved in this exercise. They would serve as distribution centers for spare parts.

Examples from other African countries

Malawi

In Malawi, Southern Africa, the water program funded by the USAID has the goal of enhancing the quality of life of the Malawian communities by improving access to, and use of potable water and sanitation facilities. The program has four components: gravity-fed piped water supply systems; integrated borehole drilling; borehole rehabilitation; and health education and sanitation promotion.

By May 1993, one piped water supply project in Central Malawi and 49 boreholes in Southern Malawi had been completed. Gravity-fed piped water projects in Central and Northern Malawi were scheduled to be completed by September 1993. In addition, project communities have received intensive education on health sanitation.

The benefits of the program have included significant improvement in health through improved access to potable water facilities and the health education and sanitation promotion. The incidence of water-borne diseases has been significantly reduced and housing conditions improved. The project stood the severe drought of 1992 and, unlike elsewhere in the country, very few cases of bloody diarrhea or cholera were reported. In addition, the project has reduced the time it took women to fetch water from 4 hours to less than 30 minutes. This has enabled women to have more time for other productive activities. The water supply also benefits livestock.

Senegal

In Senegal, West Africa, World Vision International has undertaken a multi-sectoral integrated development program in the Louga region, one of the eight political regions in Senegal, located about 100 miles south of the desertification line. The most pressing need is to increase access to clean water.

The Louga program was an outcome of the extended programming that occurred as World Vision orchestrated a multi-faceted response to the Africa drought crisis in 1983. The program was designed and implemented not only to bring relief to pockets of severe famine, but also to offset the effects of drought in the future, and to see that communities become self-sufficient in water and food.

147

A development strategy was prepared to focus a set of integrated interventions around water as the critical resource in the region. The five main project interventions were Water Extension Training (WET); Potable Water Development; Health Care; Agriculture and Education. All were started in July 1985, to benefit a population of over 200,000 in various villages in the Louga region, with the exception of the Education Project that began in October 1990.

The water supply project involves drilling a borehole in a selected village and installing a modified India Mark II hand pump, and supporting pump maintenance and repair. As of July 5, 1993, 400 boreholes had been drilled and fitted with hand pumps. The pumps are actively used by the villagers to provide adequate potable water to households in the villages. The water is also used to irrigate vegetable gardens that have been established near the pumps, and that provide a thriving business for village women, as well as to provide nutritious food for improving the nutrition of children, women and their families.

Under the Water Extension Training Project, a World Vision Senegal multi-disciplinary team of technicians is in permanent contact with the population and other partner organizations. The team carries out background studies, takes care of training for village organizations, and sees to the setting up of various community networks of voluntary assistance. The strategy is to develop networks of local people who will facilitate various development activities in clusters of villages. The bush technician network is a group of persons trained by program staff to repair the hand pumps. Persons with some mechanical aptitude, a desire to serve nearby villages, and a willingness to make some adjustments in ways of earning a living are selected after observation by program staff over a period of time. The repair activity is a part-time activity for a cluster of 6-10 villages, with enough compensation to make up for time taken away from farming. The term technician was chosen deliberately to convey respect for the function.

In the Louga region of Senegal, water is sustaining life and health in village communities.

Zimbabwe

In Zimbabwe, Southern Africa, a water, health and agriculture project, funded by the Australia International Development Assistance Bureau (AIDAB) and World Vision Australia, is aimed at supporting the Zimbabwe Government's efforts to enable people in one district to experience improvement in health, particularly for children under five years old as well as for women of child-bearing age; improved access to safe drinking water and good sanitation; and increased production of crops for consumption, and for sale.

The district, in Northeast Zimbabwe, covers 2,660 square kilometers and has a population of 93,000 people. The area is remote and under-served in all forms of development.

Since its inception in 1990, the project has gone a long way in addressing problems inherent in this area. Water and sanitation improvement activities that began in 1990 have been implemented in all four wards of one sub-district.

Twelve shallow wells were rehabilitated and fitted with pumps during 1991. Water committees were established by communities and trained by the project to maintain and sustain the water pumps. In addition, 417 Blair toilets were constructed by the community with World Vision assistance during the same period.

Transformed lives and communities in Ghana

The Ghana Rural Water Project has gone a long way, not only in transforming the life of individuals residing in rural communities of this country, but also in sustaining their very life and health.

Testimonies from the community of Oku

Oku is one of the beneficiary communities visited during the January 1993 mid-term evaluation. Augustine Kwasi Dapaah, a thirteen-year-old boy from the village of Berem, told a member of the evaluation team:

> The water we now have because of World Vision has really changed everything in my village. We children can now go to school, because we do not have to walk long distances to "hunt" for water during the dry season. Normally, we do not go to school for about three months

during the dry season because everyday all we do is walk into the bush in search of water. Now we can wash our clothes, bathe and go to school. We do not get tired anymore because we have water right here in the village.

Kwasi, a very intelligent and inquisitive boy, wanted to know why the World Vision evaluation team had paid a visit to his village, and were asking so many questions. They explained that the information was for the donors who needed to know if the water provided has had any positive effects on their lives.

Oh yes. Tell them they should continue to help us and other villages like ours who need water. Please, add that we need teachers!

From Brebi-Dogo Akuraa, Dogo told the team that:

Life is much better now because of the water World Vision has given us. Before we had water, I used to hire a tractor to fetch water from Ejura (about 60km away) during the dry season. This is no more necessary and I can now use the money more profitably. Moreover, guinea-worm has completely disappeared from this village. We realize that most of our diseases were all because of the bad water we were drinking. Now we are healthy and we can spend more time on our farms, and that has improved our harvest.

We are maintaining the borehole very well. It is always under lock and key. There are times when it is open and everybody obeys the rules. You see, we don't want to waste the water.

Dogo ended by saying that their most pressing need was a school for the children, who are now healthier than before. He himself is educated and speaks English.

In Oku village, about 48 km. from Ejura, the chief spokesman was among the original settlers who migrated from Ejura, Amantin, and other villages some twenty-five years ago.

They were originally hunters but changed their profession to farming because of the richness of the land.

The spokesman said that in the beginning, when they were few, they did not have to go far along the stream during the dry season. As their numbers increased, however, they were forced to walk as far as eight kilometers to search for water along the Oku Stream. Concluding, he said:

> Now thanks to World Vision, we have water all the year round. It is amazing how guinea-worm disease has completely disappeared from our village. Some years back, around this time of the year, you would have been sorry at the sight here. Most of us would have been totally incapacitated by swollen limbs and aching bodies. But now, look at us! We are different and we can work on our farms. Our problem now is with bees! They compete with us to drink the water from the boreholes and sometimes we have to abandon our bowls and buckets of water when they chase us.

Whatever conclusion one may draw from this trip to Oku, one cannot deny that water has indeed transformed the lives of our rural people.

Testimonies of God's power
Provision of clean potable water has improved the health status of the people and enabled them to spend more time on their farms and with their families. But it has also transformed the religious perspective of the people. Members of the beneficiary communities have grown to know the God whom those of us at World Vision International Ghana worship, the God on whom we call before the beginning of any drilling process, and to whom we render our sincere thanks whenever we drill a successful borehole.

Mr. Gabriel Mensah from Otsirikomfo (which means "I abhor the fetish"), a community in the Eastern region, says that he remen^ ... holding hands to pray before uiey embark on any drilling activity. As he gives this testimony, Mr. Mensah can see them through his mind's eye as they

151

sing choruses during the drilling until they hit the water table and the way and manner they render their appreciation to God for enabling them to drill just one borehole.

> Anyone who witnesses this exercise goes home a changed man. The importance and power of prayer is manifested to the members of the community as well as the fact that those of us at World Vision serve a faithful God.

A teacher by the name of Graham related a story about the work in Afranguah:

> I was a teacher at Cape coast. Any time I went home to Afranguah [in central Ghana] and saw the water my people drink, my heart ached within me. Our drinking water was almost black in color and over 95 percent of the population, both adult and children, including babies were infected with guinea worm, rendering them completely incapable of any meaningful work. How could they work on their farms in that condition? How could anybody do anything in that hopeless, pitiful condition? But then God moved in and showed us that with Him all things are indeed possible. Oh, how our lives have changed!

After seeing the World Vision drilling team and their equipment move past his community many times to areas beyond, he set out on his own to find out the purpose of the water project. Mr. Graham began his own investigations and discussed the possibility of World Vision rendering assistance to his village. When the necessary negotiations were completed and World Vision moved in to drill, the people gathered around, anxious to see what would happen; according to Mr. Graham, a previous attempt to give them water by another organization had failed. To the community members, World Vision's attempt was doomed to fail from the beginning.

The chief of the village and his elders arrived at the scene to perform customary rites to facilitate the second attempt at drilling. They believed the pond they drank from was a god which had to be appeased. Mr. George Nkrumah, leader of the drilling team gathered his men and held hands to pray before starting work.

Within forty-five minutes of drilling, water gushed out of the depths of the earth at almost the same spot that had been tried before.

Mr. Graham witnessed this scene and remembers the blue-clad men holding hands to pray and the water later springing from the earth. He said:

> The picture is still very vivid in my mind and it has changed my attitude towards God and prayer. Now when I pray, I do so confidently because I know God is real. I never start any venture without committing it to the Lord.

With the potable water now available, guinea worm and yaws were eradicated within a year. The people are now healthy enough to work on their farms and are interested in community work. The improvement in their health and its effect on their lives is so striking that they have developed confidence in God and also in the World Vision program.

The story of Afranguah has spread to neighboring villages, and so great is the impact on these villages that they all look up to the chief and people for advice, inspiration and direction. To quote Mr. Graham on this point:

> God has been kind to us and we have now become the eye of the district. Other villages, for example Odonase, Bando and Ekuhiakokodo, come to us for direction. Thanks to God and World Vision, our lives have really changed.

Conclusion

From the Old Testament, we learn that when the children of Israel were thirsting desperately for water in the desert, after their exodus from Egypt, God ordered their leader Moses to use his rod, to fetch water for their supply. God provided them water from a rock—as a miracle of mercy. God used Moses to perform a hydrogeological miracle, for without any heavy drilling equipment being available, the mere striking of the rock broke loose the aquifers, and released a stream of abundant water for the people to drink. This same God has given people knowledge and wisdom to design special drilling equipment that is being used to provide potable water to thousands of people around the world.

Steve M. Hilton, Vice President of the Conrad N. Hilton Foundation, put it this way in a personal communication dated March 9, 1993:

> Water is so important to life itself, as well as being central to human existence.

It is indeed a privilege for World Vision International to be involved in this exciting ministry of providing water to sustain life and health for thousands of poor, rural people in the Third World.

10
The healing congregation in whole-person ministry

E. Anthony Allen

Community-based organizing, consciousness raising, advocacy and self-help approaches may help an oppressed community move toward spiritual and social liberation.

To be effective, the church's mission to evangelize and serve must reflect accurate biblical teaching and promote human well-being. However, the dualistic or "either-or" stance in Western thought tends to separate religion and health. The church is called to be a healing community, with the poor as its priority. In order to do so, it needs to take an integrative or "both-and" view of human reality. This perspective, derived from Scripture, sees aspects of the person (body, mind, spirit, community relationships) held together in a dynamic tension of wholeness.

Creative efforts should seek to meet the totality of human needs by addressing the realities of the nature of the person as reflected in biblical theology and elaborated in scientific discovery. This would result in establishing a comprehensive primary health care program involving an approach that is *whole-person* in scope, oriented to *community participation* and involving the *congregation as a healing community*.

This strategy can be called community-based whole-person health. In Jamaica over the past twenty years, several churches in most denominations have established varieties of healing ministries based on this renewed vision. In this chapter, I will describe the approach of Bethel Baptist Church as an example of what one local congregation can do.

The Jamaican context

Socioeconomic conditions in Jamaica are harsh. For example, in 1991 per capita income was below US$400 and unemployment was 15.4 percent. Adequate health care is beyond the reach of many. When available, it involves unbearably long waits in the lines and on the lists of public clinics and hospitals.

Truly community-based, preventive health care remains inadequate despite significant strides over the past three decades. In fact, early work in proper health care is endangered by a lack of political will.

Unfortunately, community-based consciousness raising, advocacy and empowering are becoming increasingly rare. The legacy of slavery, colonialism and divisions of class and race, along with more recent political patronage and tribalism, has fragmented family and social structures. Religious denominationalism and American-influenced sectarianism also contribute to social disorganization.

More than 70 percent of Jamaican children are born out of wedlock. Women tend to be heads of households, with men being marginal. Internal and external migration have further split families and communities. Violence is a way of life in Jamaican ghettoes, increasingly involving unsupervised teenagers. Eight hundred people died by the gun during a year-long political campaign in 1980.

The financial dominance of a small white-brown commercial elite creates a color-class oppression by a minority seen only in South Africa and the Caribbean. Beyond this, external political and economic constraints imposed by First World bankers and worsened by inadequate local economic management have stifled social justice.

Health professionals and community workers have tended to inherit the authoritarian and condescending attitudes of the colonial system. Black self-hate from slavery undermines togetherness and solidarity. Furthermore, increasing North American values of materialism expressed in a "media colonialism" have undermined commitment to the poor, even in the church.

Indeed, the physical, emotional and spiritual suffering of the Jamaican and Caribbean poor calls for these brethren to be the priority of the church's ministry to the whole person. The whole gospel involves both preaching and healing. This is what Christ sent His disciples to do (Luke 9:1-2).

Community-based whole-person health ministry

In 1972, Bethel Baptist Church of Kingston, Jamaica, began a period of theological reflection and planning. The pastor and church council were concerned about having a meaningful outreach program that would minister to the whole person both within the church and in the wider community. The healing ministry began in 1974 as an evening activity, and in 1984 it became established on a full-time basis.

The philosophy and program is basically a primary health care program with a *whole-person* approach, that is, having medical, mental health, pastoral and socioeconomic service components. It is *comprehensive;* within each of the above components are curative, rehabilitative and promotive-preventive aspects.

As a *community participation-based* program, the target populations are clients drawn from the public using the church's holistic health center, an under-served inner city community called Ambrook Lane, and the local congregation. As a *congregation-sponsored* program, Bethel Baptist Church oversees the ministry and more than fifty members contribute their time to this ministry.

Curative Services

The Bethel Healing Center (also called the Whole-Person Healing Center) is the main locus of full-time curative services. It consists of medical and mental health facilities along with pastoral and prayer ministries. Each day the healing center begins with devotions in which patients and staff invite God's presence and activity.

157

Patients see the nurse-interviewer, who listens to complaints and explains the purpose and philosophy of the Center. After using a holistic assessment questionnaire to help the client to share about problems in all dimensions of life, the nurse performs medical screening. With the patient's consent, the nurse may work with a theological student and a lay person to provide basic mental health and pastoral counseling and pray for healing. A holistic reassessment is carried out on second or third visits of patients.

Next, as needed, clients go to general practitioners and psychological counselors for pastoral counseling and prayer. These professionals may refer patients to the Center's social worker or part-time psychiatrist (the author) or, by special arrangement, to outside diagnostic and specialist hospital services. There is also a specialist and general practice evening clinic run by Baptist volunteer doctors, including those from the church.

Clients then purchase any prescriptions at reduced cost at the Center's pharmacy and pay a consultation fee based on ability to pay. Though contributions are welcomed, the counseling service is free.

At the healing center, patients receive prayer as well as a prescription. Beyond the prayers of all the staff are those of special prayer counselors from the congregation. A group of parishioners meets weekly to intercede for clients who ask for prayer. The group also prays for the empowering of staff and the resource needs of the ministry.

During 1990 to 1991, the full-time curative medical service had 5,162 patients. The counseling service had 930 clients making 1,324 visits. Use of both services has been growing continuously.

More than 90 percent of attendees are non-members of the church; more than 75 percent are non-Baptists. Though most come from urban areas surrounding Bethel, some clients come from rural areas. The ministry serves a wide constituency.

According to surveys, most medical patients find the service at the healing center very satisfactory. Reasons include the approach of the Center's staff and the combination of medical and spiritual care.[9]

Case study: Mary S.

Years before, Mary S. had heard about the Whole-Person Healing Center on regular visits to church services at Bethel. When her own doctors failed to help her, she decided to seek help at the Center.

> I started experimenting chest pains, nervousness, and weakness, and I lost a lot of weight, so much so that my husband became alarmed. He sent me to have a thorough check-up. I had blood tests and a chest x-ray, but nothing was found and the symptoms continued. Finally, I decided to try the Bethel clinic. I thought that since the doctors there are Christians, they might be better able to help.

Mrs. S. describes her visit to the clinic:

> I first went to the nurse, who asked me some questions. I remember she prayed with me and gave me some advice. Then I went in to see a doctor. It was a female doctor, and she was just as friendly. She encouraged me to talk and listened patiently. I shared with her about a very distressing problem I was having at home. A relative had come to live with us and was making my life miserable.

> I made two other visits to the clinic. The doctor helped me to see that my problem was caused by emotional stress, the tension in my home environment was not only a physical one.

> I found the clinic a place where people really cared. I felt free to share my problems, which I had not been able to do before. I used to keep everything inside of me because I have no close friends and my husband is very busy so there is no one to talk to. At the clinic, I found friends who listened and prayed. My situation is now changed. I am well again. I have regained the weight I lost, and the pains and nervousness have gone. I am so thankful.

Mrs. S. is now a volunteer worker at the clinic, passing along to others the help she received.

Case study: Angela P.

Angela P. valued the opportunity to receive counseling. She was referred to the Bethel Center counselor when she sought help in controlling her 14-year-old son. The 36-year-old mother of three had been separated from her husband for nine years. She explains,

> I was having a very hard time with my son Michael. He had serious behavioral problems. His father and I separated when he was five, and I think this had a bad effect on him. I tried my best with him, but I was not reaching him.

At the time that Ms. P. visited the counselor, she had not been in touch with her husband for years. The counselor suggested she contact him to discuss Michael's problems.

> I didn't take kindly to this suggestion at all, but eventually I decided to try it. As a result, Michael was able to see his father again. This seemed to help him; they developed a relationship which has strengthened to the point that Michael now lives with his father to attend school. He visits me on holidays and some weekends. He is much happier, and his behavior has improved.

Although her immediate problem was resolved, Ms. P. continues to see the counselor. Her regular sessions help her cope better with life.

> I still have many personal problems to work out since my separation and also other areas of my life. Talking one-to-one helps to clarify things for me and guides my decision making. I am particularly happy about the Christian aspect of the counseling given at Bethel. I remember that from my very first visit, and ever since that, the counselor prayed with me even before we started talking. I was very impressed with that.

Ms. P. is part of the church now and recommends counseling to others who have problems.

> Counseling has helped me cope with the pressure I face as a single mother and also with the difficulties of trying

to relate my faith to daily life. If I had counseling earlier, maybe my marriage could have been saved. I know counseling works.

Other clients have reported divine or miraculous healing. One woman's ovarian cyst disappeared, as confirmed by X-ray. A man well known in his village for his disability dramatically regained movement in his right arm. Other practical results of prayer, such as employment and housing, have been reported.

Individuals have also come to find new purpose and meaning in a commitment to Christ, and several have joined various congregations.

Rehabilitative Services

The church provides several opportunities for the rehabilitation of clients with socioeconomic, chronic physical and mental health problems. Offerings include skill training, craft production, literacy and sign language classes, and legal and other social services. Church members visit the sick and elderly shut-ins to offer prayer and support.

Bethel has become widely used in the Kingston community for its social rehabilitative opportunities. Hundreds of people have received skill training, remedial education and employment.

Five mentally ill persons have been in our rehabilitation program. Two such persons who had been homeless were able to join our staff. Most important, several no longer act out the social role of begging and being alien and disruptive. They have been integrated into the church and have become productive members of the fellowship.

Promotive and preventive services

The promotive and preventive services have become a major thrust of the Bethel healing ministry. In the healing center, medical and counseling clients participate in wholeness education. The congregation is educated by means of church worship bulletins. For the public at large, there is a letter-answering service in the island's main newspaper.

Twice a year there is a healing Sunday; God's healing activity and prayer are highlighted as a reminder to the congregation. The day includes a health fair for the public. Once a year health fair activities are extended into a health week. This includes immunization and wellness education as well as screening and education for such ailments as hypertension, diabetes, refractive errors, breast lumps and overweight. Prayer, counseling and referral are provided as appropriate.

Several preventive services are provided weekly for members by the healing center:

- For the congregation, there is first-aid training, health education, and family life and personal growth education. These activities include wellness awareness and are promoted through special interest groups such as youth fellowship, women's federation, men's brotherhood and Sunday school.

- Training in counseling is provided for deacons of the church as well as for 90 leaders of the church-sponsored Caring Teams. To each of these leaders a given number of church members are assigned for visitation, pastoral care, support, community building and early problem detection and referral.

- Special home health workers have been trained from the membership to visit and care for the sick who are elderly, confined or disabled.

- Couples and individuals from the laity are also trained to offer premarital counseling.

- Single adults and Marriage Enrichment groups carry out self-help educational and support activities.

- Other support activities include house prayer fellowships, intercessory prayer groups and telephone prayer chains.

- A keep-fit class run by the church is available to all.

Thus every member of the church, as well as the public, has access to some promotive and preventive healing activity.

The Ambrook Lane Community

Ambrook Lane is a low-income community of 500 to 600 residents located near the church. It has several problems typical of urban Third World cities. There is a sense of transience, fragmentation, normlessness and lack of formal organization.

The residents have health needs typical of the poor in Jamaica. These include the following:

- Untreated or inadequately treated common ailments of hypertension and diabetes
- Childcare problems, including under-nutrition, gastroenteritis, inadequate nursery care and early education
- Insect and rodent infestation, uncollected garbage
- Unemployment contributing to under-nutrition and inadequate access to health care
- Inadequate youth and sports activities
- Drug abuse
- Juvenile delinquency

In collaboration with residents, several promotive and preventive services have garnered community participation:

- Health activities including education, medical screening, child welfare and growth monitoring, first aid training, immunization, family planning, community health worker training as well as informal counseling in nutrition, hygiene and parenting
- Community self-help organization and advocacy in socioeconomic and spiritual areas, with the help of a community organizer
- Informal counseling and prayer sessions for problems such as drug abuse and child abuse

There is evidence that the initial apathy and resistance of the people of the Ambrook Lane community is being overcome.

- Aged and ill persons are being visited by community health workers.
- A holistic health promotion committee has been formed and community health action has been initiated, including health worker training, child welfare, family planning, community hygiene and nutrition and drama.
- Groups have cleared garbage, fixed pipes and completed a public bathroom.
- Representatives asked city authorities to improve community amenities.
- Residents organized Christmas trees, treats and outings for the children.
- Residents cleared the play area, gained permission to use nearby church grounds and formed a sports club.
- Some residents have begun backyard gardens.
- The community sponsors fund-raising activities.
- Individuals have started small businesses with government help.
- A sewing class for girls has been started and individuals have sought skill training and employment.
- A basic school has been built by residents, over 50 children enrolled and a Parent Teacher's Association formed. Mothers are helping to maintain facilities, and a resident has received training as a teacher.
- A Sunday school and monthly religious services cater to spiritual needs.
- Residents have begun accepting Christ and becoming part of his body.

In addition to the above, parents have demonstrated an increase in knowledge, attitudes and skills in caring for their children. This has been shown in their nutritional status and immunization rate.[1]

Natural community leaders have begun emerging. The self-esteem, self-discipline and self-reliance of community members have improved.

Case study: Monica J.

Monica J. has lived in Ambrook Lane for nine years. She is a twenty-two-year-old mother of three small children ranging from one to six years. What is life like in the Lane for Monica?

> Not very good. We have many problems, especially housing. Another problem is the lack of water and the surroundings in general are poor.

Monica J. worked as a voluntary health aide in the clinics, run fortnightly by Bethel in Ambrook Lane. Because of her interest and ability, the church sponsored her attendance at a six-month community health aide course. Among the skills learned were how to take blood pressure readings, temperatures and apply dressings. Monica gives voluntary help on clinic days; on other days she often gives help to community members who visit her home.

According to Monica, the clinic has made a big difference to mothers in Ambrook Lane.

> Some mothers do not like to go to clinics outside the community and many of them have big children who are not yet immunized. When the church clinic comes, they are willing to go there. Many children have been immunized and the adults get help with their medical problems and medication.

Monica, now a leader and caregiver, has gained a new direction in life. She is getting closer to making a commitment to Christ.

Administration

Several elements of the ministry's administrative style help promote its philosophy:

- Mutual consultations, case discussion session and overall case management responsibilities are arranged between staff of the various whole-person disciplines. This ensures integration and continuity of care.

- Congregation members volunteer as administrators and workers; more than 50 people serve at a given time. The full range of talents are used. The physician or professional counselor provides professional services. Others may give lay counseling to pre-marrieds, prepare drinks, make posters or provide transportation for sick visitation. Spiritual gifts in ministering and healing are also recognized. The congregation and its leaders are regularly informed of activities and involved in decision making.

- Patient participation in the healing center services is encouraged. They are involved in evaluation surveys and relevant suggestions are made.

- Twice yearly, there are staff retreats for spiritual inspiration, learning, and reviewing the ministry's philosophy and activities.

- Staff minister to one another in informal prayer groups and have group sharing sessions led by a chaplain/adviser.

- Despite the need for grants, financial self-help is pursued. Patients are discouraged from expecting totally free service. The church has begun an income generating program starting with a low-cost lunch service, a thrift shop and friends program.

A model for healing ministry?

Through consultations and primarily by example, the program at Bethel has influenced the setting up of whole-person health services within most denominations in Jamaica.

Copeland[2] reports that in the Kingston and St. Andrew metropolis alone there are at least 29 (mostly part-time) church-related clinics. In addition to volunteers, professional medical workers include 69 nurses, 31 physicians, six dentists, eight dental nurses and seven pharmacists. Some 72 percent of clinics use the whole-person model, involving counseling and prayer. Some 57 percent indicated some form of community involvement.[10] Clergy and other staff from these centers have come together to form a national Inter-Church Association of Health, Healing and Counseling Ministries (IA-HHCM).

It is vital to recognize that most healing ministries can function without doctors and professional counselors providing direct services. Nurses, physicians and counselors can train volunteer lay persons to do a tremendous amount of ministering through health education, screening and referral, first aid, home care, promoting healthy lifestyles, family life education marriage enrichment, sharing groups, lay counseling and prayer and visitation activities.

In the Jamaica Baptist Union, for example, more than 20 churches have been able to sustain services largely based on lay counselor and church health worker training programs. The IA-HHCM has been seeking to equip church members in a similar way.

Conclusion

The Bethel Baptist healing ministry has been described as an example of church-sponsored, community-based, whole-person health care—an unconventional model of health delivery. Alongside other such efforts in Jamaica, the Bethel work helps offset the distortions of Western thought on the church's and medical profession's view of the person and well-being.

The whole-person approach results in a much wider range of needs being met among client, community and congregation members than would occur in conventional approaches in medical care, community service or church-based ministry. Community-based organizing, consciousness raising, advocacy and self-help

167

approaches may be the start of the spiritual and social liberation of an oppressed community.

The ministry's multifaceted whole-person care and comprehensive primary health care emphasis is significantly aided by congregation sponsorship and involvement. Several opportunities are provided for those in the congregation, both professionals and non-professionals, to employ their many and various talents and gifts including those given by the Holy Spirit.

Whole-person healing and thus true mission and evangelization is possible because it can involve the priesthood of all believers.

Many other Jamaican churches (often independently) have developed healing ministries with varying components of the community-based whole-person health model. This seems to support the viability of this renewed understanding of the church's ministry.

What if every local church in the Caribbean were to start at least basic nonprofessional whole-person promotion activities? What if they would recruit and train two lay community health workers and two lay counselors who would integrate whole-person work into their evangelism and local mission outreach? What if every denomination would send whole-person health-related professionals to urban ghettoes, rural villages and to other needy oppressed countries? Then we would be much further on our way to achieving both "health for all by the year 2000" and "the whole church taking the whole gospel to the whole world."

Notes

1   Allen, E.A. "Ministering Through Medicine, Counseling and Prayer—a Congregation's Health and Healing Ministry." Unpublished paper, 1989.

2   Copeland, S. "An Analysis of Church Related Clinics in Kingston and St. Andrew and Their Contribution to Healthcare Delivery." Kingston: Unpublished Dissertation. University of the West Indies, 1992.

Further reading

Allen, David F. "Whole-Person Care: The Ethical Responsibility of the Physician." *Whole-Person Medicine.* Edited by David F. Allen, 41-42. Downer's Grove: InterVarsity Press, 1980.

Anderson, Robert G. "A Model for Liaison with Clergy." *Hospital & Community Psychiatry.* 29, 800-802, 1978.

Anderson, Robert G. "The Role of the Church in the Community-Based Care of the Chronically Mentally Disabled: Reclaiming an Historic Ministry." *Pastoral Psychology,* 28, 38-52, 1979.

Griffith, Ezra E.H., et al. "Possession, Prayer, and Testimony. " *Psychiatry,* 43, 120-128, 1980.

Griffith, Ezra E.H., et al. "An Analysis of the Therapeutic Elements in a Black Church Service." *Hospital and Community Psychiatry,* 35, 464-496, 1984.

Kelsey, Morton T. *Healing and Christianity.* London: S.C.M., 1973.

Lambourne, R.A. *Community Church and Healing.* London: Darton, Longman & Todd, 1963.

Tournier, Paul. *A Doctor's Casebook in the Light of the Bible.* London: S.C.M. Press, 1973.

11

Primary health care in an industrialized country

Peter A. Boelens

To promote any degree of community health,
one must attack the root problems of poverty.
Without meaningful and adequate employment,
a family is deprived of financial resources, hope
and self-worth.

In recent years there has been a renewed interest on the part of the Christian medical establishment in the United States in reaching out through primary health care to the poor, under-served, and marginalized in the United States. A variety of approaches are being applied. Some draw from the experiences of community health development programs in nonindustrialized countries. My personal practice experiences in both post-war South Korea and in the Mississippi Delta provide the basis for the following primary health care discussions.

I began my medical missionary career as a generalist with a strong commitment to community health and prevention. This was in the early 1960s when people in the health care system could only think of hospitals and hospital-based care. The impetus for my approach came from the Scriptures. My life had been changed through a personal encounter with Jesus Christ during my internship at Cook County Hospital in Chicago, Illinois. I couldn't read enough of the Scriptures. One verse took on special meaning:

> Jesus went through all the towns and villages, teaching
> in their synagogues, preaching the good news of the
> kingdom, and healing every disease and sickness
> (Matthew 9:35).

This became my call to community health. It described a blend of curative medicine, preventive care, health teaching and the gospel of Jesus Christ. I wanted to pattern my medical career after that of the Great Physician.

From Korea to the Mississippi Delta

My first field of service was post-war South Korea. As a physician working in the slums of Seoul, country villages and the islands off Inchon, I soon discovered that although medical treatment was what people wanted from a physician, education in disease prevention was what they needed most and what would improve their health to the greatest extent. This was vividly portrayed through the experience of our Christian paramedic-community health worker on these islands. The people in this area were steeped in animism and superstition. Only when our health worker was able to make inroads through medical care were the minds of the people opened to education and to the gospel. It was then that meaningful change took place in attitudes, health and spiritual belief, and later in economic realities.

My experience in Korea enabled me to return to the United States with an interest in two specialities I would not have considered earlier—pediatrics and public health. After residencies in both, I felt God was leading me to put these new skills to practice in the Delta of Mississippi.

The Delta is still one of the poorest regions in the United States. It is like a Third World country within the First World. In the early 1970s, it was similar in many ways to post-war Korea. Respiratory illnesses, diarrhea, pneumonia, meningitis, and premature birth were the most common health problems. Forty-eight percent of families lived under the federal poverty level, housing was substandard and unemployment reached 22 percent. Functional illiteracy was 20 percent.

About 70 percent of the population was black. Over 20 percent of pregnant women were in the high-risk category, and most did not receive prenatal care. All of these factors contributed to an infant mortality rate twice the national average. It also meant that 15 percent of deliveries at the charity hospital resulted in premature or low birth-weight infants.

Cary Christian Health Center

In 1971, through the Luke Society, a primary care clinic was established in Cary, Mississippi: Cary Christian Health Center. But it soon became clear that opening a primary care clinic in the Delta did not guarantee that the multifaceted problems of poverty would be addressed. Often the patients who needed the services most never made it to the clinic. Those who did make their clinic visits often needed more than curative medical care. We needed to establish an outreach program to bring these high-risk patients into the health care system and also meet their diverse needs.

The need for this outreach service was demonstrated to me in a very graphic way. I was examining a young child with heat rash and secondary infection on a humid Mississippi summer day. The case was so severe that I asked one of our nurses to make a home visit. She discovered that the family was living in a small trailer without air conditioning or running water. In fact, the entire community was without water.

The community had been depending on a well that was now dry. We notified the health authorities, who brought in trucks with potable water. We also mobilized the community and, with the assistance of outside resources, connected this community of about 50 homes to the nearby city's water supply. Through the whole process, the community not only received water but also experienced a sense of accomplishment and satisfaction. The incident emphasized that it is often impossible to adequately care for patients without knowing the constraints under which they live. After this experience, we began including regular community and home visits as a vital part of our clinic services.

On these home visits, we became acquainted with the serious problem of inadequate housing. Often I treated children and infants for rat bites they received while sleeping. To provide decent housing, skilled volunteers from churches were recruited to repair old homes and build new ones. This proved to be a very powerful outward manifestation of the love and concern Jesus Christ had for the poor and oppressed. Many community people were so touched by these acts of mercy that all they could do was cry.

But there were still more needs to be met. Parents frequently told me in the clinic that they were not sending their children to school because the children lacked shoes and adequate clothing. It became clear that a store was needed where residents could purchase clothing, shoes, appliances and other household items at a very nominal cost. We established a thrift shop that sold used items at a low price. This gave mothers the opportunity to purchase these items and provide for their families while maintaining their dignity.

Perhaps one of the most depressing and frustrating clinic experiences for me was in dealing with mothers who had minimal parenting skills. In many instances children were abused through neglect. They had little if any stimulation from the mother and as a result suffered from environmental retardation.

The ministry of the Cary Christian Health Center began to provide these mothers with the skills they needed through classes specifically designed for them. Some women who attended these classes were motivated and caught a vision for their community. Some went on to receive additional training at the Center. Several became lay community health advisers. They visited homes of mothers with newborns, taught about health in their churches, in local factories, and in their neighborhoods.

An important concomitant effect that occurred among the health advisers was that they gained a sense of self-worth. In the process, some saw opportunities for a career and personal betterment that they had never seen before. Many of these women are now enrolled in college courses. Several are presently in training for nursing degrees. One young mother is committed to returning to work as a nurse in the health center that was instrumental in expanding her vision.

As our experience at the Cary Christian Health Center demonstrates, to promote any degree of health, it is necessary to attack the root problems of poverty. However, the most difficult problem to address, in my experience, has been the lack of meaningful and adequate employment. Without this, families are deprived not only of financial resources but also of hope and self-worth.

When I first arrived in the Delta, I went to worship in a black church. After the service I stepped outside to talk to a group of men. I asked the question, "If you could have anything you wanted, what would it be?" The answer came quickly. "We need jobs. We do not want to send our young people to Chicago or Detroit. We want work here."

To my dismay, we were unable to attract industry into the community and did not succeed in our attempts to initiate businesses ourselves. Our best alternative is to provide apprenticeship training programs in which young people from the community are brought together with volunteers from around the country in various building projects. These young people are taught skills and good work habits. They are prepared in the community but they move out of the community and find jobs elsewhere.

One of these young men is Phil. He started out as a carpentry apprentice under our work program. He continued working at our health center for a short time. Later, we were able to help him find a job with a lumber company in a nearby town. He started by building dog houses. Phil is now head of the company's home truss construction department.

Phil, through his association with our health center, also grew spiritually. There can be no genuine change in a life unless the individual is touched by Jesus Christ. Many of the problems we saw were rooted in spiritual and psychosocial ill health. The antidote is the gospel of Jesus Christ presented to people in a culturally relevant way. Early on, we began offering Bible classes at the Center for both children and adults. As the attendees came into a personal relationship with Christ and began to grow spiritually, they became teachers themselves. Today, the Center's spiritual program is a growing and vital outreach directed by two people from the community whose lives were changed by it in the early days.

As I look back at the history of the Cary Christian Health Center, I see the spiritual growth of community members as one of two major accomplishments. Programs are only as good as the people who operate them. The program at Cary Christian Center has brought together a cadre of committed local Christians addressing the needs of the poor. And more than this, it has brought about reconciliation. Whites and blacks now work together to bring about change in their community.

The other major accomplishment is that the Cary Christian Health Center has become independent of my direction. It stands on its own as a viable community organization with its own board of directors and support base. All of us in health and development hope to see organizations owned and operated by members of the community that address the whole-person need of that community.

The U.S. context

The Cary Christian Health Center is one example of a Christian community health program in the United states. What is its significance as we view the country as a whole?

Presently the United States is doing some soul-searching in regard to its health care system. For those who can afford to pay, the United States has the best system in the world. The problem is that 35 million people have no financial access into this system. Some 14 million pregnant women (one out of four) are uninsured. Most of these women do not receive adequate prenatal care. As a result, significant numbers give birth to high-risk infants. Adequate prenatal care costs only about $660 per pregnancy. High-risk infants are often cared for in neonatal intensive care units at the cost of $1,000 per day.

Under the current system, technology is worshiped and prevention receives little attention or funding. A graphic illustration is that only 40 percent of preschool children in most states are fully immunized. (China succeeds in immunizing 95 percent of its children.)

At the same time as the U.S.A. is being confronted with these problems, we are also seeing a renewed interest among members of the U.S. medical establishment in defining the spiritual factors that affect health.[1,2] Studies show that hypertension appears to be mitigated by religion, and the risk of dying from heart disease is much less for men who attend church weekly.[3] The risk of dying from heart disease among women is about twice as high among infrequent church attendees as compared to those who attend church weekly. Other studies demonstrate that drug abuse is related to absence of religious commitment in a person's life. Also, individuals who regard God as a source of strength and comfort and attend religious services frequently are much less depressed.[4] Further, individuals in intensive care units who received daily intercessory prayer had much fewer life-threatening events and complications even when they did not realize that they were being prayed for.[5]

Further, this new respect for the positive effects of religion on health among members of the U.S. medical establishment is accompanied by a resurgence of a sense of responsibility to one's neighbor. Voluntarism is increasing among charitable organizations nationwide. More and more individuals are interested in addressing the needs of the poor in their communities.

For example, a 1991 national meeting of the (U.S.) Christian Medical & Dental Society that focused on health care to the poor was one of their best-attended recent conferences. More than 100 physicians made commitments to investigate the needs of the poor in their communities. As a result, a variety of new programs have sprung up around the country. The U.S.A. is experiencing a time of great need; it is encouraging to see Christians addressing these needs.

Community orientation, spiritual dynamic

Most of these programs, however, are based on a medical model of care and address the immediate curative health needs of the poor.

We have already explained that medical care embraces only one aspect of health. What we need is medical care with a community orientation and a spiritual dynamic.

This community orientation is not a new concept. It was first proposed by John B. Grant in the 1920s, developed by Sidney L. Kark in Israel[6] and recently given renewed emphasis by Mullen in the New England Journal of Medicine[7] and Madison in the Journal of the American Medical Association.[8] It is described and promoted under the title of community-oriented primary care. The proposal is based on the concept we have discussed, that personal medical care is only one of several determinants of health. There are many others, such as economic, environmental and cultural.

Thus we need a method to appraise community needs through soliciting the concerns, opinions and observations of community members. Programs need to be developed addressing these needs with a periodic evaluation of their effectiveness. This is what has been done at Cary. This is what is meant by community-oriented primary care, which is a continuous, dynamic process.

However, the approach described in the scientific literature lacks a spiritual dimension. It is, therefore, incapable of delivering holistic or total person care. We need to incorporate the spiritual dimension if we are truly to have a significant effect in the lives of people and communities. The church, as a body of believers, holds the key in providing the poor and marginalized with this total person care.

In order to facilitate this community-oriented primary care, which adds a spiritual component to existing medical models of care for the poor, the Luke Society is providing funding and consultation for the development of these outreaches. In doing this, the local body of believers plays a vital and strategic role in the health of a community.

To minister to the total person's need within the context of a community requires a multifaceted approach and a multidisciplinary team. A physician, no matter how talented and energetic, cannot do it all. Nor can we expect to meet all needs by adding professionals; the cost would be prohibitive. We must incorporate a broad spectrum of personnel and involve the people of the community themselves. Then we have a much greater chance for success in improving health.

An approach that works

I can personally attest that this approach works. At Cary Christian Health Center, we trained lay health personnel from churches in Sharkey and Issaquena Counties to provide health education, visit pregnant women and do follow-up home visits on newborns. In 1992 these lay home visitors made 3,106 home visits with minority pregnant women and mothers with newborns. Through their efforts, an astounding 70 percent of the high-risk population was brought into the health care system and received intensive follow-up care.

The home visits had a measurable impact. Statistics from Mississippi's Department of Health reveal that Sharkey and Issaquena are the only two counties in Mississippi where the five-year average infant mortality rate among blacks is markedly lower than among whites. We are presently in the process of linking death and birth certificates for the infants who died during these five years to see if they were within the system of care and if the data is statistically valid.

To equip these lay health workers, educational modules have been developed on a variety of topics. The most recent teaches lay health workers how to identify spiritual needs and provide spiritual assistance. This new curriculum is presently being field-tested in both rural and urban settings in the United States.

The lay health workers also become the built-in mechanism for soliciting concerns, opinions, and observations from the community. They provide a continuous source of feedback on program effectiveness at the grass-roots level. Much more, their involvement shows that the community can take responsibility for corporate as well as individual health. Rather than being spectators, community members have become participants.

At times the problems of rural and urban poverty in indus-trialized societies may seem insurmountable. But, as we have illustrated, a difference is being made by God's people in these settings. An effective strategy is being implemented. People are receiving care, lives are being changed and the church of Jesus Christ is growing.

Challenges ahead

This does not mean that we have arrived. There are still great challenges confronting us as Christian health care professionals. Let me list a few:[9]

- The grass-roots involvement of health care professionals reaching out to the poor in their communities needs to continue and expand. Through the efforts of some professionals, the underinsured are being brought into the system and the poor are receiving quality care within a spiritual context. But the needs are still great. Through conferences, articles, and face-to-face discussion, we need to encourage other Christian health care professionals to become involved by highlighting the effectiveness and value of this type of ministry.

- We need to reach out to students in the health professions and involve and encourage them to participate in this ministry to the marginalized. We also need to work with these students to remove barriers such as high educational debt burdens which prevent a ministry among the poor.

- We need to move beyond the medical model of providing care for sick people toward a preventive model which includes community involvement. This is key. Preventive care is less expensive and often more effective, particularly when individuals take responsibility for their own health and when health is addressed in the context of their community.

- As health professionals, we realize that many of our patients' physical problems are directly related to spiritual ill health. Recent articles have documented the important link between spiritual and physical wellness. But we often do not have the time to address spiritual needs.

- The challenge for professional caregivers is to link with and support a variety of nonprofessional caregivers so that people are reached as total persons within the context of their own communities and families and across racial and ethnic boundaries. When the church is also brought into the linkage, God's kingdom is advanced on earth.

- We need to cooperate with one another and enlist the cooperation of other health care organizations and agencies in focusing on meeting the needs of the poor. It is a sad commentary that people in Russia and East Europe are bewildered at the competitive spirit among Christian organizations from the West who have come to minister. It seems some are more interested in carving out turf than in seeing needs met. We need to pray for ourselves and for other Christian leaders, that we keep our eyes on Jesus Christ while we work together in bringing God's healing to those who are hurting. The focus of the ministry should be on improving the total-person health of the poor and suffering in Jesus' name, not on who is doing what or which activities will bring funding.

- Those of us involved at the grass-roots level need to share our ideas and voice our concerns at the county, state and national levels. We need Christians working at all levels of society. And if those Christians can speak from personal ministry experience, it will be a much more powerful testimony.

We can thank God for a cadre of Christian health professionals who are leading the way through example and servanthood. They are paving the road for a new generation of leaders. We need to develop those leaders who, through the Spirit of God, have a burning zeal to serve both their Lord and their neighbor. It is this type of servant leadership which our industrialized societies so desperately need—and which God demonstrated through the life of his Son who went from village to village, preaching, teaching, and healing.

Notes

1   Larson D., Larson S. "Clinical Religious Research." *Christian Medical and Dental Society Journal,* 1992; Vol. 23, No.2.

2   Levin J.S., Shiller P.L. "Is There a Religious Factor in Health?" *Journal of Religion and Health,* 1987; 26(1): 9-35.

3   Comstock G.W., Partrige K.B. "Church Attendance and Health." *Journal of Chronic Disease,* 1972; 25:665-672.

4   Gartner J., Larson D.B., Allen G. "Religious Commitment and Mental Health: A Review of the Empirical Literature." *Journal of Psychology and Theology,* 1991; 19, (1): 6-25.

5   Byrd R.B. "Positive Therapeutic Effects of Intercessory Prayer in a Coronary Care Unit Population." *Southern Medical Journal,* 1988; 81:826-829.

6   Kark S. *The Practice of Community-Oriented Primary Health Care.* New York: Appleton-Century-Crafts, 1981.

7   Mullan F. "Community-Oriented Primary Care." *Journal of the American Medical Association,* 1983; 249, 10:1279-82.

8   Madison, D.l. "The Case for Community-Oriented Primary Care." *New England Journal of Medicine,* 1982; 307:1076-8.

9   Boelens P.A. "New Direction for Health Care in the 90s: A Christian Challenge." *Christian Medical & Dental Society Journal,* 1993; Vol. 24, No. 2.

12

Health care and indigenous people

Annette de Fortín

> Hear their petitions to their god, as they prayed;
> and this was the plea of their hearts: "O you,
> beauty of the day! You, Hurricane; you, Heart of
> the Sky and the Earth! You, conferrer of the
> riches, and conferrer of the daughters and sons!
> Turn toward us your glory and your richness;
> grant to my children and my subjects life and
> advancement; may those who are to feed and
> maintain you multiply and grow, those who
> invoke you on the roads, in ravines, under the
> trees, under the reeds. . . ."   —Popol Vuh

For more than 17 years, World Vision Guatemala has developed part of its ministry among the indigenous population. These people have several disadvantages in relation to the Ladino population in Guatemala. For historical reasons, they are settled in the worst land of the country, they have little government support and, in general, less access to the country's possibilities and resources. We work with more than 120 indigenous communities. Among them are the Cackchiquel, Kekchi, Quiché, Mam and Chortí groups.

The work has not been easy, due to a lack of knowledge about their cultures and significant language barriers. From the Christian point of view, there is a great gap: evangelism strategies promoted by the church lack an understanding of Mayan theology.

We have used several strategies for ministry among these people. These include:

- Doing anthropological studies to better understand specific cultures
- Hiring indigenous staff to work in the projects to enhance communication and provide acompaniment to the communities
- Using educational and awareness processes to preserve indigenous knowledge, feeling and identity
- Hiring personnel with a strong Christian commitment so they can develop a significant Christian presence and promote the church's holistic mission

Of all the indigenous groups, the Mam group is one of the most isolated and with the least opportunities. Seven years ago, we initiated a relationship with several Mam communities in the municipality of San Juan Atitán in the state of Huehuetenango. In this chapter, we discuss three stages in the relationship between World Vision and the Mam communities.

As an organization, we thank God for giving us the opportunity of growing along with communities on the margin. We thank God for the daily satisfaction of seeing how much living conditions have improved for our fellow human beings who have endured subhuman conditions for much too long.

Good news

News travels fast in small indigenous communities. Eight years ago, one man heard of an organization that could help his community. He quickly told this to the community leaders who, considering their difficult living situation, decided to find the organization. The leaders from Tuiscap, a village of San Juan Atitán, asked Lorenzo García to go for them. He had visited Guatemala City several times. He was one of the few in the community who could read and write and who also spoke Spanish.

Lorenzo descended to the main road. As he walked, he admired the stupendous view of mountain ranges, rivers and the many other natural riches in this corner of Guatemala. After a two-hour walk and a six-hour bus trip, he arrived in the big city. All he had with him were a few pennies, a piece of paper with the name "World Vision" on it, and the certainty that he would find the support his community so badly needed. He walked through the city for two days, inquiring of people who crossed his path. He saw a sign on a building and could hardly believe it: he had finally found the office.

Initial contact

The Guatemala office of World Vision (WV) usually establishes contact with communities by looking at the main needs of the people. We were dismayed at the living conditions that socioeconomic research revealed. Housing was poor—only one room with little or no furniture, no latrines, and no water. This affected the people's health, especially that of the children and women. The farming land was insufficient and of bad quality. Traditional farming techniques would not permit proper production levels.

This situation forced the people to seek other work sources, making migration for short periods a common way of life. Throughout the year, people travel from San Juan Atitán to Guatemala's southern coast seeking work on the big plantations there. Each trip lasts about three months. The entire family migrates together and takes part in the coffee harvest.

Due to subhuman living conditions in these plantations, the indigenous people of San Juan Atitán contract local diseases such as malaria and a type of tropical fever. Gastrointestinal illnesses and other diseases spread easily in crowded buildings with poor sanitary conditions. The first victims are the children, who sometimes do not survive.

First stage of World Vision's support

The first step the local committee took in cooperation with World Vision's technical team was to address the main problems found by the preliminary investigation. Support to the Tuiscap village began with the On Bil Cye Cual child sponsorship project. Components included health programs, housing improvement, formal education and nonformal education.

Health and Nutrition

A nutritional recovery program focused on the children with the greatest deficiencies. The other children of school age were given a nutritional supplement. WV staff worked with the mothers, teaching them to prepare balanced meals.

A family garden program was introduced due to the limited variety of foods being grown in the region. At first, the people cultivated a collective garden, where they learned special farming techniques for the steep and rocky ground. They learned to grow radishes, cauliflower, potatoes and other crops.

A community doctor was hired to visit seven of the 21 communities of San Juan Atitán. He was responsible for training health monitors and midwives in hygiene, promotion of immunization and control of diarrheal diseases.

The communities did not have piped water to their homes, but their mountainous area had many water sources. Water was piped to the homes in a combined effort of WV, CARE and the community people.

Housing

Materials were supplied for roof and wall improvement to make the existing houses adequate. The labor was provided by the community. The work was accompanied by a health education process.

Formal Education

Even though the community has had a school for ten years, the level of illiteracy was very high; in the women it was nearly 95 percent. The WV facilitators encouraged the parents to send their children to school. Also, WV gave school supplies and paid for enrollment of all school-age children.

Nonformal Education

All parents received technical orientation to improve their crops. There was a program for reforestation and protection of natural resources. In addition, the community's Christian leaders were trained.

Second stage of World Vision's support

After three years of working in San Juan Atitán, we were present in seven communities and could identify many accomplishments:

- The health care program continued
- Most children had access to education
- Children received Christian education with material written in Mam, the indigenous language
- Mothers were cultivating family gardens
- Fathers were learning new agricultural techniques
- Organization and participation increased in each community

Toward the end of 1989, Guatemala suffered a measles epidemic that had high mortality rates among children. For three months, the disease killed some 290 people each month in San Juan Atitán. This made us realize that the child sponsorship program needed to expand to everyone in the supported communities. We moved toward a project with a holistic focus.

We proposed to the project committees of the seven supported communities that they combine their efforts. We worked with them to develop a program based on their needs and valuing their traditional practices, knowledge and customs. The following elements were included:

Adding preventive aspects; a permanent health unit

Preventive actions had been developed partially through health monitors. There was one monitor per community, but they did not have the necessary health training. The doctor (only one for the entire supported population of about 20,000) visited by turns the people of the seven communities, mainly for curative attention. Unfortunately, access to the communities was difficult, and the territorial expanse and population was too vast for one doctor to provide all the support needed.

We suggested to the communities of the seven projects to provide operating costs for a permanent health unit to provide curative attention, health promotion, prevention and rehabilitation.

The unit was built in a strategically positioned community. It had facilities for training, including a demonstration area. It includes two small rooms for bed confinement, a laboratory and equipment for dental care.

Priority: infant-maternal care

In San Juan Atitán, the infant-maternal population includes more than 60 percent of the inhabitants. The socioeconomic conditions and the community's structure strongly affect children and women, but the most affected are children under five years of age (mainly in regard to nutritional status and infectious illnesses).

Many children have low birth weight; 50 percent of them are born weighing less than five pounds. Many women die for causes related to pregnancy, due to lack of pregnancy control and poor childbirth and postpartum care.

At first, we thought the men of these communities would oppose this effort. The privileged would be the children and women; in some groups of our society, men are considered to be the fundamental work force in the family. But the Mam indigenous people view the family in a holistic way. This facilitated support for focusing attention on the infant-maternal group.

Most of the people readily accept health actions such as immunization, which is sometimes even demanded. The training of monitors and midwives has met with great success. We worked with UNICEF to develop appropriate educational methods. Eight midwives have been fully trained, but more need to be brought into the program. (See box, "Midwives and Doctors.")

Control of illnesses

Due to a cholera epidemic in 1992, groups were organized in each community consisting of a network of health monitors responsible for epidemiologic vigilance. They were also trained to educate the mothers on diarrhea prevention and oral rehydration treatment.

Further, in regard to the control of acute respiratory diseases, the monitors were taught how to manage cases and to support communities in implementing small pharmacies with basic medicines. The pharmacies were located in the project's headquarters or in the community's school. With the financial support these communities have, they acquire basic medicines and sell them at a low cost.

Health education

The health education program included a community doctor to visit the villages frequently, a permanent doctor in the health unit who also makes house calls, two nurses, five monitors and several midwives. The monitors and midwives are from San Juan Atitán. We preferred to work with them because they knew the conditions of their communities and could also speak the Mam dialect; most of the inhabitants are monolingual.

Through this program we attempted to better the people's self-esteem, retain health-related cultural knowledge and values, and foster health promotion and illness prevention. In short, we sought to help the people discover for themselves their health care responsibilities and also become aware of their rights before the state.

Community sanitation: water, latrines and home improvement

During this stage we introduced water to the homes, mostly from uncontaminated sources. But the water did not go through any purification treatment, so families boil it. We provided latrines for the houses of one community and are working on the others.

Home improvement is for sanitary reasons. Included are separating cooking spaces from sleeping spaces (to prevent smoke from causing respiratory infections and harming the development of fetuses), introducing improved wood-efficient stoves and

---

Midwives and doctors

In August 1994, World Vision's child health care unit began a training course for the midwives of San Juan Atitán, in order to train them to detect at-risk cases and also to improve linkages with this important region of San Juan.

"The main causes of mother mortality in San Juan Atitán are delivery and post-delivery infections," says Dr. Edwin Rodas of the children's health care center. "The main cause of infection is the lack of hygiene on the part of the midwives when they help the mothers. The patients lie on the floor, which usually is a dirt floor. Most of the time the only thing between the mother and the just-born and the dirt floor are some rags that are usually dirty. Hence, the midwives were motivated to improve their techniques".

"In the training, new hygienic alternatives were used and the midwives were motivated to use them," he continues. "They learned to wash their hands, cut their nails, use clean towels and boiled water, receive the baby in an hygienic way, cut the umbilical cord with a clean and sterilized knife, and so on."

The training was not an unilateral learning process but rather a time to exchange experiences between the doctors of the unit and the midwives. "The purpose was not to teach them what we know, but rather to learn from each other" says Dr. Rodas. "Even the most experienced midwives shared what they knew with the least experienced, and together we drew our own conclusions. We also shared with them the experience of other areas. A group of midwives from Aguacatan arrived. Aguacatan is a county located in Huehuetenango. These women have already organized an association, hence, they have received more training."

One of the most important accomplishments was to gather sixty of the seventy midwives in San Juan. From these, fifty-six obtained a diploma for attending the training, despite barriers of language and accessibility.

continued on next page

---

putting in cement floors (which reduces the frequency of gastrointestinal infections).

This process has recently been initiated. Only ten percent of homes in each community have been improved because the process is slow and costly. At least three more years will be needed to achieve 60 to 70 percent coverage in each community.

For home improvements, the organization donates the materials and the community provides the labor. This is done collectively according to their common practices. The community even gets together to build the future home of the couple whenever a marriage is planned.

continued from previous page

Another of the important accomplishments of this training was the unity gained in the exchange of experiences. Many of the communities are located far from the health care unit. Some of the women had to leave their community at dawn in order to attend the training on time. These women arrived earlier than the rest of the women and were able to talk and share with the staff of the unit. This transformed the event into a place to make friends. *(One photo on the cover of this book was taken at a midwife training event. —Ed.)*

World Vision has supported the midwives in order to improve the relation between doctors and midwives. Many doctors reject the practice of the midwives. Many midwives do not trust the practices of modern medicine and Western culture.

At the end of the session, the midwives requested some follow-up training. "This shows that we have gained credibility among the people of a traditional culture" says Dr. Rodas. "Now the midwives meet at the unit every Friday to share their experiences and to learn new techniques from the doctors. They also refer their pre-natal care patients to the unit in order to provide them with vitamins and tetanus inoculations."

Another example of the credibility gained is that now the midwives trust the doctors of the unit. In the past, when the midwives had problems with a delivery, they would call the doctor of the unit but did not wait for him because they were afraid to be scolded or treated unkindly. After this training, the midwives wait for the doctor and solve the problem together.

by Rubén Cabrera
World Vision Guatemala

A health recovery program: attention at three levels

Through this program, specific health concerns are addressed, as appropriate, in the community, at program headquarters and by case references to state hospital. All malnutrition cases were detected and supplementary feeding was given to restore normal weight for size. As the health monitors became able to resolve basic problems such as the control of diarrhea-related illnesses, they received essential medicines. Subsequently, they began to identify and resolve cases of children with special needs such as heart problems, deformities or problems that required surgery. The health unit has become a special element for the treatment of these cases and is well coordinated with the public health department and many major hospitals.

In general, the health monitors detect exceptional cases and refer them to the unit's doctor, and they try to convince the parents to allow their children to receive the proper medical treatment. Many times the treatment cannot be provided within the community and the parent's authorization is needed for the child to attend a hospital. Since most parents have never traveled to a big city, the monitors accompany them and translate for them. (See box, "Special help for Ana.")

Special help for Ana

Ana Diaz Domingo is an 18-year-old girl from San Juan Atitán. Like most of her older sisters, she began to help her mother at an early age, taking care of her brothers and tending to the house chores such as cooking and cleaning. This situation prevented Ana from going to school.

One day Ana realized that something strange was happening to her belly in the way it looked. Desperate, she told her parents about it. They took her to the children's health care center supported by World Vision. Dr. Edwin Rosas, after seeing Ana thought she was only pregnant. Ana's belly looked like that of a lady who had been pregnant for four months. But Ana's parents told the doctor that despite her age, Ana did not have a husband. (In San Juan most girls of this age already have a couple of kids.)

Dr. Rosas then continued his checkup and felt a mass of flesh. He sent Ana to the general hospital in Guatemala's capital city for a more detailed exam since the health center lacked the equipment needed. The girl traveled with her father, Mr. Manuel Diaz, and was admitted to the general hospital where an upper and lower abdominal tomography was taken.

The tomography detected a mass in one ovary. It was removed by surgery, but it tested positive for cancer. Ana had to be sent to the National Institute of Cancer (INCAN) to give her the treatment needed. At INCAN she underwent additional surgery and is receiving chemotherapy in hopes of curing the cancer.

Although Ana is not a one of World Vision's sponsored children, the health center took her under its care to provide treatment. As there are many special patients in San Juan Atitán, the communities which are part of the project in San Juan have joined efforts to contribute to a fund to provide emergency support in situations like Ana's. It was through this type of support that her travel, food and hotel expenses were paid. The expenses incurred at the general hospital and INCAN were also covered. (The first surgery was paid by the government since the hospital is a public service). The chemotherapy treatment is being paid for by the special patients' fund of the San Juan Atitán project.

by Rubén Cabrera
World Vision Guatemala

Regional organization

An increased emphasis on regional organization was initiated with the participation of seven communities.

Third stage of World Vision's support

In January 1993 we evaluated the intervention model we had used in San Juan Atitán. The use of the Primary Health Attention (PHA) strategy was affirmed, and the program components for essential sanitary assistance were clearly defined. We found three main aspects to be considered:

1. **Strategic issues** We outlined several issues that need to be addressed in properly implementing the PHA strategy.

Community organization and participation

Given the living conditions of these communities, it is necessary to strengthen community, local and group organization. They need to have the capability to take actions in order to confront the centers of the power of the government and other institutions. They need to be able to identify alternatives that will allow them to solve their problems. This is, in other words, the search for empowerment. Elements include:

- Stretching, growing, maturing
- Democratic decision making
- A permanent process
- Response to the community's genuine interests
- The search for the common good and solidarity
- Conscious, critical and active community participation
- A potential movement for social change that will protect the rights of all, based on community organizing, consciousness-raising and a process that will merge popular knowledge with scientific knowledge
- Capability to produce and acquire goods and services for and from the community. One effective means is creating roads to improve transportation.

193

Permanent health attention process

The community's social action and procurement process, in constant negotiation with other social entities, seeks the holistic satisfaction of needs for better living conditions. Elements include:

- Promotion of the community's critical awareness regarding the many determinants of holistic health
- Participative search for equality and justice
- Consideration of effectiveness and feasibility of actions
- Increased control by the community over the immediate conditions of their existence
- Participative evaluation and feedback
- Linkage with other social movements
- Systematization

Alternative technology

This involves gathering together alternative techniques, methods, knowledge, material and equipment to address needs and solve problems. Alternative technology can help improve the community's environment in accordance to their economic, social and cultural context. Elements include:

- Manageable costs
- Democratization of knowledge
- People identifying priority needs and taking responsibility for them
- Use of available resources
- Helping to improve ecological, economic and social resources
- No specialists required for implementation
- Scientific validity
- Subject to ongoing review

2. **Model for applying PHA** We developed an application model for Primary Health Attention (PHA). It ensures consistent

criteria in applying the PHA strategy. We refer to the model as we work with communities.

The PHA application model has enabled us to focus the work appropriately and achieve concrete results, such as:

- The base community's enhanced social organization
- Women's participation in decision making
- Immunization and environment sanitation coverage
- Control of diarrhea-related diseases

Attention to primary health care issues occurs at *four attention levels*: the household, the sector, the community and the group of communities. Embedded in the four attention levels are *three levels of community organization* for addressing health problems.

Household
The home is the basic place for the development of the PHA model. It is the family's center for health self-care. It makes possible the self-sufficiency necessary for the model. It also takes advantage of existing knowledge and practices. The key players in this level are the parents and other members of the family who must share the responsibility of the family's health care.

Sector
The sector consists of households grouped according to the community's criteria. It is the *first level of community organization* for addressing health problems. It is coordinated by a sector representative. The key players in this level are the sector representatives, sector leaders and leader mothers.

Community
The importance of the community lies in the capacity for social mobilization—the possibility for facing and solving deeper problems and producing a real impact in health conditions. It is the *second level of community organization* for addressing health problems. The key players are the committee members, sector leaders, health promoters and midwives.

Group of communities

World Vision Guatemala has adopted a community clustering strategy. A clustered project is formed with the participation of various communities that share common problems and contexts. The communities combine their efforts to solve problems. In the case of PHA, the group of communities is very important.

The coordinated communities group is the *third level of community organization*. It is represented by regional or district boards that strengthen the capacity to confront or negotiate with other social players such as formal authorities, private initiatives, and government organizations. Its functions are the same as the community level, extended to the group of communities.

This group facilitates the process of seeking justice in health-related areas. Also, it has potential for participating in the Local Health Systems (SILOS) concept.

3.   **Reflections about implementing the model**   To implement the model in the communities, we integrated the community into institutional processes. We built a team that includes community leaders, local and regional authorities, personnel from international organizations (OPS, UNICEF) and World Vision personnel.

World Vision is responsible for coordinating this team. To reach the proposed goals, World Vision's staff developed a process that includes strengthening institutional participation and using work-study methods in the continuous education process.

It is satisfying to see the good disposition and enthusiasm of the communities and of the local and institutional leaders. This has allowed the development of short-term, concrete actions that have improved the lives of people in the communities.

Conclusion

The working experience in holistic health care in San Juan Atitán has been complex but also enriching, both for the communities and for World Vision. We are enthusiastic and committed to continued learning. We want to improve the use of the mentioned model. It is a good reference point for work on holistic health.

We have begun to systematize some important processes that may help improve our effectiveness. We soon hope to evaluate formally the impact of our holistic health work. But we can already mention some definite results:

Community participation and organization
We aim to strengthen organizations such as community and regional committees and local interest groups. Assemblies and regional boards may include representatives from each community. The people are highly involved in program development.

Improved health status
Direct health care services to the communities have produced good results. For example:

- Immunization coverage has increased to 85 percent.

- Infant mortality has decreased.

- Infant malnutrition has been reduced; all children receive nutritional care. Growth and development monitoring is more systematic.

- The people consume a variety of foods that they did not grow or eat in the past. There are vegetable gardens and medicinal herb gardens.

- Most medical care is provided at the project's health care unit.

- Supported communities contribute to programs for latrines, home improvement and water supply.

Trained personnel
The communities contribute trained personnel, plus several people are in the process of being trained.

- Our goal is to train people from the communities who will progressively take over the positions in the project. For this reason, we have identified trained health promoters, monitors and midwives to promote health attention and disease prevention activities. People with problems they cannot resolve are referred to the health unit.

- Some Christian leaders are involved in program and training components related to holistic mission and holistic health care.

Research, Bibles

Two research projects were carried out, one on women's participation and the other on the status of the Mam church. This was done in coordination with the Evangelical Service for Latin America (SEPAL). Working with SEPAL, WV also supported the printing of 10,000 Bibles in Mam. Some of these Bibles will be used in teaching new readers.

Economic development and education

In relation to other transforming development programs, economic activities have started that seek to make it unnecessary for the people to migrate for work on coffee plantations. As we have seen, migration affects the health of entire families but mainly that of women and children.

Education programs have been reinforced, and some special programs for children under 5 have been created. In coordination with UNICEF and Guatemala's Ministry of Education, WV is promoting a new educational model that adapts to the needs of migrating children. This model takes into account the fact that these children must speak Spanish. It also addresses problems of grade repetition, school desertion and lack of full participation by girls.

Finally, the search for sustainability and transcendent changes must be made through short-, medium- and long-term processes in which the community plays a leading part. Organizations such as World Vision play an accompanying part, facilitating the process without interfering with the culture.

References

World Vision Guatemala, Monographic Study of San Juan Atitán, 1989

Statistics Office of Guatemala (Direccion General de Estadisticas de Guatemala), Bulletin, 1990

World Vision Guatemala, Monthly and Quarterly Reports of the San Juan Atitán Project, 1994

World Vision Guatemala, "No mas Angeles con Hambre" (No more hungry angels) Video, 1989

Popol Vuh, *The Quiché Histories*, First Edition 1947.

13

Medical Ambassadors Philippines: primary health care

Eleazar O. Sarmiento

> Moses was a great primary health care worker
> trained by God himself.

Medical Ambassadors Philippines (MAP) is an interdenominational medical missionary organization. Through MAP, doctors, nurses and other professionals pursue the compassionate ministry of healing the sick and sharing the Good News of Jesus Christ. In 18 years of medical missionary work, we have experienced the bliss and the pains of growth. This chapter will share these experiences for the sake of better medical missionary service.

History

As a young man, I felt the call to serve the Lord. I began by sharing the gospel among tribal people in Benguet, Philippines; many of them became Christians. During one of many trips to the northern mountains, I got very ill. There was no medical help available, but local Christians showed their love and concern for me. They carried me through rugged mountains to reach the nearest road, and a truck took me to the city hospital. God used that incident to challenge me to become a missionary doctor and help bring health care to tribal communities.

I entered medical school and, by God's grace and provision, obtained my degree. Soon after graduation I answered a call to head up a medical missionary hospital in Banaue, Ifugao,

201

Philippines. The American doctor who had started the work and built the hospital had to return home for an indefinite furlough. It was an opportunity for me to train as a medical missionary.

About this time my wife-to-be (Elma G. Franco) had just arrived from Chicago with training in internal medicine and cardiology. She was already an assistant medical educator, had come to the Philippines only for a short vacation and had planned to become the partner of a prominent internist. Well, I proposed marriage and told her that I was going to be a medical missionary to the tribal people in the northern mountains of the Philippines. It was a very hard decision for her to make, but "love conquers all." We were married and became medical missionaries in Banaue, Ifugao.

The hospital we took over was a beautifully built facility, although small (just twelve beds). It was like a Stateside setup in the remote mountains. Foreigners and city people admired it, but it was not practical for the communities that we served. For instance, one day we admitted patients to the ward and the nurses neatly fixed their beds. The next morning, the patients were under the beds lying on their own mats. Also, we did not need to have a dietary department because the patients preferred that their relatives cook for them. For every patient that we admitted, one to three relatives would also want to stay. Somehow we had to rethink how to run the missionary hospital in the local context.

We saw that many people who were sick and needed health care did not come to the hospital because they lacked money or did not consider it a high priority for spending money. We were not improving the health status of the communities this way. The few that came to the hospital got well enough to go back to their villages and get sick again.

However, this was a great opportunity to reach people with the gospel. Before they were seen by doctors, they listened to preaching in their own dialect. Many of them professed faith in Christ. They became familiar with the Bible and the person of Jesus Christ.

We were busy with curative care. Surgical cases would come in; I had to do emergency surgery without training. Anything elective I sent to the city hospital, which is a whole day's bus ride through the mountains. After four years, I decided to go for some surgical training, which the Lord made possible. I was accepted into the surgical residency training of the University of the Philippines, Philippine General Hospital medical center (UP-PGH).

I trained in surgery. But what God accomplished during my stay with UP-PGH was more than just that: he gave me a vision of a medical mission. In UP-PGH I met Christian medical students and nursing students who were looking for ways to serve the Lord. On vacation breaks we would take them to the mountains and expose them to the needs of the people we worked with. This helped the people but also enabled the medical students to see what they could do for God.

When I finished my training in surgery, I was ready to go back and operate on people. While visiting a certain tribal group, I saw that most of their health problems did not have surgical solutions. I felt useless; something was missing.

One day, a Summer Institute of Linguistics (SIL) missionary invited me to visit a tribal group, noting that the people were willing to forsake their pagan ways if a doctor would come to help them with their health problems. Without thinking I said I would go if they built an airstrip. I thought it would take them at least six months to build one. They built it in three days. I had to go.

My next excuse was lack of funds to build even a small clinic. Meanwhile, in the city hospital, my wife was in consultation concerning a business executive who was fatally ill. Before he died, we had a chance to minister to him and his family. His wife eventually accepted Christ and donated a considerable sum for the clinic in the mountains in memory of her husband. God used the death of one man to bring health services to an entire tribe.

So began Higendorf Memorial Clinic, the first medical station of Medical Ambassadors Philippines (MAP). We had four volunteer nurses and a doctor. At first we ran the clinic as a curative health care service. We kept on getting repeated problems and practically the same patients. We saw that to promote health status in the community we had to change our emphasis and do more health education and preventive care.

This approach was working in the first community, so we tried it in one place after another. In five years we had five medical stations doing mostly primary health care rather than curative care. Just about this time, we came across Dr. and Mrs. Sison, who were involved in the same kind of work in Mindanao. We joined forces and shared learning experiences.

At this point the government decreed that all medicine and nursing graduates must spend their first six months in rural areas supported by a small allowance. We harnessed this available manpower. We invited Christian graduates to work with us, providing funds for food and housing in addition to their government allowance. However, the next year we had a problem. The government would not allow us to select our workers; they would have to draw lots. We encouraged our graduates to pray. When they drew lots, they drew our stations.

The time came when the government could no longer afford to support these graduates. We had to look for ways to support workers ourselves. Our family used to sing short concerts (our three children were then 11, 8 and 7 years old). One day the executive vice president of World Concern heard us and invited us to sing for churches and organizations. I do not think that our singing was that great, but people thought the kids were cute. Starting that year we were able to get support from the churches through World Concern. We employed a small office staff and started to learn how to do detailed reporting based on milestones and programs.

At first we were favored with air transportation. The Civic Action Group of the Philippines Air Force provided monthly helicopter trips to our stations. (The Air Force pilots needed flying time for their training.) This went on for a few years until the worldwide oil crisis set in.

Within the first ten years we developed twelve medical stations on Luzon and Mindanao, with 30 nurse practitioners, six doctors and an office staff of five. Additional churches and organizations like USAID and Christofell-Blinden Mission from Germany contributed to our work. We continued to open other medical stations. We also turned over to the respective communities some of the older stations, which we still visit regularly. In 1992 we opened ten stations in new areas.

For the last 18 years Medical Ambassadors Philippines has extended primary health care services to remote ethnic communities. Through this experience we have developed programs for the joint goals of providing compassionate healing services and sharing the gospel of Jesus Christ.

Biblical basis

Jesus' prayer for his disciples in John 17:18-19 is the most comprehensive scriptural basis for this ministry:

> {Father,] as you sent me into the world, I have sent them into the world. For them I sanctify myself, that they too may be truly sanctified.

God has always been involved in this kind of work. It was not an easy job to lead a whole nation from Egypt to the Promised Land through the wilderness. Moses had to take care of more than 600,000 men, not counting women and children, plus their animals. Whether he liked it or not, Moses had to address health and sanitation issues for this wandering community. He had to teach the people certain measures to prevent sickness and some basic nutrition rules. He had to provide potable water. This was all a part of the ministry to which God called him. Moses was a great primary health care worker trained by God himself.

Other servants of God were also involved in this kind of ministry. Elisha not only proclaimed a message of returning to God but also helped feed the people in times of hunger. He provided potable water for communities and taught health measures to prevent the spread of disease. Health care was very much a part of God's program through his prophets.

Jesus read his commission as he started his ministry:

> The Spirit of the Lord is on me, because he has anointed
> me to preach good news to the poor. He has sent me to
> proclaim freedome for the prisoners and recovery of sight
> for the blind, to release the oppressed, to proclaim the
> year of the Lord's favor (Luke 4:18-19).

His life and ministry was characterized by attending to both
spiritual and physical needs of the individual. The life of our Great
Physician perfectly reflects the manner in which he was sent, as
portrayed in Isaiah 61. His ministry was certainly holistic in
approach. He was interested not only in the salvation of the soul
but also in the relief of physical suffering. He taught his disciples
this ministry and sent them into the world to be his representatives,
his body on earth.

Status of medical missions

We regard highly the work of medical missions in the past and
have learned much from their experience. We believe in certain
basic things, such as the holistic approach. The word for health in
Hebrew is *shalom* or peace. It depicts the holistic concept very well.
Physical health is actually homeostasis of the individual and the
environment. Psychological or emotional health is attained when
there is peace between the inner and outer self. Social health means
peace between the individual and society. Spiritual health comes
when the individual has peace with God.

Health covers all aspects of one's life. Hence, our approach
to human health cannot be dichotomized. When the scientific
world advanced so rapidly, medical missions also tended to stress
the physical aspects of health; many of the mission hospitals placed
the spiritual aspect of the ministry on the side.

Today the big mission hospitals in the Philippines have little to do with spiritual things. Any remaining spiritual aspects have
become a ritual and are not integrated into the treatment of the
patient as a whole. In some instances the spiritual aspect is left for
the chaplain or the visiting ministers, as if to say that only medical

personnel are responsible for the physical aspect of the patient's illness.

Misconceptions of medical missions

The concept of medical missions has been reduced to the material level. Some hospitals may be called mission hospitals since they offer charity beds or good discounts. A few mission hospitals have kept a Christian training program for nurses and benefit from maintaining the humane aspect of their service to people.

This tendency has spread to medical missionary outreaches. They render free curative services and give free medicines from time to time. Doctors and nurses travel to remote areas for two to four weeks per year and demonstrate acts of kindness and love. This is good and Christian in outlook, but we do not think it is medical missions as God would have us do it. We may have eased our consciences by helping some poor patients. But have we been instrumental in bringing about a significant change in individuals and communities through the holistic approach?

To enhance their idea of medical missions, some doctors join forces with an evangelist or a church effort for a limited period of evangelism. Free medical services are offered and the people are drawn in for evangelistic meetings. This may help the results of evangelistic efforts, but it certainly is not a good health care service. Few patients would get proper follow-up.

Jesus did not take this approach. Medical professionals should not use health care as bait to get people to believe in Christ but should sincerely imitate Jesus by expressing God's love and concern for the individual.

Current Strategy of the MAP ministry

When we go into a community, we work closely with the government. We come through the *barangay* (village) officials and get the cooperation of the people. When we offer our services, we ask them to provide a building or house to use as a station. We lead them in identifying their health problems and then ask them for possible solutions. The health care system therefore becomes their project.

Our personnel agree to live with the people for three years, during which time we should be able to develop village health workers and health promoters. Curative care can immediately begin. Our nurse practitioners are trained in the five most common illnesses in the area. In effect, they act as local doctors but refer to our circuit or regional doctors any problematic cases or diseases beyond their training. For patients who need to stay for a day or two for treatment, we have asked each village to build a hut within the perimeter of the medical station. Patients maintain their own huts and stay for free.

This approach is cost effective. It is not a hospital, so there are no requirements for permits, licenses or fees, building specifications, or a minimum of three shifts of nurses. The doctors and nurses just make house calls. What is more, gospel sharing is easily integrated in this activity.

A village pharmacy is established as the community's project. We donate seed money to purchase medicines and keep the shelves supplied. We ask people to pay for their medicines unless they are extremely poor. (We used to dole out medicines to people, but many of them feigned sickness to obtain medicines and sell them to their neighbors.) We sell the medicines with a 10 percent mark-up for handling and services. We teach the people that this is necessary to keep medicines available for their use.

Within the three-year project period, the nurses also train people hand-picked by their own community to become village health workers and health promoters. These barangay health workers (BHWs) work alongside the nurses as assistants in the clinic and in lecture groups. They learn about the common diseases in the locality, get acquainted with the common medicines used and run the pharmacy themselves. The nurses' responsibility becomes supervisory.

The doctors and nurses also perform an evangelistic and discipleship ministry. The health care program includes active witnessing and personal discipleship efforts with the village health workers.

To safeguard the work of the BHWs and the running of the village pharmacy, the nurses and doctors organize a local health committee. Members are elected by the villagers. The committee's responsibility is to oversee the health care work done by the BHWs. At the end of three years the village is ready to run its own primary health care station with periodic visits from their own former nurses and doctors. Through all these activities, BHWs are told about Jesus Christ and trained to be lay leaders in the local churches, if and when they become Christians.

Programs

Nutrition   Identifying third-degree malnourished children age 0-6, feeding them one good meal a day (five days a week for two to three months), providing Bible teaching for those old enough, training mothers to prepare proper diet for the children, and aiming to convert a certain percentage to adequately nourished children in three years.

Tuberculosis   Identifying advanced TB cases by sputum smear, treating them with triple drug therapy for one year, aiming to cure a certain percentage within three years.

Malaria   Teaching the preventive measures against malaria by eradication of breeding places for the vector, planting plants that have repellent properties, encouraging use of mosquito nets and treating cases of malaria.

Goiter   Identifying endemic goiter patients and treating them with long-acting lipoidal, following them up for three years.

Oral rehydration   Teaching mothers and health workers the importance of early diagnosis and treatment of dehydration due to diarrhea, teaching them how to make a homemade oral rehydration formula, aiming to teach a certain percentage of mothers in the community to make and use the formula.

Immunization   Aiming to immunize a certain percentage of the children against DPT, polio, measles, BCG and other diseases.

Preventive dental care Teaching school children the proper way to brush, floss and rinse, deputizing school teachers to follow-up, grouping children, and assigning and training a student as a dental health promoter.

Environmental sanitation Teaching the importance of having a sanitary toilet and using it, giving incentives for getting a water seal toilet, aiming to have a certain percentage of households owning one or sharing one, teaching each household about potable water.

Primary eye care Providing preventive eye care education on blindness secondary to measles and proper eye care of children with measles, immunizing with anti-measles vaccine, identifying vitamin deficiency and supplementing diet with vitamin A, identifying candidates for cataract operation and referring them to clinics and hospitals for surgical management, case-finding of patients with refraction errors and supplying glasses, teaching school children eye washing.

Maternal and child care Organizing mothers' classes, teaching prenatal care, perinatal care, family planning and breast-feeding.

Levitical health care Identifying patients needing secondary and tertiary health care, referring them to city hospitals or clinics. We also partially or fully subsidize needed services for indigent patients, pastors, Christian workers and their families.

Livelihood Not actually a health program, this effort provides incentive to the volunteer BHWs. For instance, they are given a stake of hogs or fish to start hog raising or fish ponds. When they make a profit they give the stake back to MAP so others can receive an incentive to multiply livelihood projects.

Christian education Each member of MAP staff is involved in Christian witnessing such as personal evangelism with patients or relatives, home Bible study groups, Sunday school, daily vacation Bible school, Bible clubs with school children or children in the nutrition program, Bible teaching with BHWs or mothers' classes. These are all done in cooperation with local gospel-preaching churches. If there are no such churches, a church planter is invited to work in relation with MAP. We have a full-time Christian education minister, a chaplain that oversees this work. Occasionally, volunteer ministers are invited to help.

Staff development Conferences are held for members of MAP staff to update them in their health care knowledge, encourage spiritual growth and develop skills in sharing the gospel. There is one national and two regional conferences each year.

Training and research Training and research is the emphasis of the ministry and covers a large portion of the work. It involves the doctors, nurses, and health workers. Research work is stratified: the BHWs record data, nurses gather and collate it, and office staff analyze it. MAP has written a book for training mothers and BHWs.

Church lay workers health care This is a fairly new program being tested to see if we can work through local churches to spread out health care work in the country. Lay volunteers are invited to attend health care classes for five days at a time about three or four times a year.

Missionary personnel Our nurses and doctors are recruited from nursing and medical schools. They must be born-again Christians. They must have a calling and a commitment to serve the Lord as medical missionaries. They must understand that they are not being employed by MAP but that Jesus is their direct Chief Physician. (Legally, however, they are enlisted as employees of MAP.) They are encouraged to be members of local churches. The churches are encouraged to send them as their missionaries to specific tribal groups through MAP. The churches therefore have a responsibility of commissioning them, praying for them and supporting them as their missionaries, even with a small amount each month. Thus MAP becomes a coordinating and overseeing agency.

New direction of MAP

The past three years we in the Philippines have been faced with multiple natural calamities: droughts, earthquakes, floods, storms, volcanic eruptions and lava flow. We have felt helpless during these times; the resources we could offer immediately are meager. We actually need a "superman" to answer this need. But we do have a "superman" in the person of Jesus. But some would argue that Jesus is not here right now.

But Jesus *is* here bodily. He left the church, his body, to do his work. However, his body has been busy doing other things. The Great Commission is more than just a spiritual work. It has to do with giving physical relief as well as saving the soul. Toward the end of Jesus' ministry he said that our service to him can be expressed by our service to those in need:

> The King will reply, "I tell you the truth, whatever you did for one of the least of these brothers of mine, you did for me" (Matt 25:40).

With the recent natural calamities in the Philippines, even our government cannot meet the needs of the people. We face the same problem as the disciples faced in John 6:

> Andrew, Simon Peter's brother, spoke up, "Here is a boy with five small barley loaves and two fishes, but how far will they go among so many?" (John 6:9).

But Jesus knew what he would do. He took the loaves and fishes and gave the hungry people as much as they wanted.

A possible solution

- If we could train people in our local churches in primary health care as well as disaster relief and rehabilitation, the needed personnel would be all over the country right where they should be when calamities come.

- If local churches would realize that this is part of the Great Commission, each church could make it part of their financial responsibility. They would be ready to meet the material needs of the communities around them, as done in Paul's time.

We are convinced we can help our country at this point of dire need by allowing God to use his body, the church, to meet human need.

Strategy

- We will challenge the churches to do health care work among the people in their communities or in the evacuation centers.

- We will ask the pastors to identify volunteers in their own churches who have medical aptitude. (Those with management skills can help with administration.)

- MAP will train volunteers as health care workers for their communities. There will be as many health care clinics as there will be churches willing to participate in this ministry. We believe in the separation of church and state but not in the separation of the church and health care.

Scope   We will select three to five top causes of mortality and morbidity. The training of lay health workers will focus on diagnosis, preventive measures and treatment. The management of these illnesses will include compliance with prescribed treatment and monitoring the effectiveness of the program. As need arises, some amount of curative care, both elective and emergency, will be taught and given. Other conditions can be referred to our secondary or tertiary care ministries.

Procedure   Each church will ask for volunteer health workers. These workers will be trained for two months in primary health care to function as health workers and promoters. The volunteers will receive refresher training every six months. This work of primary health care will be the undertaking of the local church and their gospel outreach, so its continuity and growth will be ensured.

Finances   At the start of the project, we will ask help from churches that are able to contribute to this cause. Local beneficiary churches will be responsible for maintenance and growth.

Primary needs

- Seed money for church pharmacy
- Support for health trainers
- Nutrition needs for two months
- Training expenses and transportation

Medical mission and
the body of Christ

We in MAP will continue to strive toward doing authentic medical missionary work that is holistic in approach and meets the needs of the individual and the community, just as Jesus did. More and more we feel that medical missionary work must be church-based, serving the community. Every program and activity must be closely related to the local church; recipients must be directed to it. The community should see the good that the work does as coming from the Lord and his body, the church.

14
Christian witness through community health

Stan Rowland

> Without Christ, we are only treating the symptoms of our separation from God, not the disease of sin. Our role in healing is to show how people can receive Christ and appropriate his healing wholeness.

Community health evangelism (CHE) is a strategy to restore harmony or wholeness in individuals. The purpose of CHE[1] is to transform individual lives physically and spiritually in local communities by meeting people at their point of need. These transformed individuals are then involved in transforming their neighbors, thereby transforming the community from the inside out. This is multiplied to other areas, eventually transforming an entire country for Jesus Christ.

The CHE strategy combines three essentials: first, the integration of physical and spiritual ministry; second, multiplication through the training of national leadership; and third, community ownership of a program directed by villagers themselves with a minimum of outside resources.

Many community health projects aim to change the whole community. If the community as a whole does not participate or implement projects, then people are dissatisfied. Our emphasis is on transformed *individual lives*. We do not focus on the community as a whole but rather rely on the multiplication effect of neighbor influencing neighbor.

"My passport to heaven"

Early in a Uganda CHE project, we met a 92-year-old man named Samwell. Samwell greeted us outside his house and warmly welcomed us inside.

One of our staff trainers started sharing the gospel with Samwell using "The Four Spiritual Laws Picture Book." Samwell listened intently. By the end of our conversation, he was sitting on the edge of his chair with tears running down his cheeks.

When Samwell was asked if he would like to invite Christ into his life, he said, "Yes, yes." After his prayer, he held up the booklet, turned to us and said in English, "My passport to heaven. My passport to heaven."

Samwell then explained to us that normally by that time of day (11:00 A.M.) he was drunk and fighting with his neighbors. Now he understood why he had not started drinking that day. God had ordained this meeting.

More than a year later, Samwell remains strong in his walk with the Lord. He has not had another drink of alcohol since the day he received Christ. He has others read to him daily from the Bible and has memorized many Scripture passages. He cannot walk long distances and so is unable to attend church services. But he has built a small shelter outside his home under which he "preaches" to family members and friends.

Samwell was trained as a community health evangelist (also "CHE"), learning to tell his neighbors how they could live a healthy life, both spiritually and physically. He regularly visits his neighbors to share what he has learned. Because of the tremendous changes that have taken place in Samwell's life, especially the joy he shows, he has become a strong witness that Jesus Christ changes lives, both physically and spiritually.

Samwell exemplifies the reason spiritual values must be integrated with any village health program. The need for transformed lives is as necessary as the need for improved health care.

Biblical basis

Christian community health care should be based on the Bible. We are commanded in Luke 10:27 to love God totally and to love our neighbors as ourselves. If we love our neighbors as ourselves, we will truly be concerned with their physical and spiritual welfare. We will want to help them live a more abundant, meaningful life here on earth and to share how they can have eternal life. Because of God's love for us, we desire to share that love with others.

From the very beginning of his ministry, Jesus was concerned about the whole person. In Luke 4:16-21, just after he returns home to Nazareth, Jesus reveals why he came: to fulfill the prophesy found in Isaiah 61:1-2 concerning the coming Messiah. The Messiah came to preach good news to the poor, bind up the brokenhearted, release the prisoners and proclaim the year of the Lord's favor. Jesus said that the Scripture was fulfilled that day. As the Scripture foretold, he came to deal with the whole person.

Jesus made a startling statement in Matthew 25:34-40. He asserted that as we give food and drink to those in need, take in strangers, clothe the naked, visit the sick and those in prisons, we are doing these things to him. Most of us would find it easy to do these things for Christ and even for our own family, but Jesus says we must do them for the lowliest of people, including those we don't know or who may even despise us. We are called to serve all people!

Jesus commands us in Matthew 28:19-20 to go and make disciples of all nations. We do this in the name of God and under his authority. This is not an option for the Christian; it is a command. In addition, Jesus says he will be with us now and always. We should do these things in God's strength made available through the Holy Spirit, not in our own power. The emphasis of Christ's Great Commission is on spiritual needs.

We are told in II Timothy 2:2 to find faithful men we can teach to teach others and who, in turn, will teach still others. This verse speaks of multiplication. This should apply both spiritually and physically, because we want to see the world physically improved as it is reached for Christ. As we pour our lives into faithful men, they will catch the vision for teaching others who in turn help others.

When Jesus walked this earth, he was concerned about the whole person. He healed the sick as he preached and taught. As Christians, we too must be concerned for the well-being of the whole person. This involves meeting both physical and spiritual needs. When Jesus sent out his twelve disciples to minister to others in Luke 9:1-2, he commanded them to heal the sick and to be concerned for the physical needs of others as they preached the Good News.

Good health is wholeness

What is good health? God's Word uses the word *shalom* to mean peace, wholeness, soundness, well-being and good health. In the Old Testament, *shalom* is used when there is harmony between people and between people and things. To be in harmony means to live in peace with someone or something. To be in good health, a person must live in harmony.

But with whom must we live in harmony? First God, then oneself, then others, then nature. But what does it mean to live in harmony with God, oneself, others, nature?

Living in harmony with God begins by establishing a relationship with God through Jesus Christ. That relationship is nurtured by reading his Word, as we speak to God regularly in prayer, and as we praise God and give him the glory. We try to live righteously as we seek God's will and obey it. We look to him to meet our needs as we submit ourselves to God and desire to please him.

Living in harmony with ourselves means to be happy and at peace, to see ourselves as God sees us. It means to understand ourselves as we accept the reality of sin in our lives and realizing our need to ask forgiveness. Also, we know that good health is physical, spiritual, emotional and social well-being. Not to say disease will never attack us, but we will still be at peace no matter what the situation. We must know that many times our behavior and attitudes negatively affect our health, giving us ulcers, depression, headaches, and other ailments.

Living in harmony with others means to live the commandment to "love your neighbor as yourself" (Luke 10:27b). Our love of God should result in our loving others as we minister to their physical, spiritual, emotional and social needs. This means being helpful in every way possible. We have to realize, though, that others affect our health by what they do to us. They can give us diseases; we can give them diseases.

Living in harmony with nature means to know that God created the natural realm with its laws. Winds, earthquakes, and storms are part of the natural order. Viruses, bacteria, and parasites affect us. To have good health, we must live in harmony with the natural things around us. Also, we need to know that most of our physical ill health is caused by living in disharmony with nature, such as stripping our land of trees and causing drought and starvation. Pollution of our air and water causes many health problems. We must respect God's land and animals and not destroy nature around us.

If good health is living in harmony with God, ourself, others and nature, then what is illness? Illness is being out of harmony with God, others, self or nature. A break in fellowship with one of these causes illness.

Healing, then, is bringing restoration or wholeness to the person as we restore our relationship with God, ourselves, others and nature. Remember that Christ came to bring healing. The Old Testament deals with laws for being pure so we can worship God. Also remember that Christ died to make us whole.

In the case of Samwell, for much of his 92 years he was living in disharmony with God, himself, others and maybe even nature because of his drunkenness. He was continually harming his physical and mental health with alcohol. He harmed his social health because of his fighting with his neighbors. He did not know God, so he could not live in harmony with God. But Jesus changed him.

Without Christ, we are only treating the symptoms of our separation from God, not the disease of sin. Our role in healing is to show how people can receive Christ and appropriate his healing wholeness.

Does CHE work toward wholeness?

The preventive side of health care is development. Christian development is helping people become all that God intends them to be. It brings lasting benefit and freedom when people develop themselves under God's direction. CHE is God's love in action.

The CHE strategy is one way that Christian development can take place in local villages. It begins by training nationals who are mature Christians and capable of teaching. A team of trainers, one of whom usually has a medical background, enter a cluster of villages where the CHE program is introduced. The villages then elect their own committee, which becomes the administrator of the program. The people also choose their own community health evangelists (again, "CHEs"—see note 1), who will be the front-line workers.

Training community health evangelists

Both the local committee and the CHEs are trained over the ensuing six months by the training team. The CHEs are taught the following:

- To recognize the signs and symptoms of key diseases found in their area.
- To use simple, locally available methods for cure.
- To prevent disease in the first place involves protecting their water sources, building pit latrines, and growing and using the right crops.
- To put what they learn into practice in their home.
- To take what they learn and teach their neighbors.
- To trust Jesus Christ as their personal Savior and grow in their faith.
- To share this Good News with their neighbors.
- To follow-up and disciple new believers.

During this training, nearly all who are not already believers come to faith in Jesus Christ. Then a fascinating thing occurs. Since all committee members and CHEs are volunteer workers, those who do not come to Christ lose their motivation to go on with the program. Non-Christians drop out of the program, leaving an inherently Christian organization, which at the same time has the essential quality of being truly representative of the community. Thus the program is both community-owned and Christian.

Each CHE regularly visits up to 50 neighboring families, impacting more than 400 people. When CHEs share Christ with their neighbors, up to 40 percent accept Christ as their Savior. Since CHEs are sharing with their neighbors, it is easy for them to help others begin and mature in their walk with Christ.

CHEs use 17 picture books on physical and spiritual topics when they teach in homes; this helps to make all their learning transferable. A Bible study is used to deepen CHEs' walk with the Lord as they learn ministry skills that they put into practice in a chosen target area. The CHEs then lead their own Bible studies using the same materials.

Once CHEs graduate from the six-months' training program, they begin to share what they have learned with neighbors in their villages. For instance, they organize the people in their communities to protect local springs. This brings the people good water and greatly reduces sickness and death. Vaccination programs are begun in the villages. The villagers are encouraged to start vegetable gardens and improve the nutrition of their children.

The same process is then begun in surrounding areas. Teaching success is not measured by the projects in and of themselves, nor by people putting into practice what they have learned. Again, the CHE process is concerned with multiplication. Success is measured in terms of people using what they have learned and then teaching others to do the same.

CHEs and the community

Many Christian development organizations are excited to teach people to do something that changes their lifestyle. They see success when the people are using what they have learned in their daily lives. If they are planting gardens and eating the vegetables, this is success. But many times this focus becomes project-oriented.

CHEs teach the people to plant a garden, eat the vegetables, teach their neighbors what they have learned, and then see their neighbors put the teaching into practice and teach their neighbors in turn. Simply putting into practice what a person has learned is good, but not good enough. Multiplication takes place through the use of transferable materials such as "The Four Spiritual Laws Picture Book" and 17 other picture books.

When people talk about health care, they are usually talking about curing a disease after someone has gotten it. But it is also important to talk about preventing the disease in the first place. The concept of cure versus prevention applies in spiritual truths as well. When people sin, they need to be cured of their sin, which is done by confessing to God and accepting his forgiveness. Sin can be prevented from entering our lives by reading and memorizing God's Word, breathing spiritually[2] and praying.

Available curative care is critical to the success of a CHE program. But such clinics do not need to be run by the same organization doing CHE. We are more concerned with prevention than cure, although the CHEs know how to deal with a problem when it affects others. Many of our projects have a clinic that acts as a training and referral center for nearby CHE projects.

A foundational principle for a CHE program is that the community sees the project as their own, not as started by outsiders. Too many times organizations have come from the outside to do something for the people, but when the outsiders leave, their accomplishments disintegrate; there is no sustainability. The people expect the outsiders to provide the funds, parts or labor to maintain or repair the project.

When outsiders do things for people in a community, the people always see what has been done as belonging to the outsiders. From the beginning, the emphasis must be on the community saying, This is ours and we will make it happen. We need to enable people to take more responsibility for their health, under God's direction.

If the program is to continue after the training team leaves, it is critical to involve a cross-section of the community, the broader the better. Otherwise, one small group within the community may be seen as controlling the project, and the rest of the community sees the project as belonging to that group. If the community as a whole never takes responsibility for the project, the likelihood of its sustainability decreases.

To easily implement CHE, there need to be training materials to train the three groups of people involved in a project: the trainers, committee members and CHEs. One hundred lesson plans equip the trainers during the training of trainers (TOTs) in our learner-centered approach. The trainers then choose from more than 250 lesson plans on physical and spiritual topics to equip the CHEs and committee members.

Not one action but many enable community ownership to take place. We work alongside the people, never doing for them what they can do themselves. The people must be actively involved from the beginning and at all times in planning, budgeting, implementing and evaluating the program. They must see themselves as responsible for their success or failure.

Churches and CHE

A program may begin from a church base in areas where the community is fragmented. The community may have so little sense of unity that the churches may be used to initiate a CHE program. Such a case might be in an urban slum area. Or in like manner, Christians may be in a small minority in a community dominated by anti-Christian groups.

The committee members and CHEs will probably be made up of church members. If there is more then one evangelical church in the community, there should be equal representation from all churches regarding the committee and CHEs.

The churches must view this strategy as a means to reach out to their non-Christian neighbors in a holistic way, rather than exclusively using it for their own church members. For a successful program to be started, the local congregation must have a missionary vision for evangelism and a desire to minister physically in the community. The Christians must be concerned with man as a

223

whole and not just his spirit. They must see CHE as a way to win people to Christ and to help them grow as whole persons.

Churches must view development as being important for the community. They must be willing to give up control in order to see community involvement and commitment. Initially, the change agents may be church members who multiply themselves physically and spiritually in the community. The church must minister with, not to, the community.

Multiple churches in the community should work together in the program as a cohesive unit. Working with one small congregation generally dooms the program to slow growth and little impact, as there are not enough resources, manpower or money for the program to spread.

The church-based model is especially useful in an urban slum setting. In general, slum dwellers do not have a sense of belonging but feel they are just there temporarily. They also hold very few things in common since they are from all over the country. So the community is very fragmented. A church can be a community within a community: it has recognized leadership, some sense of unity, and members hold their Christian faith in common.

We are developing such models in the slums of Guatemala City, Manila, and Kampala, Uganda. From these experiences we have found that we must follow the above guidelines or we will never gain community acceptance and ownership.

CHE in California

We in the CHE ministry are also developing a model on the west side of Modesto, California, U.S.A., a city with great ethnic diversity. (Our headquarters is there.) Part of our team has been holding a Good News Club for two years with the children of the local Cambodian community. They have also held several practical outreaches, distributed clothes and helped to build a playground. We now have the credibility and acceptance to begin a more whole-person approach to ministry.

The first phase focuses on 2,000 members of the Cambodian community who live in two large apartment complexes. We are involving the Cambodian church as well as another local churches. We are working from an apartment in the major complex. We are going through the steps that we have found useful in establishing such a program. We hope to train the people to meet their felt needs, which may include health, English as a second language, and tutoring of children.

The second phase involves 25,000 African-Americans, Asians, Native Americans and Hispanics on the west side of Modesto. In a sense, the Third World has come to us at our U.S. headquarters. While we are beginning the work with the Cambodians, we are also contacting other churches within the target area to gain acceptance and involvement. We are also gathering information on services already being offered and what the people feel their needs are.

Christian organizations and the whole person

Most Christian organizations are concerned with either fulfilling the Great Commission, meeting spiritual needs (Mt. 28:19-20); or "Great Concerns," meeting physical needs (Mt. 25:35-40). They forget the Great Commandment (Lk. 10:27): loving your neighbor as yourself.

The evangelical church may concentrate on the spiritual side of man while the liberal church concentrates on the physical and social side. Both groups dichotomize man; God does not. They fail to deal with a person as a whole.

Some churches that want to eliminate this dichotomy develop parallel ministries with different people doing the two functions. They claim to have a balanced ministry. An evangelist may minister spiritually while a nurse or agriculturist ministers physically. Often there is a tendency to be stronger on one side than the other. If asked what they would choose if they could only do one thing, they revert to their strengths.

It is important to understand such factors when seeking an integrated ministry. The same person can, in fact, minister to both the spiritual and the physical and social aspects of people's lives. This may happen simultaneously or at different times, depending on the needs of the individual. Community health evangelism

(CHE) aims to have a balanced ministry that truly integrates the physical and spiritual.

Many secular development projects are initiated by a large organization that imposes its ideas on a community. This is a top-down approach of the superior to the inferior. One who knows more is helping one who knows less. One who has greater access to resources provides for one who has limited access to resources. This is the general approach of governments. Success is measured in terms of quantity, not quality or relationships. Governments want to change their country in the shortest time possible, getting as many communities taught as quickly as possible.

The more typical approach for Christian organizations is to work alongside the community. They have the attitude of learning together. Much emphasis is on developing relationships. Without relationships, true change does not take place. Relationships bring results.

Projects that are community-based desire full participation and ownership of the community for all that is done. This is bottom-up or grass-roots development. This often results in a good project that is owned by the community. However, the organization may not see or want accomplishments multiplied elsewhere.

CHE is concerned with bottom-up development that can be multiplied elsewhere, something that can fit in with government programs when and if they reach the community. One successful project is necessary as a model but that, in and of itself, is not enough. We want to see success happen again and again.

The whole-person approach

It is one thing to talk about having a whole-person approach to ministry; it is quite another thing for it to happen. Several assumptions underlie this type of ministry:

- We have Christ's example, command, promise and authority to deal with people as whole beings.
- People want to be dealt with as whole beings, not separated into parts as we in the West tend to do.

- Everyone has a sinful nature that only Jesus can change through a personal relationship.

- People cannot change themselves or others by their own efforts.

- The world is not becoming a better place through human self-effort.

- Man is destroying the world because of disharmonies within himself, with others, between mankind and God and between mankind and nature.

Taking the above assumptions, then, a number of elements need to be in place to facilitate an approach to the whole person. The main point of integration of a physical and spiritual ministry is that one person deals with another as a whole person—physically, spiritually, emotionally and socially. Such ministry tasks are not delegated to specialists. One must have love for all, not just part, of the whole person.

From the first entry into a community and throughout the program, we talk about a holistic approach. In introducing the CHE program or a gospel presentation, we begin by noting that God is interested in a person's whole being. Most other religions readily accept this fact, so we can teach spiritual truths. We start where the people are, moving them from the known of the Bible to the unknown of Jesus Christ.

It is critical that all of the training team members have a personal relationship with Jesus Christ because they will be the models for the program. They must have the common objective of integrating a spiritual ministry into a community health program with the desire to deal with the whole person. Each training team member must know how to share Christ and follow-up new believers as well as to deal with health problems.

The trainers should all be trained with the same materials so there is consistency when they train others. They need to model a balanced life. As they do home visiting with CHEs, they model what is expected of CHEs. In addition, they teach in the style that they expect CHEs to use. All trainers should do both physical and spiritual teaching regardless of their professional training.

When teaching a physical topic, we are always looking for ways to apply biblical teaching to the physical topic and vice versa. For example, a foreign body in a wound will fester and become infected and must be removed. It is the same with unconfessed sin in our life: the sin festers and becomes worse.

We pray continuously that the work will be holistic as we look for changed lives, both physically and spiritually. But talking about spiritual integration is not enough, nor is providing high-quality health care and teaching or living an exemplary Christian life. We must expect physical and spiritual integration and then evaluate our efforts.

Ministry in closed countries

So far we have been talking about a strategy that was developed where people are not antagonistic to the gospel. But can we minister to the whole person in closed countries where people are antagonistic to the gospel?

The answer is yes. But we need to make some modifications while adhering to the core values of the strategy.

We have used a strategy to work in Muslim communities. Here the CHE physical ministry provides entrance into Muslim villages. The strategy combines the spiritual emphasis of calling people to repentance with the physical emphasis of caring for the physical person through demonstrating Christian love in action.

The program is called community health *education,* not evangelism. The strategy allows Muslims to inquire about Christ in nonthreatening situations. It exposes the village to the gospel during a period of time that gives room for the Holy Spirit to work and provides the individual more time to respond.

Working with a Muslim community

One model for work in Muslim countries is community-based:

- From the beginning, we talk about dealing with man as a whole person—physical, spiritual, emotional and social.

- We may spend 12 months developing relationships and learning the language if necessary. During this time we hold informal classes to sensitize the community and prepare them for the work.

- The training team chooses and trains a community committee (who are probably all Muslims) on physical and spiritual topics. The spiritual teaching is on *moral character topics from the Bible*. Those who show interest in spiritual matters are invited to join an inquiry class covering topics like creation, Adam, sin's beginning, and Isaac, but not Jesus. We start with what Muslims accept from the Bible (Torah, Prophets, Psalms), and then move on to Jesus.

- The committee chooses community health educators (also "CHEs").

- Each day, the CHE training covers both health and character topics. The character teaching is the same as is done with the committee, since the committee members are used to help in the training.

- After a health topic such as scabies, we may transition to a spiritual topic such as sin.

- The intent is to build relationships and bridges showing that the Koran and Bible contain some of the same stories. Whenever possible, it is good to show where the Old Testament verses are found in the Koran.

This model has worked slowly, but the people have been open to the training team. One time, when Muslims from the outside came to discredit and possibly harm the team by saying they were trying to convert the people, the community protected them. The community said the team was there to help them, which was more than what their brother Muslims did.

When individuals come to Christ, care must be taken that a number are baptized at the same time to give them a community within a community, as they will probably be thrown out of their homes. At some point, Christ will become an issue and problems will probably arise, but we continue to pray that this happens only after a number have come to Christ and the community has begun to change positively.

Starting with one Christian family

Another model is based around a Christian family as a precursor to establishing a more conventional CHE ministry. This is used in an antagonistic, non-Christian area devoid of any Christian churches. The program may be initiated by finding or planting a Christian family. They invite their non-Christian neighbors to their home for holistic training on health and spiritual topics. They then encourage them to share what they are learning with their neighbors.

This Christian family becomes a nucleus for the future development of a CHE program. The husband and wife must be a highly committed and mature couple. Their goal will be to fill the role of CHEs themselves until their work bears fruit and they make disciples who in turn become CHEs. Then the couple takes on the role of training in a more conventional CHE program.

If such a committed family is not found to act as CHEs, any Christian family can be used. This family must be willing to call their neighbors together for an outside Christian trainer to do both physical and spiritual training.

Successes in Northern India

This family approach has worked very well in an area of Northern India with Hindus and Buddhists. One family starts in a village ministering to people at their point of physical need. They pray for healing and provide simple health care. They take opportunities to teach individuals from the Bible. They invite people to come to a group study on physical issues as well as on Bible topics.

In one village, a man who was told he had a fatal illness came to live for three months with one such Christian family. After curative care and prayer, praise be to God, he was totally healed. Because of this, 16 of the 18 families living in the village became Christians. The families saw the love of Christ in the Christian family. They witnessed the healing and recognized that Jesus was more powerful then their gods.

This ministry has spread to 68 villages, where some 2,500 Hindus and Buddhists have accepted Jesus Christ in the last three years. Sixty-eight church fellowships have started; some have as many as 250 members. Four full-time clinics with medical staff care for more than 10,000 patients a year.

Four English medium schools, from nursery through fifth grade, have been established for Hindu children. The children learn Bible verses, Christian songs and stories. Their parents accept this because it is desirable for their children to be taught in an English-speaking school.

Is CHE seeing results?

Ministering to people at their point of need and then taking every opportunity to verbally share the gospel fosters an approach to the whole man.

When investing in God's kingdom, we are all interested in the results. In the CHE program we look for results at four levels:

- Individuals changed, both physically and spiritually.
- Individuals who change the lives of others, multiplying the results throughout a community and changing it from the inside out.
- A program that continues after outside assistance ends.
- Entire nations changed, both physically and spiritually.

Changed individual lives

The story of Samwell and his "passport to heaven" is only one example of thousands of individual changes that take place when Jesus comes and transforms lives from the inside out.

Changed lives multiplied

A good example of how a CHE project is changing communities is seen in our project in central Zaire, done in conjunction with the Presbyterian church. The project area is 40 by 60 kilometers in size; 62 CHEs are helping 36 villages.

After four years, the number of churches has grown from two to thirty-two. In one year, God changed communities in several spiritual and physical ways:

- Spiritually, 1,619 decisions for Jesus Christ were made, with 508 people baptized. The CHEs followed up 2,936 people and led 42 Bible studies for 2,936 people.
- Physically, 20,834 women and children were seen at ante-natal and well-baby clinics; 6,441 children were vaccinated.
- CHEs made 9,704 home visits to their neighbors.
- Some 1,775 new pit latrines and 1,258 new rubbish pits were built.
- Finally, 1,457 families received a "healthy home award" for having completed five major health interventions with their family in the year.

A program in Uganda continues on its own

In Uganda, a parish pastor in the Church of Uganda caught the vision. Initially, an outside team spent 16 months with him establishing one CHE project in his village. Then the team left.

Since that time, the pastor motivated people in 18 surrounding villages to become involved in CHE. He also mobilized the people to build, equip and staff their own clinic, which is self-funded. Currently, they are building a 40-bed health center.

The pastor has trained 100 local people as CHEs, who make 50 visits to their neighbors, monthly. Approximately the same numerical changes took place physically and spiritually as in the Zaire project.

Multiplication by training other organizations

A major way that CHE concepts are multiplied throughout a country is by training Christian organizations in establishing their own integrated community health program. This is done through a training of trainers (TOT) seminar.

This training is done in three phases, spread over one year. Each training phase is one week and emphasizes a different stage in the development of a CHE program. The participants gain knowledge and then go back to their home areas to put it into practice.

Over the last six years, 1,000 people have been equipped as trainers from more than 140 Christian organizations. They have put into practice what they have learned by starting more than 175 CHE projects. They have trained an estimated 10,000 CHEs.

To God be the glory

This Christian ministry to the whole person is having results beyond our wildest dreams. The Lord calls each of us ministering in his name to deal with people as whole persons. The starting point and center of good health is our Lord Jesus Christ.

Community health evangelism is a strategy that works. To God be the glory!

Notes

1   According to the context, the acronym CHE may stand for community health *evangelism*, community health *evangelist*, community health *education*, or community health *educator*.

2   One approach to the spiritual discipline of confession is breathing out sins and breathing in God's forgiveness. This is known as spiritual breathing.

Part three

Building
Healing
Communities

15
Healing: the church's birthright

Karin and Wesley Granberg-Michaelson

> *Shalom* is never individual but corporate, known
> in community. It is never just between people,
> but always incorporates a right relationship to
> all creation. Its purpose is not human mastery
> and dominion, but the praise and glory of God.

We can probably all think of examples of people who have become ill right after some psychic blow, such as a woman who first evidences cancer shortly following her husband's death. These people may be literally embodying their pain and sense of loss. Holistic or whole-person care assumes that health is a composite result of emotions and spiritual orientation as well as physical condition. This concept is expressed in the Old Testament unity between body and spirit and is part of our Christian heritage.

Holistic medicine is clearly a concept and practice whose time has come. With the widespread divergence in holistic health care and practice, it may be clarifying to explain that church-based holistic health care confines itself to traditional medical practice with a special emphasis on the emotional, spiritual, and perhaps nutritional factors in illness. Secular expressions of holistic health care often include Eastern religious practices and paramedical approaches to healing such as yoga, herbal remedies, or megadoses of vitamins. A primary commitment of Christians involved in whole-person health care, however, is, to return health care to the domain of the church. People should not be treated medically apart from a holistic approach.

In practical terms, whole-person care treats each person's illness as multidimensional, particularly focusing on the emotional and spiritual factors that have contributed to getting sick. It recognizes the close connection between a person's sense of well-being, or lack of it, and physical health. Feelings of alienation from God and from significant others, of anger, of guilt, and of frustration eventually find expression in bodily and emotional illness if they are not attended to. Whole-person health care takes particular interest in the range of psychosomatic illnesses in which soul and body appear to be divided and working against the total health of a person.

Paul Tournier's medical experience convinced him that spiritual unrest underlies many chronic and acute illnesses. When this unrest reaches great enough proportions it throws the body's systems out of balance. So he encourages his patients to probe deeply into the feelings that accompany their physical or emotional illnesses. In doing so, they often discover a need to make restitution to someone, perhaps a parent or a spouse. When patients pursue the roots of their illnesses and properly mend broken relationships, their balance is restored. Then a measure of healing takes place.

In the affluent Western world, traditional medical practice is being reexamined by various forces in the culture, reflecting the breakdown of the worldview inherited from the Enlightenment and the scientific revolution. The person can no longer be neatly divided into physical, mental and spiritual parts. The personal relationship between the health care provider and the patient is central to the healing process. Resources for health are not merely external to the patient, delivered through a technological process, but are also internal, within the patient's total person. Disease, while having intensely personal effects, is not an individual phenomenon, but is linked to a web of biological, social, environmental, nutritional, economic, and even political factors.

Growing sensitivities such as these have spawned a plethora of theories, books, movements, organizations, and innovative approaches to healing and health. Some are foolish and perhaps even dangerous. Others are insightful harbingers of future health care. Some trends move within the safe boundaries of the medical establishment, such as wellness centers promoted by hospitals. Others, like the hospice movement, are on the fringes. Still others, like the rapid growth of various healing ministries conducted by noisy evangelists, or practiced quietly in committed prayer groups, are generally regarded with skepticism—if not disdain—by the medical establishment.

Consider the dramatically changing attitudes in Western culture toward the experience of giving birth. Thirty years ago, giving birth was regarded as a health problem demanding a technological solution, resulting often in the mother being made numb to the process. Today, giving birth is regarded by parents as a natural life experience to be savored, shared, and even enjoyed. Home births have increased to such an extent that hospitals are rushing to provide birthing rooms designed to convince the patients that they are not really in a hospital.

All these trends reflect how a changing world view is affecting medical practice today in Western societies. Fundamentally, these developments illustrate the folly of approaching the healing process from a thoroughly secular framework, assuming that health can be narrowed to a purely physical, scientific, technological and individual framework.

Christians involved in health care encounter a rich and open opportunity. To put it bluntly, the governing assumptions of secular medicine have stood in a distinct but often unspoken conflict with biblical insights. Now, as a new level of dialogue over the meaning and practice of health is emerging, the church should play a critical role.

The time has come in the life of the church to rejoin the separate roles of doctor and priest. Practically and literally this task may seem nearly impossible. Robert Reeves, Jr., points out the common reality:[1]

> Although we talk a great deal about "total patient care"
> in actuality we show little evidence of believing in it. We
> seem quite content to deal with a patient as if the only

thing that mattered was the welfare of his body, if we are doctors, or of his spell, if we are clergy. We do, of course, tip our hats to each other as a gesture of courtesy, and sentimentalize about the importance of both the body and the soul — and then go right on as we were before, preoccupied with laboratory findings, the mechanics of surgery, stomping out disease, or with the rituals of religion, pious reassurance, bombardment of God with prayer.

The trouble is, we are stomping on human beings in the process. The bombardment backfires. We sometimes wind up with sicker patients than we had before, neither healed nor saved.

Symbolically, at least, there must be a deep wedding of medicine and religion. Our ministers must become wise in the way of the human psyche and our doctors must become well-acquainted with the spiritual world.

Biblical foundation

The New Testament pictures the healing acts of Jesus, and then of the early church, as signs of the kingdom at hand. The accounts include critical details of who is healed, when they are healed, and how they respond are always critical. The unclean lowly woman, the despised and outcast leper, the isolated paralytic, the blind beggar—these experience the dramatic embrace of God's love. Once thus loved and accepted, their experience threatens all those powers, traditions, and people that have ignored, rejected, and suppressed them. Healing is part of creating a new order in society. It announces salvation. It demonstrates justice. It points to shalom, God's intended wholeness for all creation.

After Peter's Pentecost sermon, a forty-year-old lame man lying at the gate to the temple was healed. Peter proclaimed that the resurrection power of Jesus, which was active to restore all things, had healed the cripple, and that this Jesus was to be worshiped as Lord over all. The threatened authorities arrested Peter and John. They understood that this healing was no mere good deed, but rather a challenge to their power, a call for a new allegiance, and an assault on the prevailing system.

By contrast, much of our healing has been co-opted by the system. Rather than witness to a new order based on God's justice, we make an uneasy truce with the prevailing system even as we treat its victims.

Too often we remain locked in narrow, parochial, self serving definitions of health care that are clearly unbiblical and reinforce a compartmentalization of life that denies the wholeness of the gospel's message. When we restrict health to the individual, when we are imprisoned by the glittering promises of technological mastery, when we conveniently ignore connections between health care and social justice, and when we deny that healing has any intrinsic relationship to taking care of the earth, then we are resisting the Bible's own definition of health, healing, and wholeness.

From the outset of the Bible, we know that all creation is one, proclaimed as good, and intimately dependent on its Creator. God's intention for creation is expressed in the rich Old Testament vision of *shalom*. The term indicates a wholeness, fulfillment, harmony, and peace characterizing the earth and all its inhabitants. This is the root of the Bible's understanding of health; it provides a basis for the Old Testament understanding of salvation. This *shalom* is never individual but corporate, known in community. It is never just between people, but always incorporates a right relationship to all creation. Its purpose is not human mastery and dominion, but the praise and glory of God.

Jesus Christ comes as the Prince of this shalom, or peace, and his body is to be the sign that creation itself has been redeemed. God reigns. Shalom will be restored. The kingdom will come on earth. Here is the foundation for all the church's ministry of healing—healing of the person, healing of the community, healing of the earth, for the glory of God.

This discussion of the healing community is rooted in the belief that it is a global and ecumenical reality. While communities may have different visions and ways of working together to accomplish their mission, ultimately they all exist for the healing of the

241

nations. Healing communities from the North and South need each other to find the wholeness God intends for us all.

It is obvious that communities in the developing countries are forced to concentrate on practical survival needs, while those in the more developed nations may have the luxury to focus on theological, ethical and philosophical issues. The division between rich and poor is in the end perhaps more powerful than those of race and sex. The developed nations, too, have their pockets of poverty where people starve in the midst of plenty. This division between rich and poor certainly creates different kinds of communities in different corners of the world. Yet they are all needed because the body has many parts and each is indispensable to the other.

The call for interdependence is a far cry from the reality most of us know. We have separated ourselves from this reality in the world today. The North in fact is arrogant and cannot imagine what it needs to learn from the experience of the poor in traditional cultures of the South. Yet it is in the cries of the people for liberation from all forms of injustice that we are all awakened to the vision of the kingdom of God and the need for the church to respond in a peaceful revolution so that righteousness and peace at last will join hands.

The contribution of South to North is contained in part by the Liberation Theology that comes from Latin America and is echoed in repressive countries of Asia and Africa. The response to Liberation Theology in these regions has caused the people of God to come together in the ecclesial base communities to say no to death and disorder and to build communities of hope who read and interpret the Bible with new eyes—the eyes of wounded healers. The Bible they read together instructs them to rise up and be free from all that is holding them back.

These communities of liberation are sounding a call to the rest of the church to respond to the cries of all people. But what does the South have to teach the North about creating healing communities? And how can this dialogue take place?

The Christian Medical Commission of the World Council of Churches believes that traditional societies have an inherent understanding of health, that disturbances in beliefs and feelings are root causes of illness. Many of these societies have preserved the sense of belonging to the community that the developed nations have lost or are in danger of losing. The sense of identity and place provided by traditional cultures protects individuals against the isolation and alienation that are a bitter reality for many living in industrialized nations of the North. Progress is a comfortable disease that has spread the sickness of the modern age throughout all of the world's cities, but traditional societies do not so quickly succumb to the breakdown of life in community.

The church needs to take hold of this message that we were created to be people in community—not isolated individuals pursuing our own futures. Traditional concepts of health and sickness support the view that disharmony in relationships with God, neighbor and significant relatives leads to separation, brokenness and sin. This lack of well-being occurs in all cultures and calls for gifts the church has to offer. Confession and forgiveness restore a person to life in community. In Africa and Asia, the family or a community elder deal with broken relationships.

Not only can much be learned from a dialogue between traditional healers and Western medical practitioners, but the church can learn from these traditional models of caring community. Things might look very different in many churches in the North if elders in the community saw it as their responsibility to mediate troubled relationships where necessary. In many parts of the North, particularly in large cities, the heritage of being part of something larger than oneself has been lost. There is no community. There is no longer an elder with the authority to bring wounded parties together to seek reconciliation. Pastors who are themselves isolated and alienated cannot create community out of nothing and are not prepared in many cases to intervene in the lives of people in their congregation.

People in the North have moved very far away from their roots in earlier traditional communities where people knew where they came from and to whom they belonged. It is no wonder then that so much of the disease prevalent in affluent societies represents disorder of the soul and stems from this lack of community.

Healing communities

Although communities in the South struggle against seemingly insurmountable obstacles of poverty, disease and war, many have preserved a sense of belonging that promotes well-being and combats illness. What do these communities look like? How can the whole church benefit from their example? Do they bear any resemblance to the community experience of the North?

East African revival

Dan Kaseje, a former Director of the Christian Medical Commission of the World Council of Churches, comes out of a community experience in his home of Kenya. He and his family participated in the East African revival that swept the country from the early 1930's and 1940's and still exists in a modified form today.

The East African revival began in Rwanda and quickly spread throughout the whole of East Africa. Initially, the revival was a threat to the organized church, but eventually many pastors joined in, and its impact was felt by the mainstream of the east African church. Today it exists in four camps with differing emphases.

The revival was centered around personal conversion and giving public witness to that experience. In Dan's view, the outstanding gift of this revival was the way in which the Scripture was applied in the local context. Each Bible study meeting would lead the group to a specific form of response, particularly to confession or needed repentance. People would then seek to restore the broken relationship on the spot. Repentance was central in order to maintain their walk in the light.

Members felt a constant need to put right their relationship with God and others. What this meant to participants in the revival was what they called a repeated journey to the cross to make confession and be restored in fellowship. The repeated self-examination meant that people had a strong sense of personal responsibility for their faith and did not tend to blame others for their failures. They also took personal responsibility for being reconciled with others in the community when things went amiss.

What can the world church learn from the East African revival's attempt to be a healing community? As a former member, Dan Kaseje believes it is the role of confession and forgiveness combined with the deep sense of belonging to a community. Additionally, the clear-cut, life-giving entrance requirement of "walking in the light" calls the church back to its origins described in Acts and the Epistles.

Ecclesial base communities

The *ecclesial base community* movement of Latin America is another model of healing community that can enrich the world church. The base communities, which are a major force in the remarkable political change taking place today, are the result of people being empowered by the faith and community that, in turn, comes directly out of experience with poverty and political injustice. As some thinkers have said, those who read the Bible on an empty stomach draw different conclusions from those who read it in comfortable surroundings. In countries with a debt crisis that hurts poor people already groaning under the burdens of hunger, malnutrition, illiteracy and political violence, reading the Bible from the perspective of *favelas* (slums) has given rise to new communities that are shaping a grassroots theology and impacting the ecumenical church.

Bruce Menning and Gene Beerens, two Reformed Church in America pastors, are well known to the authors. These two pastors have been profoundly affected by seeing that many of the same struggles confront both urban poor people in North America (where the pastors work and live) and people in ecclesial base communities they have been regularly visiting for five years. Bruce has written about the base communities he has visited in Latin America; Gene has written about the base community he is experiencing with ex-prisoners in the inner city where he ministers.

Bruce Menning sees the base communities as a new reformation in the church—a living sign that our theology must lead to political and economic action. He suggests that the poor see God most clearly because they have fewer idols than the rich. This should lead the church to trust what the poor say about God and be suspicious of how the rich use God to defend the status quo. In Bruce's words,

> There is a conversion that comes from nontourist travel to the Third World countries. It challenges one's theology, ecclesiology, politics, economics and lifestyle. . . . The Word of God has been rediscovered by the people. They have claimed it as their possession, both in its reading and its interpretation. It ties all of life together and gives it meaning. Furthermore, the Scripture has called forth a priesthood of all believers, producing leadership for church and society.

> Pope John XXIII sought a church that was more than hierarchy. He sought a church actively made up of the whole people of God. Nowhere is this vision of the church more clearly realized than in the base communities.

Base community gatherings may be planned by a nun or priest, but there is strong lay participation. Small groups come together informally to pray, read the Bible and apply it to their own life situation. They take time to share their insights with one another. One theologian from Brazil says that biblical texts are often used as a background to analyze common problems the community faces such as poor housing conditions and lack of drinking water. In this way, Christian faith is being translated into the everyday reality of poor people. For many of the women involved in the church base communities, Bible study has been the first step toward a self-awareness that has led them to become active in political issues outside the church as well.

A base community in Michigan
Gene Beerens made several trips to Latin America to dialogue with base community leadership. This caused him to make many compar-

isons to his own ministry with recently released prisoners in inner city Grand Rapids, Michigan (U.S.A.). Gene has shared his reflections in an informal newsletter from his ministry, Cross Road Correctional Ministries. He notes that the Third World exists in the First World—and vice versa—wherever people are held hostage to injustice by their national and cultural systems. This insight has challenged him to participate in a form of Christian base community among the volunteer staff and ex-prisoners with whom he works.

Gene found that the weekly support group has challenged his assumptions and values and empowered his formerly imprisoned sisters and brothers who are trying to re-enter North American society. The growing base community will soon "multiply by division." The small percentage of people who have chosen to be part of this group are all being converted and rehabilitated.

In adapting many principles of the base communities of Latin America to his own inner-city context, Gene is demonstrating what our churches could do on a larger scale to share ways of forming communities where all forms of healing—physical, emotional, spiritual and societal—can take place. Gene concludes,

> It is not only the prisoner or former prisoner who needs to hear the forgiving and liberating gospel of Jesus Christ. We as well need to hear it—from their unique vantage point—as it impacts that "space" where structural evil and personal sin has deeply entangled and damaged so many lives. Perhaps they have more to offer to us than we to them, if we really care to learn about how the demons and idols of sin and death affect us all.

The Medical Mission Sisters

Describing the journey of the Medical Mission Sisters who have been involved in the healing ministry of the church for over sixty-five years, Sarah Summers and Mary Pawath report that they began to sense a call to create caring communities in which people became aware of their own right to life and health. Their programs became more community-based. The people themselves began to identify needs and make decisions about responses. The sisters

247

wrote, "We knew that we could no longer remain silent in the face of unjust local, national, and international systems and policies that affected life and health."

The Medical Missionary Sisters moved into public life to help people exert pressure on government hospitals in the Philippines and in South India to provide accessible health care. They are learning again and again that the process of healing is essentially one of building relationships and so building one world. "Healing is a way of life in which all of us recognize that our humanness is being drawn by God into wholeness," they said.

As Catholic priest Thomas Merton put it in *New Seeds of Contemplation*, "The whole idea of compassion is based on a keen awareness of the interdependence of all living beings that are all part of one another and all involved in one another."

Christian ashrams

In another corner of the world, some Indian Christians have adapted the wisdom of their indigenous religious traditions to the creation of Christian ashrams (spiritual communities). These ashrams, located all over India, promote healing community by encouraging their members to practice a simple lifestyle focused on the Spirit. An atmosphere of tranquility is maintained through daily prayer and devotion. Counselling or spiritual direction is provided by experienced members.

The ashram community seeks to develop an attitude of detachment that frees them from the distractions of life and allows them to concentrate on communing with God and reflects their roots from many faiths.

Some Christian medical institutions in India, such as the Church of South India's college and hospital in Vellore, are making use of the ashram principles in the treatment of medical patients. The former hospital chaplain at Vellore, A. C. Oomen, wrote about his experience in an informal communication:

> In almost every aspect of healing recorded in the New
> Testament, there is a community present either bringing

the patient to the Lord, or coming with the healer. Health is far from individualistic. It is realized in relationship.

Nearly every disease described in the New Testament has a symbolic value as the disease of the community. The blind man points out those who cannot see the truth, the deaf, those who are insensitive to the voice of God. To forget this representative aspect both of sickness and of health is to miss the centrality of the meaning of the *koinonia* in the New Testament.

An institute in Papua New Guinea

Sister Mary MacDonald is a member of a Melanesian pastoral and socioeconomic institute in Papua New Guinea. She described healing in the community of the South Kewa people by saying,

As for the people of Jesus' time, so too, for the people of Mararoko today, sickness is viewed in terms of damaged or broken relationships, in terms of sinfulness. Traditional society provides for confession of sins on occasions of illness and danger of death, and a preliminary task for healers is to discover what wrongdoing or broken relationship of the sick person or his or her family has caused the illness. This may be openly confessed or suggestions or accusations may be made. The damage must be recognized and put right so that the sick person can be restored to health and reconciled to his or her community.

Using their own traditional healers and Western nurses, the people of Mararoko anoint their sick with oil and the laying on of hands. In some cases the traditional healers may even choose to anoint the whole body of the sick person.

A common thread

There are many such examples of healing communities and healing practices throughout the globe. As churches continue to pursue their healing mandate, they should recognize the common thread in these examples and consider them carefully:

- All communities require commitment and self-sacrifice, whatever their context.

- People belong in community, whether in the extended family or in the church.

- Finding one's place, and experiencing solidarity in the struggle for justice and liberation is empowering and thus healing.

- Reconciliation within community life always creates wholeness and sometimes even cure.

- Community and a sense of belonging significantly improve health.

Note

1   Robert Reeves, *Healing and Salvation*, unpublished manuscript. Unless otherwise noted, the direct quotations in this chapter come from personal communications, newsletters and other informal sources.

16
The healing ministry and the local congregation

Murray Robertson

> Healing is a sign of the kingdom, but because the kingdom is not yet fully come, not all will be healed. When the kingdom comes in all its fullness, we will experience total healing in the presence of the Lord.

My own spiritual upbringing began in a liberal Presbyterian church in New Zealand. As far as the healing ministry is concerned, this was a major disadvantage. From the vague recollections of my early years, I have memories of sermons on the supernatural aspects of Jesus' ministry. These were often explained away as being unlikely coincidences, or having some other natural explanation. In hindsight, I suppose it had one advantage. At least I was not locked into the dispensational viewpoint which is so crippling for many evangelical Christians, when the healing ministry of Jesus and the apostles is divided off from the rest of the Christian era.

My journey to personal faith began at a Billy Graham crusade in 1959. I began reading the Bible and sharing the new faith I had found. A year into this experience I came in contact with a charismatic group at the local Baptist church, who prayed for me to experience an empowering of the Holy Spirit. Since then I have never had any serious doubts that healing is an important part of Jesus' ministry in the world today.

I completed a degree in philosophy at the University of Wellington. Then Marj and I were married and we spent three years in Edinburgh where I undertook a degree in theology. Coming back to New Zealand at the end of the 1960s, we were called to a small church in a working-class suburb of Christchurch.

Spreydon Baptist Church

Spreydon Baptist Church started in 1865, 15 years after the European settlement of Christchurch began. In its early decades the church had a very effective ministry. But when we arrived over a century later, although the surrounding suburban area had grown to a community of over 30,000 people, the church had dwindled to a tiny, mostly elderly, congregation of about 50.

Tragically, the church typified the plight of Protestant congregations in working-class areas in most Western countries. Although many younger pastors begin their ministries in churches like this, they quickly move on to more prestigious congregations in middle- and upper-middle-class areas. However, twenty-five years later we are still here.

In spite of wanting to move on many occasions, and often having the feeling our time was completed, the Lord has kept us here. Over the years we have been on a journey of faith with this community. Most of the things I have learned about ministry I have learned in fellowship with the people in this community of faith.

My initial concerns for the congregation did not center around the healing ministry, but rather the ministry of evangelism. It didn't take much perception to realize the church had what seemed to be a terminal illness. Unless new people came to faith, it seemed unlikely the congregation could survive.

I began with an expository series of messages on Luke's Gospel that took about two and a half years to complete. I have remained committed to an expository preaching model. I think it is the only approach that allows for the development of a long-term ministry.

I now believe passionately that if local congregations are to go on significant journeys of faith they need leaders who will be committed for the long haul. There are very few large Protestant churches in New Zealand, and there are also very few pastors who stay very much beyond the customary five to eight year period of ministry. But God in his good purpose has kept us here, and so we have been able to share in a faith journey of discovery.

The adventure begins

My first recollection of a healing experience in the ministry here occurred when a man had to take several days off work because of a back condition. I remember visiting him, putting my hand on his back and praying for God to heal him. He rang me the next day to say that the pain had left him and he was back at work. Over the next few years there were a number of intermittent experiences of that nature. I had not seen the healing ministry as a priority. It was something that happened along with a number of other things.

Then about seven years into our ministry, David Watson came to Christchurch. He had come to take a mission at the local university, and I was invited to be the assistant missioner. I spent the week with him. During that time he shared with me about the journey of St. Cuthberts Church in York. In many ways this is what I had been waiting to hear.

Although my wife Marj and I had both had a charismatic experience in the early 1960s, we really had little idea about how to integrate it within the life of an evangelical congregation. In the mid-1970s in New Zealand, there had been a number of spectacular relationship explosions in churches that had tried to move into the charismatic dimension. Many people talked about powerful encounters with the Spirit. But there didn't seem to be any churches testifying to what could happen with an openness to this area of spiritual life.

Now here was David Watson talking about a church that had been open to the Holy Spirit, had effective ministries in evangelism and healing and was growing while relating together in unity. It gave me the confidence to believe this could actually happen and marked the real beginning of our adventure with charismatic gifts.

One unexpected outcome of this new life in the Spirit was that we started having a weekly Communion service, which is unusual in a Baptist congregation. Very soon after starting this we began inviting people to come forward during Communion if they wanted prayer for physical or emotional healing. We have been doing this for nearly twenty years now and have seen many people touched by the grace of God.

A short time afterwards we began a Friday noon healing service, and this too has continued to the present. The service begins with a time of reflective worship and praise, then people break into teams to pray for those who have come. In our healing ministry we have been committed to having people pray in teams of two or three with individuals who come seeking help. People come to this service with a variety of disorders, both physical and emotional.

About seven years ago, John Wimber paid his first visit to New Zealand. I was strongly challenged about the healing ministry. Subsequently, I experienced a power encounter that left me laughing for a long time. I was asked to write about the experience in the book *Riding the Third Wave*. This was a turning point in my willingness to more imaginatively trust the Holy Spirit to raise up ministries in our community, without the need to be in control of what was happening.

An inhibiting factor for many of us in ministry is our need to feel that we are in control of what is going on. And extensive ministerial training can end up creating people who are more interested in managing organizations than in creating a climate where the Holy Spirit is free to raise up the kind of ministries he desires.

A healing ministry takes shape

Subsequently we have seen the development of an extremely diverse and varied number of ministries operating from our church into the surrounding community. The healing ministry plays an important part in this. We have seen development in six areas.

1. Personal healing

In addition to giving opportunities for healing prayer at Communion and in the Friday healing service, we have seen the emergence of other prayer healing groups. One of our pastoral staff members takes overall responsibility for the healing ministry.

We are not simply pragmatists. We have felt that throughout the development of the healing ministry, it has been important to engage in theological reflection. We see the healing ministry in terms of a theology of the kingdom of God. In the ministry of Jesus the kingdom has come, but it has not yet fully come.

In his ministry Jesus mentioned healing as one of the signs that God was at work (Luke 7:22). I would understand this to mean that because the kingdom is with us now in the person of Jesus, some people will be healed in response to prayer. Healing is a sign of the kingdom, but because the kingdom is not yet fully come, not all will be fully healed. Some will not be healed at all. This is part of the tension of living "between the times." The kingdom has come, but not fully come. There will come a day when the kingdom comes in all its fullness and we will be in the presence of the Lord. Then total healing will be experienced.

One alternative to this kingdom view of the healing ministry is the "faith teaching" that if we have faith we will be healed, and we will see healing in others. As well as being pastorally devastating, this teaching is biblically unbalanced. I cannot see where Jesus sent people away condemned because of their lack of faith. If there was anyone he confronted about their lack of faith, it was not sick people who came seeking healing, but the disciples.

To the faith teachers who condemn other people for their lack of faith, I say that in the Gospels it is people like them who received a hard word from the Lord, not the sick people who were being prayed for. Pastorally, it is not difficult to find people who have been spiritually crippled by this teaching. People have been told they must always make a "positive confession" and then have terrible difficulty facing the reality of what is going on within and around them. They can end up struggling to live with unreality. We need a theological framework that helps us understand the healing ministry and in itself helps people to be whole.

2. *Spiritual and medical healing*

Our church lies midway between the two main hospitals in Christchurch; over the years many doctors have worshiped with us. One of them was Gareth Tuckwell from England who spent a year with us over a decade ago. When he and his family were here we enthusiastically discussed developing a church-based healing center that Gareth would lead as a member of the church staff. But Gareth was not able to get long-term residency in the country, and eventually a very important healing ministry opened up for him at the Burrswood community in England. (*See chapter nine – ed.*)

But a few years later, a similar kind of center eventually came into existence: the Arahura Christian Medical and Counseling Center. A group of three people had a vision for this: a general practitioner, an allergy specialist and a counselor on our pastoral staff. There are now other full-time staff in the center. A four-year training program for Christian counselors has been developed.

The Center's work is finding a widespread acceptance in the secular medical community. Its main faith journey has been exploring the relationship between medical work and counseling and the spiritual dimensions of healing. One growth area has been the interaction between pastoral and medical people in the healing process, although some doctors are keener than others to be involved with people outside their own profession. Although it is an overtly Christian center, many non-Christians are willing to pay for counseling.

One special area of ministry has been working with people from churches with a strongly triumphalist emphasis. Many have come because in their own churches they have not been able to acknowledge spiritual struggles and have been prayed for without being physically healed. These denials have produced real difficulties for them. The center has had an important role in enabling people to come to a more holistic appreciation of the faith. It has enabled some people who might have left the church to stay in fellowship.

3. Psychiatric healing

Over the last few years, we have developed a community help center. This has come through the vision of one man whose wife had been under psychiatric care. After he had come to faith in Jesus in the mid-1980s, he had a vision for developing the community help center, which is located not far from our local mental hospital. A variety of ministries have grown out of this center, including an opportunity shop, meals on wheels, practical help for incapacitated people and other ministries.

Early on, a Bible study group was established for a number of needy people, many of whom were psychiatric patients. This group very rapidly outgrew the room in which it was meeting and began meeting in our church hall. It has now grown into a Tuesday night congregation of about 130 people worshiping in our church building. It is unlike any other congregation I have ever seen. Many who attend have psychiatric needs and other forms of disability.

This is one of the best examples I know of a contextualized congregation ministering to people who have come from this kind of background. But it is better experienced than described. Last year a journalist from Radio New Zealand spent a week with us preparing a documentary on our church. At the beginning of the week he described himself to me as a Christian humanist who had pulled out of attending church. At the end of the week he said that the time with us had given him back his faith. When I asked him what specifically had caused this, he said it was attending the Tuesday night congregation. "It was like being at a party," he said.

In addition to the community help center, we have two houses for the rehabilitation of psychiatric patients. These are government-funded operations. Also, a family in the church operates another large house for people with a broad range of emotional needs. This is a privately funded ministry.

4. Healing the demonized

It seems to me that evangelical Christians tend either to ignore the controversial area of healing the demonized or go overboard with it. In our journey with this area of healing we have come to see demonization as something of a "secondary infection," to use medical terminology. Something happens to a person that results in them opening their life in some way to the powers of darkness. These powers may be expelled through healing prayer, but long-term healing will not result if the root cause of the problem, the place of entry to the enemy, is not addressed.

The story that Jesus recounted in Luke 11:24-26 illustrates this. A demon had been expelled from a person. It eventually comes back and finds the person's life cleaned out but nothing put in its place. The demon then goes and gets seven others worse than itself and in this last state the person is worse than the first. This understanding of a secondary infection can help make sense of some deliverance ministries. Often, claims are made about demons being expelled, but after a period of time the person's life seems to be no different from what it was at the beginning. Sometimes in these deliverance ministries the secondary infection is cured but the root cause is not dealt with.

I have found David Pytche's understanding of the Apostle Paul's terminology to be helpful at this point. He notes that Paul uses a variety of terms for the work of demons in people's lives, such as fiery darts, footholds, strongholds, bondages and possessions (*Come Holy Spirit*, 1985, pp. 198-199). It is not possible to systematize these terms (the source material isn't extensive enough), but we have a picture of various degrees of demonization. What is a helpful healing procedure in one situation may not necessarily be so in another. Basically, in the healing of the demonized, we are seeking to let the light of Christ expose the powers of darkness. To find the root of the problem for people who are demonized requires a context of pastoral care and healing love.

5. Healing in the community

Unfortunately, in the ministry of healing a dichotomy has arisen between those seeking healing for individuals and those seeking healing in a wider social context. So some Christians gather in small groups to pray for individuals, and others are involved in struggling for social justice. As I look at the biblical material, I don't see that it is basically an either-or option. Our concern for healing is to be a widely encompassing experience, embracing both individuals and the social context in which people live.

We have sought to create a climate in the church where people are encouraged to hear what God is saying to them about the ministry of the kingdom of God. Accordingly, we have seen a variety of ministries come into existence that have had a healing component in a broader social context.

One example is the Kingdom Bank. Since this started several years ago, nearly NZ$1 million has been lent to poor people at no interest. This has often enabled people to pay off outstanding debts, in some cases keeping them out of prison. Loan recipients have someone from the church work alongside them building a relationship of trust, helping them sort through their financial problems. Most people in these kinds of difficulties not only have financial problems but also have whole areas of their lives that need healing. Through relationships formed in these ways we have seen some people take the step of faith and become followers of Jesus.

Another example is a series of clubs for at-risk young people called Manaaki Tanga, a Maori word which means "people who love." There are also clubs for young people of high school age and clubs for younger children. The newest club is for pregnant teenage girls.

It is a hard and demanding ministry to build relationships with these young people and involve them in various activities. Virtually all of the young people in these clubs are victims of sexual abuse and have other areas in their lives that need healing.

6. Healing worldwide

In our journey of faith as a church, we have tried to be open to the Father's heart of compassion for the whole world. One of the most significant areas of development for us in the last few years was to help form the mission Servants to Asian's Urban Poor. This grew out of a ministry in the slums of Manila and is now a holistic mission with people involved from Australia, Switzerland, Britain, the United States, Brazil, France and Germany as well as New Zealand. A mission to the largest cities of Asia, it includes ministries of evangelism, healing, church planting and community development.

This mission is part of our healing ministry. The powers of darkness enslave the poor of the earth in poverty and oppression. Christians go to live in the midst of the darkness, struggle for justice, become involved with people in the development of their communities, pray for the sick and share the gospel. Some of our church's best people have pursued ministries like this and then returned to our church. This, of course, has a profound effect on our life here. It isn't possible to have people involved in a healing ministry of this kind and simply carry on back home as a comfortable, established congregation.

The journey continues

We have come a long way from the day when I prayed for the man with a sore back. However, we see this whole experience as a journey. A good journey is an exciting experience with a sense of adventure. Through many struggles and trips down cul-de-sacs, it has been a learning and growing experience. But the journey isn't over. It is continuing as we seek to be open to what God has for us.

One passage of Scripture in particular has shaped our thinking on the journey. Jesus was in the synagogue at Nazareth at the beginning of his ministry. He asked for the scroll of the prophet Isaiah and read:

> The Spirit of the Lord is up me, because he has anointed
> me to preach good news to the poor. He has sent me to
> proclaim freedom for the prisoners and recovery of sight

for the blind, to release the oppressed, to proclaim the year of the Lord's favor (Luke 4:18-19).

This is the mandate of Jesus. It is all about healing. Good News comes to the poor. Freedom is proclaimed for the prisoners, the blind receive their sight. The oppressed are released. Economic justice is proclaimed. We see this as our mandate as we seek to continue the journey of faith.

17
Burrswood Christian Centre for Medical and Spiritual Care

Gareth Tuckwell and Hugh Sansom

> All who come to Burrswood are God's gifts to
> us, in ordinary or beautiful packages. But some
> appear battered in transit despite warnings like
> "Fragile, handle with care" or "Do not bend."
> They are afraid it will hurt to be unwrapped, or
> need help to accept God's gift of themselves that
> is inside.

Burrswood is a Christian Center for medical and spiritual care. People find the healing of Jesus Christ through skilled nursing, medical expertise, counseling and prayer. Stillness and beauty provide space for the Holy Spirit's transforming work in every area of life. Many who come for a short stay are enabled to do so without regard to their means.

The community of Burrswood, with its individual gifts and abilities, is committed to bringing together medicine and Christianity and to working within the mystery of healing and suffering. It aims to keep the love of Christ at the heart of care and to be a sign of the kingdom of God in a hurting world.

How Burrswood began

Burrswood Christian Centre for Medical and Spiritual Care, situated on the Kent-Sussex border in southeast England, was founded in 1948 by the late Dorothy Kerin as the result of her miraculous healing in 1912. Dorothy was born in London in 1899, one of five children. She was devoted to both her parents, and after the death of her father in 1902, her own health began to deteriorate. The family doctor told Mrs. Kerin that Dorothy was a very delicate child who would need constant care. Despite her mother's loving care, Dorothy had a severe attack of diphtheria four years later and was sent to an isolation hospital. Although this was followed by nine months convalescence in a sanatorium, Dorothy was still far from well and soon was confined to bed by tuberculosis, pneumonia and pleurisy. Her mother said that Dorothy seemed to live so close to her Master that visitors to her bedroom were aware of a divine presence. Dorothy spent much time in prayer and intercession, and many people felt the Lord's touch on their lives in answer to her prayers.

By January 1912 tuberculosis had spread to Dorothy's brain, leaving her blind and deaf. The doctors could do no more for her, and she was not able to take any food by mouth. She was kept alive by means of starch and opium injections and other stimulants, but eventually became unconscious for two weeks.

On February 18, her pulse faltered for eight minutes. Then the family, who had been warned by the doctor that she would not live through the day, saw her suddenly sit up in bed. She announced, "Mother, I am well, I must get up now." Getting out of bed and walking for the first time for several years, she demanded and ate a proper meal. When she eventually returned to bed, she slept soundly. The next morning her family and her doctor were amazed to see that her body had returned to a perfectly normal condition and that her bones were covered with firm healthy flesh.

Three weeks later, while staying in the home of a specialist doctor in London, Dorothy received a vision with a message from God:

> Dorothy, you are quite well now. God has brought you back to use you for a great and privileged work. In your prayers and faith many sick shall you heal; comfort the sorrowing and give faith to the faithless.

It was 17 years before she was able to see how God wanted her to start fulfilling this commission. In 1929 she opened her first home of healing, St. Raphael, in Ealing. As demand for places at St. Raphael increased, she was constantly looking for ways to expand and over the next few years purchased several other houses on the same street. The money for all these purchases was given in response to her prayers of faith.

Dorothy believed strongly that there was no conflict between prayer and conventional medical treatment, and her work had the support of four eminent Harley Street specialists and several leading Anglican churchmen, including the Archbishop of Canterbury and the Bishop of London. The home at Ealing, which was officially registered as a nursing home, also had a chapel at its heart, and services of prayer for healing were held regularly.

In 1946 Dorothy bought a house in Speldhurst, Kent, and two years later purchased Burrswood, just a few miles away in Groombridge. The properties in Ealing were eventually sold, and all the work was transferred to Kent. Extensive restoration and building work was completed; Burrswood became the sole center for her work and ministry.

Dorothy's last major undertaking was construction of the Church of Christ the Healer at Burrswood. Capable of accommodating over 200 people, the church was built by a local firm in just eleven months and was dedicated in May 1960.

She died in January 1963. Soon afterwards the Dorothy Kerin Trust was set up to continue her divine calling to heal the sick, comfort the sorrowing and give faith to the faithless. The work not only continued but has also expanded and developed.

A detailed account of Dorothy's life and the fulfillment of her vision has been given by Bishop Morris Maddocks, Advisor for the Ministry of Health and Healing to the Archbishops of Canterbury and York in his book *The Vision of Dorothy Kerin* (Hodder & Stoughton, 1991), to which the authors are indebted for some of this information.

Burrswood today

With over 290 acres of beautiful woodland and meadows, Burrswood's setting brings beauty, peace and a sense of spaciousness to those who come. With about 120 on the staff and more than 100 volunteers, there is a feeling that time can indeed be given to those in need.

In addition to housing for about 30 staff and a small block of administrative offices, Burrswood has the following facilities:

A *medical center* has 31 beds and offers full medical care for all who do not require highly specialized monitoring. There are two resident doctors who work alongside two chaplains, about 30 nurses, a counselor, physiotherapists and other staff to provide closely coordinated care. The doctors have access to full diagnostic facilities, and visiting consultants provide specialist advice as necessary. Equipment includes lifts, wheelchairs and hoists, plus telephones, nurse call, color television, and a sound relay from the church in each room.

Most who come cannot afford the actual cost of their stay, but there is a bursary fund so that no one need be turned away on grounds of finance. A minimum charge of £40 per week is made.

Each year there are about 650 short-stay admissions to the medical center, the average length of stay being 16 days. People come with all manner of illness and difficulty. All come with their doctor's approval, but the referral to Burrswood may have been initiated by them, their vicar or minister, their social worker, or by their general practitioner or consultant. Some are admitted with acute illness such as pneumonia or heart failure, some come for rehabilitation after a stroke or surgery, some come for help with depression, spiritual problems, anxiety and stress-related problems, and others come for respite or hospice-type care.

The *Chapel House* at Burrswood provides a guest house for those who do not need medical care but require a time of rest or personal retreat with the opportunity to join in daily worship. Some may come at a crossroads in life, looking to rediscover their deeper selves and experience values that give meaning and structure to their lives. Others come for good food, fellowship and a break from the daily tasks of life. About 550 stay each year under the pastoral eye of a chaplain. Reduced rates are available to those engaged in full-time Christian ministry, and a number of weeks are offered free to those involved with mission to inner-city situations.

A *hydrotherapy pool* is available for both in and outpatients, and is used by about 450 people of all ages each week. Trained physiotherapists provide individual help with disabilities. A caring team is always on hand to give practical and spiritual help. A recently opened facility is a *rest and recovery room* where patients can relax over a cup of tea or coffee after their time in the pool.

The Church of Christ the Healer has services twice every day; four times a week there are services with laying on of hands for the sick. More than 1,000 people attend these public services each month. The church, which has easy-access facilities for wheelchairs, has been described as the outpatients' department of Burrswood! A ministry team is available to come alongside those in distress and spend time with them after the service. Many people come to the services to give thanks for healing. The church is at the heart of the community. On the altar is a book containing the names of those who have requested prayer.

The *playgroup* is for healthy children and those with disabilities; children come for five hours, two days a week. They learn together and enjoy all that nature has to offer on the glorious grounds. One of the chaplains regularly visits the playgroup. The children occasionally have their own special service in the church.

The *bookshop* is stocked with a wide range of books on all aspects of the Christian healing ministry, as well as calendars, cards for all occasions, and a selection of audio and video tapes. There is a steady mail order business. Burrswood's own quarterly magazine is now incorporated in the publication "Healing and Wholeness," which has a circulation of about 10,000.

Burrswood International Fellowship has more than a thousand praying members. Prayer lies at the heart of all that is done at Burrswood. Everyone directly involved in the ministry is undergirded in prayer by members of the fellowship. Many members had been patients in Burrswood, experienced the healing touch of

Christ, and pledged themselves to support the ongoing work through prayer. They receive a quarterly newsletter and a prayer diary. Many also attend an annual fellowship day in the summer.

Pioneering teamwork at Burrswood

At Burrswood every member of the staff contributes to a high standard of teamwork. Some, like the doctors, chaplains and nurses, are members of the inner team. But they know how much they rely on the work of the much wider outer team, which includes all community members—the house and kitchen team, receptionists, secretaries, administrators, the team in the hydrotherapy pool, the estate team, those who specifically give time to prayer and a large team of volunteers who help in many different ways.

Caring is stressful; teamwork is time-consuming. Sometimes it seems easier just to get on by oneself. But the strength of a team is that stress is diffused amongst the team members, and interdisciplinary and personal support is never far away. The team continually works to maintain communications and handle the conflict and pain triggered by the intensive care of suffering people.

An admissions group meets daily to pray and to seek God's wisdom regarding a response to those applying to come to Burrswood. Application papers generally say little or nothing about the hidden pain and deeper needs that are likely to surface in an atmosphere of love, safety and beauty.

The community tries to see all who come as God's gifts to them. Those who come are, in a way, wrapped up like parcels. Some are ordinarily wrapped, some are beautifully wrapped, whereas others seem to have been mishandled in the post despite warnings like "Fragile—handle with care" or "Do not bend." Many are afraid that it will hurt to be unwrapped, and others need help to accept the gift of God of themselves that is inside.

A member of the nursing team welcomes the patient and makes initial inquiries about their daily living activities, their medications and their expectations for their stay at Burrswood. The duty doctor then meets the new arrival and explains how the care team operates and how each patient is also considered to be a key member of the team.

In contrast to a normal hospital situation, the whole team shares one file of notes for each patient. Team members' comments are distinguished by the use of different colors: i.e., the physiotherapist writes in red, the counselor in green, the chaplain writes on a blue sheet. (The doctors don't need any color coding; they just write illegibly!) The nursing team also uses a daily record. The file contains all referral letters as well as the patient's own application to Burrswood and the results of all investigations.

Because patients are considered as part of the team, the doctor will explain that they can see their records at any time, if they so wish. In practice this very seldom happens, since patients feel safe in the team's holding. The feeling of safety is enhanced by a routine explanation of the boundaries of confidentiality. It is explained that whatever is shared by the patient with any member of the team will be the property of the team, and that the team as a whole is a totally confidential group.

If the patient shares something with a team member which he or she wishes should go no further, the patient has only to say, "Keep that to yourself." Such restricted information is neither recorded in writing nor passed on verbally. This team confidentiality brings its own sense of security and confidence.

Disciplinary interfaces

At Burrswood the approach of each discipline has fuzzy edges because there is a common calling. Thus the chaplain may point the way for medical insight, the counselor may suggest massage from the physiotherapist, the nurse may hear the key that unlocks the door of pain, the physiotherapist may pray and lay on therapeutic hands, and the doctor may anoint with oil and lay on hands with prayer. No team member is ever going it alone, but remains part of the whole.

Much of the creative tension of teamwork arises from the differences in training and approach that tend to belong to the different disciplines. For example, the nursing discipline tends to want to make things better, while the counseling discipline aims to stay with the pain issue. So at midday the chaplain or counselor may say to the senior nurse, "Mr. X will need lunch in his room after a heavy session with me." To which the reply comes, "You've done it again, just when we were getting him better!" Team members need to hear one another so that counseling does not simply stir things up for the sake of it and nursing does not always simply smooth things over.

One fascinating interface is with the physiohydrotherapy department. In a recent treatment a patient simply let go of support in the pool, but this act carried strong sacramental and baptismal overtones.

The use of liturgy and symbolism has an important interface with counseling work. This includes both fixed events like a daily Eucharist and services with laying on of hands, and also spontaneously arranged events for individual situations like the symbolic burning of sins and resentments, or the use of holy water to bring cleansing.

The team is always working at the interface of prayer and counseling. Sometimes "therapy" goes round in circles and prayer is needed that the Holy Spirit would intervene and move things beyond human resources.

At other times, the opposite is true. Too much reliance on prayer ministry may have led to over-spiritualizing. Unwanted personal material may get projected onto the devil—to be cast out, please! Or the individual may avoid doing his or her own work by hoping the Lord will come in and take care of it. At such times there is often a need for the human encounter of the counseling discipline to focus on the individual's situation and engage his personal resources.

Crucial to all the teamwork is the interface of the medical and spiritual. The team is most unhappy that so much deliverance ministry, for example, is undertaken without medical support or insight, especially when there is a history of mental illness. Again there are creative tensions. A doctor can expect a certain immediacy of treatment about which a pastor may be more wary. It may be implied, for example, that the chaplain should "do something about the patient's need for forgiveness," if possible by tomor-row—as if it were an injection to be administered. A spiritual response is needed to medical diagnosis and prognosis so that these do not become all-controlling. This is a very difficult balance to keep.

Hierarchies are interesting here too. Is the hospital consul-tant "god"? At Burrswood he may find himself waiting for the chaplain—or even on one occasion, a Greek Orthodox bishop—to vacate the patient's room. It would be a totally different story in a hospital. Burrswood is blessed by consultants (including a psychia-trist) who identify with this way of working and who understand the benefits of balancing spiritual and medical input.

Report meetings may also have their humorous moments at the medical-spiritual interface; e.g., "His inspiration is poor" proba-bly means he is not good at breathing in. And is "pneumatology" about understanding the lungs . . . or the Holy Spirit . . . or per-haps both? The joys and the difficulties of such real communication develop into a mutual respect for one other's contributions. After all, it is the love of God that flows among the team members and enables patients to enter deeper into God's ways and purposes. This often happens quite apart from the attention and skills offered by the professional team.

Also, Burrswood operates a placement scheme whereby a doctor, priest, counselor or person in full-time pastoral ministry can apply to join the multidisciplinary care team for a month. Board, lodging and supervision is provided free of charge, and time is allowed for individual study. Those interested usually have to apply at least six months ahead of time.

Conclusion

The work of Burrswood continues to bring life and hope to people in pain, and (in the words of the original commission given to Dorothy Kerin) "to heal the sick, comfort the sorrowing and to bring faith to the faithless." Burrswood is a pioneering ministry; there is no similar center for the physically sick in the United King-dom. Those who come are helped on their spiritual journey; they are drawn by the love of God into a deeper understanding of his ways. Life takes on new meaning and individual lives find new purpose and freedom, sometimes despite physical disability and progressive disease.

Christian healing, and Burrswood, is about much more than physical cure. Cure may or may not always happen, but at Burrswood are seen many miracles, beautiful signs of God's love. Many people receive healing of body, mind and spirit. Many find Jesus for the first time. In Isaiah we read:

> They will soar on wings like eagles; they will run and not grow weary; they will walk and not be faint (Isaiah 40:31).

For all of us, our goal is not soaring, it is not running—it is walking. The community seeks to enable each person who visits Burrswood to have the strength to carry on faithfully, whatever happens to them. Occasionally something will make their spirits soar like eagles—and now and then someone will get up and run—but more often they see people becoming whole, able to carry on more fully in their everyday lives.

Perhaps our lives are not lived on the heights with eagles, feeding exclusively on signs and wonders, nor on a racetrack with runners, running after a God found only in the supernatural, but in the day-to-day responsibilities and practicalities of work and home—in the ordinariness of life. That is surely where we need God most.

Contact information

Burrswood Christian Centre for Medical and Spiritual Care

Groombridge, Tunbridge Wells, Kent TN3 9PY, U.K.

Telephone: (01892)863637; fax: (01892)862597

Healing & Wholeness Magazine

Broadway House, The Broadway, Crowborough, East Sussex TN6 1HQ, U.K.

Telephone: (01892)652364

18

Therapeutic conversation and prayer: Making persons whole

Theodore H. Perera

"Don't seek healing. Seek the Lord Jesus Christ."

Healing function of the church

After 45 years in the ministry of divine healing (1948-1993), I affirm that the church has an important function in holistic health care. Jesus, who still walks among us, asks of the sick: "Do you want to get well?" (John. 5:6). He still empowers and sends his disciples to preach and to heal (Matt. 10:1). The church today, more than ever before, should respond to the divine charge to care for the sick to make them whole.

Wholeness is an old English word that means health. It connotes a state of well-being. The person is integrated in body, mind and spirit as an individual—an undivided person in a right relationship with God and fellow beings. When wholeness is broken, the person is ill.

Who can make a broken person whole? The answer is, and always will be, *Jesus* and Jesus alone. Jesus uses physicians, psychiatrists and clergy as his instruments of healing. We need to submit to God and cooperate with one another, supplementing skills without competition. It should be possible to bring healing and wholeness to a person, treating him in one place.

Called to heal

In 1948, Jesus bade me:

> Come out of the hospital into the church. I have a healing
> ministry for you.

I followed him, forsaking my government job and lucrative medical practice as an assistant medical practitioner in charge of a rural hospital. The cost of that sacrifice has depreciated and is not worth talking about. To the contrary, I testify to the ever-increasing ministry of healing within the church.

Unfortunately, my church took 23 years to realize the importance of the healing ministry. But God kept using and preparing me to fulfill my commitment.

In 1959, I went to England on a World Council of Churches scholarship to train in pastoral psychiatry under Dr. Leslie Weatherhead. Quite an unexpected turn of events took place. I met Dr. Weatherhead in his London office. I told him that I was at New College in London and had been sent by my church in Ceylon (Sri Lanka) to be trained by him. But he was surprised. "Somebody has brought you down from Ceylon without inquiring from us. We do not have a setup to teach. I am sorry, we can't help you," he said.

The young widower

Dr. Weatherhead was, however, willing to hear about how God had already used me. Seizing the opportunity, and hoping that he would change his mind, I began to say:

> A young widower fell ill, three months after his wife
> died. He was suffering from a respiratory illness. Difficulty of breathing kept him confined to his room for days
> on end. He was very depressed and broken. His church
> minister sent for me and gave me a history of his falling
> ill grieving over his wife's death.
>
> Prayerfully, I entered into a conversation with him. It
> then became known that they had been very unhappily
> married, so much so that when his wife was expecting
> their first baby, he had kept saying, "Let her die of this."

The wife, too, had no desire to live. It so happened that she and the baby both died during labor. He put up a good show that gave the impression to everybody present at the funeral that he was very sad and broken over her death. A few days later, he felt guilty and suppressed it. He forgot all about it, and then fell ill and did not respond to treatment.

When I showed him that his intense desire for his wife's death was equal to murder in the sight of God, he repented, knelt down and confessed his sin, asking God to forgive him. I then prayed over him with laying on of hands and he was able to breathe freely and was instantly healed.

A year later, he married again and is enjoying a very happy married life, giving glory to God.[1]

God opens a door

Dr. Weatherhead listened to me in rapt attention. After remaining silent for a while, he remarked, "You are forty years ahead of time. Keep it going." With that, he dismissed me.

I humbly accepted his assessment of my ministry and gave thanks to God as I left his office. Nevertheless, it was not much of a consolation to me in my predicament. My hopes were shattered and I was greatly disappointed. I placed myself entirely in God's hands, knowing that "He doeth all things well."

Shortly afterwards, the Lord opened a door for me to meet Dr. Frank Lake of clinical theology fame. "I will teach you just what you are seeking," he said. "I am teaching Anglican clergy and holding seminars on clinical theology at which clergy, doctors and nursers are present. I take up actual cases to teach them. I will get your scholarship transferred."

Dr. Lake took me under his wing. For six months, I received just the kind of intensive training I yearned for. He taught that the church should use the great resources of the gospel—joy for the

275

depressed person, peace and tranquility for the anxious, and the capacity to love again fully and freely—to bring healing to broken people. During a January 1960 teaching session, Dr. Lake declared:

> Allopathic medicine alone will not be sufficient to heal people. The underlying cause of the illness will be in the strain and stress of life, in the workplace and in the home. You clergy, who make pastoral visits, should be able to detect them in their early stages. You should be able to enter into a dialogue and heal them.

God's love heals

When Dr. Lake and Dr. Florence Nichols, who was at that time working in Nottingham, heard how God had used me to bring healing to people, they invited me to minister to a woman diagnosed as hysteric. She was described as the kind of patient who does not respond to treatment.

I ministered to the patient in the presence of Dr. Nichols in her clinic. The patient was restless, saying all the time, "Nobody loves me. Do you understand, doctor?"

After a brief prayer, I engaged her in conversation. She strongly protested that neither her father, mother nor anybody else ever loved her. Reluctantly, she accepted that her psychiatrist, Dr. Nichols, had loved her though she did not realize it.

I told her that God loves her. She went in to a violent tantrum, screaming and throwing things at us saying, "God does not love me. I hate God. I hate everybody."

After I continued to talk with her, she realized that God did love her. She knelt for prayer. She asked God to forgive her and she forgave others. As I prayed over her with laying on of hands, she fell flat on the carpet and became very restful. Then she sat up completely relaxed and was healed. The next Sunday she came to church, and within a week she brought a friend who also accepted Jesus and was healed.

Having had such a mountain-top experience in England, I returned home in June 1960.

A healing home in Ceylon

Eleven years later my church finally released me to labor full time in the ministry of healing. Thus in March 1971, in Moratuwa, Sri Lanka, I founded a home of healing named in Sinhalese *Dev Suwa Sevawa* (divine ministry of healing). We live here in community as a Christian family. We take patients into our home as guests. They join us in devotions—morning, noon and night—in Bible study, prayer and group spiritual therapy.

The main thrust of our ministry has been a quietly conducted service of worship, that includes a full gospel message, prayer and the laying on of hands. We have always encouraged people to seek Jesus, saying, "Don't seek healing. Seek the Lord Jesus Christ."

Ernest and Lou: God reaches out

It is wonderful how the Lord draws people to himself. Lou, a high government officer, once reprimanded Ernest, a lethargic subordinate officer, who pleaded an excuse of tiredness due to the strain and stress of work. That evening Ernest, smarting under the reprimand, felt even more exhausted and broken and was walking home dejectedly. A friend, Richard, happened to pass by. On learning what had taken place, Richard exhorted Ernest to attend a healing service at Dev Suwa Sevawa, close to his home.

Accepting this chance meeting as providential, Ernest came and found Jesus. The following Sunday he went to church after a twenty-year absence and kept coming to our healing services.

Lou was quick to notice the change and complimented Ernest. Then Ernest told Lou of all that took place. "Something wonderful happened. I found Jesus at Dev Suwa Sevawa and he has turned me around. I am healed in body, mind and spirit. I do more work than ever before."

Lou was delighted and interested, specially about his meeting Jesus, and asked Ernest: "Where is this Dev Suwa Sevawa?"

So Ernest brought Lou and his wife Wimala to our healing service. Even though they were Buddhists, they knelt in deep adoration and entered fervently into the spirit of the prayer that was offered. The Lord placed his hand upon Lou's right shoulder. Lou witnessed later:

> When I first heard of the healing ministry of Father Theodore [*the author -ed.*], I was not ill in body. Yet my mind and spirit were restless in the search for truth and righteousness. So, one Tuesday evening, I joined Ernest, my colleague, to go to Dev Suwa Sevawa. We entered a small but impressive church by a lake. It was peaceful and tranquil within, and was conducive to my own search.
>
> I was impressed by the extreme simplicity of the service, which commenced with a strong and stirring prayer by Father Theodore: "The Lord is in his holy temple, let the whole creation be still before him." We instinctively moved into a state of devotion. "The Lord God saith: Be still and know that I am God." We entered into a holy silence and I felt a touch on my right shoulder, and I turned my head sideways. There was no hand on my shoulder; it was a mystery. Soon I realized that the Lord Jesus Christ was present at this healing service. The testimonies of those healed corroborate the bold declaration of Father Theodore that the Lord Jesus was at work performing miracles in Sri Lanka. And now I believe it, for Jesus touched me and healed me in body, mind and spirit.

From then on, this family came regularly. It was evident that Lou was being drawn to Jesus. He read the Bible and asked questions, and he committed himself to Jesus. Every morning on his way to the office, he worshiped at the Colombo Fort YMCA chapel. After a few months he asked for baptism. I waited until his wife also resolved to follow Jesus. Soon their son Gehan accepted Jesus as Lord. All three were baptized.

Samanthi: Many come to Christ

People who have found Jesus at our healing services have understood that even death is healing when their loved ones die in the

Lord. Non-Christians, too, have found peace in such circumstances. Samanthi, a Buddhist girl of twelve years, passed away peacefully to be with the Jesus she loved.

Samanthi had been the eldest of several children born into a peasant family of Katiyawa, a remote village in the dry zone of Sri Lanka. Following several years of inadequate rain, her father Richard had no water for his rice fields. He eked out a living by dry cultivation. Samanthi's family lived in a wattle-and-daub hut in abject poverty. To add to the misery of it all, Samanthi had a congenital heart defect and lay on a mat, dying.

Richard, inconsolable and desperate, wrote to the newspapers inquiring where he could take her for healing. The response was tremendous—628 replies. The villagers helped him to read and categorize the letters. They found a letter written by one Swinitha of Moratuwa, saying,

> Jesus heals today. No money is needed to obtain divine healing. Bring your child to Dev Suwa Sevawa. Jesus will heal her.

So Richard brought Samanthi to Dev Suwa Sevawa. At our healing service, the whole congregation prayed earnestly for Samanthi's healing.

A couple of days later, something wonderful happened. Samanthi made a miraculous recovery. On the following Tuesday, at our healing service, people praised God when she stood up beside me. For two years thereafter she stayed out of the hospital, and her health improved daily.

Samanthi was keen to learn of this Jesus who had healed her and corresponded with us. Soon, through Samanthi, her whole family accepted Jesus as their Lord and Savior. On Richard's invitation, we conducted a healing service in their village. A large crowd heard with gladness the gospel message that Jesus heals today. Richard testified. Samanthi, of course, was a living testimony. Their baptism was postponed for the lack of a Bible teacher.

Then one night Samanthi woke up saying Jesus had appeared to her and beckoned her to Dev Suwa Sevawa to receive full healing. She insisted that they go at once, but Richard had to find the money. Four days later they set out. It was night when they reached Colombo.

Samanthi complained of severe chest pain. She was rushed to the hospital and there she died. Richard took her body home for burial.

A party of us from Dev Suwa Sevawa visited them within the week. Richard told us that he did not bury her according to Buddhist rites. In fact, for want of a Christian priest or layman, he himself had committed her body to the grave and her soul to the Lord Jesus. We were greatly encouraged to see their faith had not been shaken. We had a prayer meeting beside her grave.

Before we left, Richard asked for baptism. A month later we brought Richard, his wife and the six children down to Dev Suwa Sevawa. In the presence of a large gathering, Richard testified, moving people to tears. They affirmed their belief in Jesus, and I baptized them. They remain faithful to God and live among their people as witnesses of Christ.

Now, through their witness, there is a Christian community in the village. Samanthi's younger sister, Ramaya, was educated by us in a Christian boarding school. Today, she is working at the Colombo City Mission and is preparing to be a candidate for the Methodist ministry.

Samanthi's brother, Lalith, is also working in the church as an evangelist. His witnessing of Christ brought nearly twenty people to the Lord in a remote village. This resulted in a physical assault on him and his mate by a gang wearing robes. But he and his converts remain faithful.

Healing conversation and prayer

A successful way to use spiritual resources to heal an individual is a session of spiritual conversation and prayer. As the patient and I meet together in my room, I tell him that Jesus himself is present with us: he silently listens to our conversation and inspires what we talk about. After prayer, I encourage the patient to share with me whatever is upon his mind, saying "You do the talking. I will listen."

Jude: Forgiven and healed

One morning, a young man named Jude was brought to us from far away. Four of his friends carried him from a van to my room and laid him on the divan. After prayer, I told him of the man sick with palsy, whom four friends carried to Jesus to be healed by him. (Mark 2:1-12). I noticed that Jude stirred. He told me he was a Roman Catholic and had been taught the story of this miracle healing that Jesus had performed.

That was a good beginning. When I told him that Jesus first forgave the paralyzed man and only then healed him, Jude began to weep. With a little encouragement, he opened up, saying "I am ill because I have sinned. I am unable to confess my sin to my priest. It is so terrible; he will look down upon me. I have stopped receiving the blessed sacrament. Day and night, I tremble with fear. I have nightmares of what happened. I can't sleep. I can't eat. My whole body has stiffened and I can't walk. I can't go to work. I am doomed to die. Doctors have failed to diagnose my illness."

The Lord inspired me that he needs to confess his sin. "Did you not think of going to a priest of another parish to make your confession?" I asked.

"May I tell you of what happened?" he replied. I saw that he very much wanted to get this off his chest and told him to go ahead.

"One night," Jude began, "my elder cousin and I were alone in her home. She seduced me to have sexual intercourse with her. I had the fear of God within me and so immediately afterwards, I hated myself for consenting and breaking the commandment of God. I am unable to confess because of the shame of it. I am in great distress. Please help me."

Then, I got Jude to pray to God seeking forgiveness for himself, and to tell God that he is forgiving his cousin for enticing him into sinning with her. "There is assurance of forgiveness through Jesus," I said. I showed him the Bible text of 1 John 1:9:

If we confess our sins, he is faithful and just and will forgive us our sins and purify us from all unrighteousness.

Lying flat upon the divan, Jude prayed with tears pouring
down his cheeks. I then prayed over him with laying on of hands
and told him: "God has heard your prayer to forgive you. Accept
the forgiveness offered to you through Jesus the Savior. Get up and
praise God."

Jude stood up, smiling. He walked around a bit and then
walked out of the room. His friends were astonished to see him
walking. They all knelt to pray and thank God before they left.

Jane: Out of "hell"

God used us in like manner in our healing missions abroad. Once
when in England, I was invited to minister to a rich young woman
I shall call Jane.

She was an only child and was in the final year of studies in
a university. She had suddenly started shutting herself in a small,
overheated room of the family home, which had several large
rooms. Jane reluctantly opened the door for us, at the request of her
mother who left us with her.

Jane took my wife and me into the room and shut the door.
It was very hot inside that room. Jane didn't seem to mind the heat
at all.

"I am in hell," Jane began. "I am burning in hell."

"Why are you in hell?" I asked.

"Never mind that. You don't need to burn with me in hell.
Why did you come?"

"To take you out of hell. You remember how we affirm our
Christian faith saying that Jesus descended to hell. So we have
come to your hell to help you. Please tell me why you are in hell," I
pleaded.

"I have committed the unforgivable sin,"she replied.

"What was that sin?"I asked Jane.

After much persuasion, Jane opened up, saying "When I
was a child I had a lovely cat. After a baptism service in the church,

I returned home and baptized my cat in the name of the Trinity doing exactly as the priest did."

"Why are you now reminding yourself of that incident to torment yourself?" I inquired.

"We had a discussion on baptism at the university Christian society meeting and I told them of how I baptized the cat. They told me I had committed the unforgivable sin and that I would burn in hell," replied Jane with great emotion.

It took a little time to convince Jane that God understands her innocent act of desiring for the cat what he would do for a child.

"Animals too are God's creatures like us humans. That is why I have prayed over animals with laying on of hands for their healing, and God has healed them too," I testified for her consolation.

Jane accepted my word of assurance and we called in the aunt and the mother to join us in prayer. I got Jane to pray too. After we had all prayed, I asked Jane to switch off the electric heater as a token of accepting the assurance that all is well.

Jane did it with a smile, which meant so much to us. I then suggested to Jane that she wash herself and come down to the parlor to join us at the Bible study that was going on there.

Great was the joy of all present, to see Jane coming down the stairs, in a beautiful black gown. Her well-combed, flowing hair added to her radiance.

The next morning she had gone back to the university and, in due course, she obtained her degree in classics. She corresponded with me for a while, and expressed her desire to go to a Third-World country to teach English.

Pansy: Intensive prayer-care
We listen to our patients in a nonjudgmental way. Pansy had a problem about caring for her aged father. I was led to tell her that I read somewhere that we have a lifetime to keep nine of the Ten Commandments but only the parents' lifetime to keep the fifth:

Honor your father and your mother, so that you may live
long in the land the Lord your God is giving you"
(Exodus 20:12).

Unfortunately, some people neglect their parents but spend
lavishly to bury them. "Wouldn't it be better to make sacrifices
while they are alive?" I asked and went on to say that we should
care for them while they are alive.

Pansy thanked me for the message. Her problem was that
at a time of ethnic unrest in Sri Lanka, all her brothers and sisters
had emigrated, leaving the aged father behind with her.

Years went by and her father was still alive and very feeble.
Her husband had been offered a job abroad. That was the chance
for them, too, to emigrate, but the father's health did not permit
him to go with them.

Pansy and her husband decided to stay behind rather than
accept the job abroad. A year or so later, the father died. God gave
them another opportunity to go abroad. They went and after some
time she wrote to me saying, "You will be happy to hear that we
just bought a house in Portland. It is indeed wonderful to see the
way the Lord has been working in our lives. The words you told
me five years ago still ring in my ears—'Do your best for your
father and the Lord will bless you abundantly.' We are actually
experiencing that abundance now which the Lord is showering
upon us. We are thanking God for the guidance he gave us through
you."

Retirement syndrome

The time came for me to retire, or so I thought. In 1985 The
Methodist church had released our son, Rev. Asiri Perera, to minister
with me in Dev Suwa Sevawa. God blessed him to follow clinical
pastoral education courses abroad; he was very well equipped for
his ministry. So at the age of 65 and having completed 45 years of service in hospital and church, I retired together with my wife Delicia.

For seven months we travelled abroad in six countries,
relaxing and ministering. In England we attended an eight-day
silent retreat, "A Way of Life," conducted by Sr. Kathleen O'Sulli-

van of the Order of St. Louis. It was for me a mountain-top experience. One night, during the period of the Exposition of the Blessed Sacrament, I was in deep contemplation. I had a vision of myself standing on a high pedestal from which I could not come down. Then I saw myself inside a tower of my own making. There was an open window at the top, and I flew out through it but was pulled back in.

On the last day of the retreat, Sr. Kathleen placed some cards face down on a table. We were each asked to pick up one, which would be a "gift from the Holy Spirit." Mine read: "Be emptied so as to be filled by God." Its aptness overwhelmed me. My emptying process began.

After our return to Sri Lanka, I suffered a severe attack of urticaria (an allergic disorder of the skin). This erupted periodically in different parts of my body. After months of treatment, I was troubled in spirit. In that broken state, I went to Dev Suwa Sevawa to be ministered to by my son and successor, Asiri.

Inspired by God, tracing the root cause of my illness, he said, "Dad, you are grieving your retirement."

I recognized that I was restless without a retirement ministry. Healing was instantaneous. Soon after, I found the clue to my emptying process in paraphrasing Philippians 2:5-8:

> In your decision making, be like Christ Jesus, who though he was in the form of God, did not cling on to the divine nature, which he always had, but emptied himself (*i.e., stripped himself of all privileges*), making himself of no reputation and gave all he had, to become a slave-like servant in the form of a man and humbled himself and was obedient even to the extent of accepting death on the cross, on which common criminals were put to death.

I then accepted that the excellent quality of our Lord's humility and self-denial was perfectly reflected in his obedience and death. I emptied at a deeper level my covetous interest in Dev Suwa Sevawa. And without clinging to what was mine, I denied myself, God being my helper. Like Abraham, in obedience to God, I offered back to him my "Isaac"—Dev Suwa Sevawa. Peace pervaded my whole being.

Shortly after that, at Asiri's invitation, two of our past presidents of Conference met us in consultation. One of them said, "You have been given the charisma of healing by God. You should have never retired." The other said, "Go out and do it again."

I acted on their advice, and applied to the church for a retirement ministry. The Conference appointed me to the staff of the Colombo City Mission as a part-time worker to continue my healing ministry. On the day of the inauguration of the ministry and my commissioning by the president, I had a message from a prayer partner in England saying, "No one can truly be alive if he is on a pedestal."

In my retirement, I am engaged in a healing ministry within the structures of the church. God is filling me now out of the riches of his inheritance. I am experiencing the complete fulfillment of my calling from Jesus:

> Come out of the hospital into the church. I have a healing ministry for you.

Note

1   This happened in 1955. The young widower and his second wife are now approaching forty years of happy marriage.

Part four

Breaking New Ground

19
Traditional medicine in Africa

G. L. Chavunduka

The World Health Organization recommends that traditional medicine be taken seriously by modern health planners, modern medical practitioners and academics.

Traditional healers form the essential core of primary health workers in Africa. Hundreds of people seek their services every day. These healers not only deal with medical issues but also address a wide range of social problems as well. Many traditional healers are local historians. They help maintain social stability. Many are legal and political advisors, marriage counselors and social workers. The most respected traditional healers also perform a priestly function; they interpret for sick and anxious people the reasons for their plight and pinpoint spiritual and interpersonal influences believed to be affecting their health and well-being.

Some traditional healers also play an important role in public health. In many areas traditional healers, in cooperation with chiefs, headmen or other community leaders, control a wide range of basic health conditions. They advise, for example, on the choice of rural village sites and cemeteries. For village sites, healers typically select locations on high ground near clean water sources and above mosquito zones (they know that mosquitoes bring malaria). Traditional healers also assist some communities by isolating individuals seen as ritually polluted because they are lepers or are infected with smallpox or have other medical problems.

Suppression efforts

Although traditional healers continue to play many important roles in social life, people in modern society know little about them because of colonialism, cultural imperialism, Christianity and Western education. During the colonial period, governments and early Christian missionaries despised and discouraged traditional medicine. They attempted to suppress the traditional medical system because they did not know that traditional medicines are effective in curing many illnesses. They saw the traditional healer as a rogue and a deceiver who prevented many patients who would otherwise be treated effectively with Western drugs and surgery from reaching government and mission hospitals.

Early missionaries felt that traditional healers encouraged witchcraft, a hindrance to the gospel. They saw ancestor worship as a sin. They regarded traditional healers as devil worshipers due to their association with ancestral spirits and other types of spirits. In fact, missionaries saw both the patient seeking relief and the traditional practitioner attempting a cure as devil worshipers who were doomed to hellfire unless they turned to Christianity.

Another factor was ethnocentrism, the tendency to like what is familiar and to devalue the strange or the foreign. Ethnocentrism led many early Europeans in Africa to regard anyone not acting in accord with their own practices as ignorant and superstitious. To them, the only medical system that worked was their own. It was the only system of medicine they knew.

The last important reason for attempts to suppress traditional medicine was an economic one. Colonial administrators wanted to force Africans everywhere to depend entirely on Western medicines. This would benefit Western countries and their pharmaceutical companies.

A number of measures were adopted to weaken the traditional medical system. Provision of education, particularly Christian education, was one way to weaken traditional beliefs and practices; this, it was hoped, would make people abandon traditional religious ideas and their faith in traditional healers. Also, motives for building government and mission hospitals included the belief that these hospitals would prove to be one of the greatest instruments for keeping people in touch with the spiritual life of the Christian church. The schools, too, which in many areas were largely controlled by Christian missionaries at that time, discouraged the use of traditional medicine. In a number of countries in Africa, various laws are still in existence that are aimed, at least in part, at suppressing the activities of traditional healers. Modern medical councils and associations also had a part in attempts to suppress the activities of traditional healers. Until recently many of these councils did not recognize traditional healers as medical practitioners.

Modern medical doctors were not allowed to refer patients to traditional healers or work with them in any way. If they did so, they committed a breach of ethics and were liable to penalties through their medical council. Patients who went to hospitals and clinics after consulting traditional healers were often insulted by modern doctors and nurses for doing so. In commerce, industry and other employment sectors, some workers lost their jobs because they had missed work to consult traditional healers. (Missing work to consult modern doctors was not cause for dismissal if the worker could produce a letter or certificate; such a document from a traditional practitioner was not valid.)

Inaccurate names

The terms used during the colonial era to describe traditional healers further undermined their position in the society. The most common were witch doctor, sorcerer, herbalist, medicine man, diviner and magician.

Traditional healers are not witches or sorcerers. Witches and sorcerers are bad people whose only aim is to harm others. In Africa, witches are said to be people able to do extraordinary things beyond the capabilities of ordinary human beings. They are thought capable of travelling great distances at night, riding hyenas at night, or of going out in spirit and killing a victim while their bodies remain at home in bed. Sorcery is a technique used by an individual under certain circumstances to cause illness or other misfortune. A sorcerer may cause illness by putting medicine or poison in the victim's food, drink or tobacco or may use some other techniques to harm people.

Some traditional healers claim to identify and cure witches, but they treat other people as well. Witch-finding is not a full-time occupation. Moreover, this practice is forbidden by law in many countries. The term witch doctor is rarely used nowadays.

Although the term herbalist is still used, it does not describe the work of such traditional healers adequately. They do not confine their remedies to herbs but use other ingredients as well, such as portions of animals, insects and snakes. The term medicine man or woman is also not correct. Many traditional healers do not handle medicines but rather deal only with religious, spiritual and cultural issues that affect health.

A diviner is a traditional healer who specializes in divination. He is an expert at carrying out a diagnosis using spirit possession or other traditional methods. A magician is not a traditional health practitioner, but some healers use aspects of magic in treating certain health conditions.

The term traditional birth attendant does not adequately describe the work of traditional healers in midwifery. They provide prenatal and postnatal care and treat illnesses of mothers and children. The term traditional midwife is more accurate.

The practice persists

Despite the various attempts made by early missionaries and government officials to suppress the activities of traditional healers, many people have continued to use their services. There are a number of reasons for this:

- Traditional healers are successful in curing many illnesses. Many people are aware of this.
- Modern medical science has failed to get better or even good results in certain types of illness.

- People consult traditional healers for many reasons. Many traditional healers are competent to handle social, psychological and spiritual problems.

- Many traditional healers are influential people in their communities. The advice they give is taken seriously by many people; they are a trusted source of support and information.

- Many traditional practices are effective and empirically correct by scientific standards.

For example, for a snake bite the traditional healer might open the wound further and suck out the poison, or what others believe to be the evil spirit that had entered. In doing this, he also extracts venom from the wound and does what is essential in objective scientific terms for curing the patient.

Support from WHO

Because of the important role traditional healers continue to play in health care, the World Health Organization (WHO) took a remarkable initiative in the late seventies recommending that traditional medicine be taken seriously by modern health planners, modern medical practitioners and academics. WHO further recommended that the concept of primary health care should involve the notion of a team of workers, including not only modern physicians, nurses, modern midwives and community workers but also traditional health practitioners.

The late seventies were, therefore, a major turning point in the long history of antagonism between modern and traditional healing systems. Rather than being a disparaged subject in academic and modern medical circles, the possibility of using traditional health practitioners in modern health care systems has now received the official stamp of approval from WHO. This has become part of the official policy of many national governments as well. This policy change made a lot of sense.

Empirical research

Traditional healers possess empirical medical knowledge. This knowledge has been developed through dreams, trial and error, experimentation and systematic observation for a long time.

Dreams

Dreaming is an interesting research method—a method of discovering new medical drugs. A number of people have acquired medical knowledge through seeing in a dream the correct medicine to cure a sick person and where to find it. I have personally accompanied to the woods a number of people who had dreamt about a cure for a particular ailment. In many cases I have seen, the herbs discovered in this way have turned out to be useful.

Incidentally, I have known two traditional healers who discovered minerals through dreams. The first one discovered a gold deposit; the second one discovered an area where tantalum, tungsten and emeralds are now being mined. A number of other healers are said to have discovered minerals through dreams—minerals being mined today by large multi-national corporations in Africa.

Discovering medicines

The research methods listed above have led to the discovery of many traditional drugs and medical techniques in use today. In Zimbabwe, for example, more than 500 different types of plants are used for medicinal purposes. Besides plants, traditional healers have discovered other forms of medicine, including parts of animals, birds, insects, snakes and fish.

Traditional healers have also discovered traditional veterinary medicines in use today for cattle, donkeys, pigs, goats, sheep, dogs, and chickens. Traditional veterinary drugs effectively treat worms, constipation, burns, painful udder, diarrhea, external parasites, snake-bite and painful eyes.

Many modern scientists are now researching traditional medicines—research aimed at identifying the active principles. But research into traditional medicines is not easy. Many plant screening programs have not yielded any meaningful results. One problem is that several different plants are often used in a remedy; these plants might be cooked with various portions of animals, birds, fish, snakes and insects. Another problem is that mixtures used by traditional healers are not always intended to eliminate the symptoms alone. Some ingredients are intended to suppress toxic effects of certain aggressive drugs and enable the body to withstand them. Furthermore, some traditional healers often throw in a herb or two in their medicines as a decoy so that bystanders may not know which of the various herbs has the active principle for the illness being treated. In some cases, ingredients may be added to meet the sociocultural needs of the patient's beliefs and convictions.

For success in researching traditional medicines, traditional healers themselves must be involved in the study. Modern medical scientists must acquire some knowledge of medicines from traditional healers before proceeding with scientific analysis. Experience has shown that where traditional healers have been involved in the study, the results of scientific research have been encouraging.

Subjective knowledge

Besides empirical medical knowledge, traditional healers also possess non-scientific or subjective knowledge. A sizeable amount of the traditional healer's knowledge of medicine is explained in terms of revelations, dreams, and flashes of intuition. There is also tacit information gained through practical experience that the healer may be unable to communicate logically to others.

One major source of nonscientific or subjective knowledge is the spirit world. Many traditional healers are spirit mediums; that is, they have or claim to have the ability to communicate with spirits. When faced with a difficult medical problem, for example, such healers consult spirits. They do this while in a state of spirit possession. Before the practitioner becomes possessed, his muscles usually stiffen. Then he jerks his body and passes into what appears to be a trance. When in this state of possession, the healer carries out his diagnosis. He may remain in a state of possession for several hours.

Some healers have an assistant who conveys questions and messages between the patient and the healer. The assistant is usually necessary because healers in a state of possession may speak in a language not easily understood by a layman. Also, when the healer emerges from the state of possession, he is sometimes unaware or pretends to be unaware of what the spirit said to the patient through him. When the diagnosis is completed, the spirit leaves its medium.

Another source of nonscientific or subjective knowledge is what is generally known as the throwing of bones. These are pieces of wood, small stones or other objects that are cast in order to determine the causes of an illness. Each time the practitioner throws these objects he quickly looks to see how they have fallen and then explains the meaning in reference to the particular questions asked. Other instruments may also serve as sources of medical knowledge. Examples include a calabash, a small mirror, a religious book and a needle.

Spirits are not observable objects. It is difficult to study divination using modern scientific methods. These issues, then, belong to a realm about which the modern scientist has no accumulated empirical knowledge. Because of this, modern medical science has tried to disown this level of knowing. But all medical knowledge is, in fact, produced in a variety of objective and subjective ways; medicine deals with human beings, who have both objective and subjective dimensions.

The art of medicine

It has been shown that states of illness and health are to a large extent subjective experiences. There should not, therefore, be a tension between scientific and other forms of knowledge in the field of health. Medicine in its practice is and should be both a science and an art.

Traditional healers generally practice holistic medicine. The aim has always been to treat not only the disease that may be worrying an individual but also to identify and remove any social or psychological factors that may be associated with the illness. When consulted by patients with certain health problems, healers tend to spend a lot of time examining all aspects of the disease situation, including the many personal, familial and social factors that may promote health and encourage healing.

Healers and religion

Although many traditional healers are members of traditional religions, a large number are members of other religions. All major religious denominations have traditional healers among their membership.

A study carried out in Southern Africa showed that the majority of the Christian traditional healers are members of the Roman Catholic Church, the Anglican Church and the Methodist Church. Membership of a Christian church does not prevent an individual from participating in traditional religion or from practicing traditional medicine. Many traditional healers hold important positions in Christian churches.

Training

Individuals who wish to acquire traditional medical knowledge are usually trained by others in an apprenticeship. In the case of plant medicine, graduates of this medical system know an impressive amount about flora and fauna. They show fine discrimination in their observation and classification of leaves, stems, roots, fruits, flowers and bark. Many of these medical graduates are also able to distinguish plants on the basis of taste, touch, smell and appearance across the seasons. They also know a great deal about animals, birds, snakes, insects and fish.

Many traditional healers are selected for medical training early in their lives. The length of training varies; some are trained for two years, others for more than ten years. The length of training depends on a number of factors such as age of the student, branch of medicine, continuity of training, and attitude of the teacher. Before setting up a medical practice, the candidate must pass medical tests in many areas, followed in many cases by a graduation ceremony.

There are traditional healers who claim to have served no apprenticeship at all and attribute all their knowledge to the guidance of a spirit. Studies have, however, shown that many of them have also had a long informal apprenticeship. They may have grown up in a family with a healer and learned a great deal about medical practice before the death of the old man or woman. Since much of the training is informal, some do not regard it as training.

However, there are healers who have not served any apprenticeship. They entered the profession through dreaming. Other healers have received formal training at a school of traditional medicine.

Challenges ahead

Traditional medicine has its limitations. There is a lot of room for improvement. Many important tasks remain:

- Identifying and removing any harmful practices that still exist in the system.
- Eliminating, as far as possible, quacks and charlatans that are part of the system.
- Ensuring preservation of a high level of professional ethics and practice.
- Continuing efforts to improve traditional methods of gathering, storage and preparation of medicines.

20

Christians practicing herbal medicine in India

Sevanand Melookunnel

> One of the concepts in community health care is
> to empower people to manage their own health
> problems. Simple herbal medicines could help
> in this process.

Introduced by my mother and a mason

I owe my interest in traditional medicine to my mother and a local mason. I didn't have to look beyond myself for a proof of the efficacy of the herbal system that the modern medical system usually scoffs at as superstition. I myself am living proof.

My mother used to tell me that I was very anemic when I was born. Mr. Shankupanikkan treated me and saved my life. He earned his living by laying bricks and, in the customary manner, offered health care as a service to the community. He was well-known as a pediatrician.

It is thanks to him that the infant mortality rate was not very high in the area even before the first modern hospital came to the place in 1956. The treatment given to me, I was told, was very simple:

> Take a cup of the pure juice of lawn grass (Dog grass—botanical name: *Cynodon dactylon*). Pour the juice into a flat plate and add half a cup of fresh butter. Churn strongly both the juice and the butter with the palm of

the hand for nearly an hour. Apply this preparation (called *mukkuttu* in Malayalam) on the baby and bathe him after half an hour in lukewarm water. Continue the treatment for 21 days.[1]

Modern medicine may not find anything "scientific" in this. But I put on weight and I have been enjoying good health for the last fifty-five years. Experience—not chemical research—is the proof of the efficacy of the herbal system of medicine practiced by people like Shankupanikkan.

Traditional systems: complex and simple

When we speak of traditional medicine in India, we have to include a variety of medical practices. Some of these traditional practices have developed into complex systems.

One such system is *Ayurveda*. This form of medicine has its own well-developed pharmaceutical system that could easily compete with modern medicine in its variety and efficacy. One is struck at the enormous variety of surgical instruments used. In fact, Ayurveda was so developed in ancient times that practitioners could even conduct plastic surgeries.[2]

As early as the fourth century A.D., a well-disciplined medical education system developed in India. The renowned treatises of Ayurveda—*Susruta Samhita* and *Charaka Samhita*—were compiled by the seventh century A.D. In these seminal works, Susruta details the medicinal effects of about 750 plants; Charaka covers 500 plants. Susruta, who also wrote extensively on surgical practices, is revered even today. Atreya, another ancient authority in Ayurveda, is credited with formulating the first code of medical ethics for physicians.

Modern science has yet to find the therapeutic value of many more plants. In the eyes of traditional therapeutics, practically all plants have medicinal value. We have a story in India about this:

Punarvasu Atreya sent out his six disciples on an errand. They were asked to travel to various districts and return

300

with plants that they found which did not have any medicinal value. Five of them returned with several plants.
The sixth one, Jivaka, returned empty-handed. He could
find no plant lacking in medicinal value.[3]

Each of the six disciples wrote a compendium on Ayurveda;
Jivaka wrote the best one. His book was edited by Charaka and
Drdhabala and is extant today as *Charaka Samhita*, a source book on
plant-related therapies.

Sidha is another highly developed system. Developed in
South India, it is similar in many respects to the Ayurvedic system
of the North. A special feature of the Sidha is *marma* ("vital force
point") treatment, akin to China's acupuncture and acupressure.
Some say that China took inspiration from the marma treatment.

Today Ayurveda and Sidha have medical colleges in India
that compete with allopathic medical colleges. Some of these colleges keep promoting systematic research both on the validity of
various treatments and on possibilities for interaction with allopathy (the prevalent Western system of medicine).

These systems developed very striking and varied procedures of diagnosis called *neoteinia*. One such system deals with
nadir or pulses. A trained physician can hold a patient's wrists, feel
the various pulses with his fingers and accurately describe both
sickness and remedies. The principle is that the pulses in the hand
beat differently according to certain body conditions. Other procedures check the urine, color of the eyes, phlegm, stool, and the
nature of pain.

But we here deal mainly with herbal systems that are not
yet systematically codified and that remain simple practices by
tribal people in hill areas and poor people in villages.

In the divine plan

The first chapter of Genesis could be read as an affirmation of the
curative values of plants and herbs. The plants and the herbs the
Lord created are good for a number of purposes. We celebrate the
Creation of the Lord when we affirm in practice this goodness for
therapeutic purposes.

Then God said, "Let the land produce vegetation: seed-bearing plants and trees on the land that bear fruit with seed in it, according to their various kinds." And it was so (Gen. 1:11).

Then God said, "I give you every seed-bearing plant on the face of the whole earth and every tree that has fruit with seed in it. They will be yours for food (Gen. 1:20). God saw all that he had made, and it was very good. (Gen. 1:31).

God was pleased with what he had made and the order he had established.

Herbal practice in India

People turned to traditional practices of herbal and home remedies before allopathy became popular in the nineteenth century. Even today, in most of the remote villages and tribal areas, people survive with the help of traditional practices alone.

Tribal people in India live in close union with nature and have their own store of knowledge of traditional practice. They mostly make single preparations from ingredients readily available in the jungles; sometimes they use compound preparations, including even animal products. They pass on their knowledge from generation to generation. The medical lore of the indigenous people of India was likely taken over by the Aryan invaders from the Mediterranean. The invaders pushed the indigenous people to the mountains, where they have survived to the present tribal people.

Herbal practice in Western countries

In Western countries, also, traditional medicines were in vogue before the spread of the Industrial Revolution. Wise women (also a few men) who knew the secrets of herbs were the accepted healers. There were also university-trained medical practitioners, but they were not successful with herbal medicines.

With the coming of the Industrial Revolution, however, there was a swing in favor of the university-trained medical practitioners. The industrialists monopolized the health care system for profit motives. And in the course of time, with a systematic and a planned strategy, they succeeded in totally suppressing herbal practice.[4]

By experiment and observation

How would the tribal people have gathered such knowledge? Besides the more systematic researches of the masters of the more developed systems like Ayurveda and Sidha (details of which would have percolated down to tribal people), their own chance encounters with plants and consequent experimentation and observation also matter.

The case of a well-known bone setter in Northeastern India could be a pointer. Almost everyone in this region knows this bone setter. It was by accident that he came to learn about the effect of a certain plant in joining bones, which he keeps as a family secret. His story:

> One day, he came home with a rabbit after a hunt. He asked his wife to cook it. His wife had been nursing the baby. So she asked him to skin and clean and cut it into pieces and get it ready for cooking. He quickly did the job and went out.

> After about an hour or so when his wife went to cook the meat she found that the skinned rabbit was just one piece. She didn't cook it.

> When her husband returned and asked why she did not cook the meat, she retorted, "Why didn't you cut it into pieces? You think I will cook the whole animal in one piece?" He checked where it was kept. He was surprised to see that the bones that he had cut had joined together. Although illiterate, he could conclude that the leaf on which the meat had been kept had made the pieces join together.

He identified the source of the leaf and began to experiment with animals to further establish the efficacy of that particular plant for joining bones.

A few years ago, one of my priest friends, Fr. K. A. Thomas, a missionary in Mizoram, had a very serious Jeep accident that left many bones badly broken. He went to the same bone setter for treatment. Fr. Thomas recovered about two weeks later.

Though chemical analysis is not done in the herbal system of medicine, this example shows that close experimentation and observation takes place before a herbal medicine is advocated for public use.

Where allopathy fears to tread

Though allopathy is supposed to be very much advanced and has tall claims, it has no effective treatment in many cases. Twenty-nine years ago, my friend Augustine was admitted to one of the best-run hospitals of Bihar, India. He had jaundice. A few days later, he fell into a coma for three days. All we got from that allopathic hospital was the news that our Augustine died. The best-equipped hospital could not save him.

Nine years later, I came across a wonder medicine for jaundice which has saved scores of people. If only I had known this remedy before: my friend Augustine would not have died! The remedy is very simple:

Gather a handful of the tender leaves of Castor oil plant, (Bot. name *Ricinus communis*) Make sure the bud and tender leaves are greenish, and avoid the red variety. Wash them well. Crush them and squeeze out about half a glassful of juice. Add plenty of sugar. Drink on an empty stomach early in the morning. Continue for three to nine days, according to need.

The hospital has changed. Today, it uses mostly herbal medicines for jaundice. The result: hardly any casualties from jaundice.

I have found from experience that for paralysis, chronic gastric problems, asthma, skin diseases and a number of other diseases, traditional treatments with herbal medicines are more effective than modern medicine. Herbal treatment may take more time. It uproots diseases rather than suppressing them.

A service, not a profession

I believe that modern medicine, though highly developed and scientific, has unfortunately become a form of exploitation protected and patronized by politicians, bureaucrats, medical professionals and the business community. It has become a cut-throat, competitive business beyond the reach of common people. Patients become experimental subjects, helpless and passive victims of profit-oriented doctors.

In view of such exploitation, we need to demystify medical care. We need to make people less dependent on profit-making experts and professionals and enable them to take responsibility for their health. We need to give them alternative systems that are within their reach, simpler and less expensive. We need to empower people with the required knowledge regarding traditional herbs.

Fortunately, this is not difficult. I have had the joy of seeing many people, even not so learned ones, who learn medicinal preparations with ease, pass on the knowledge to others and help patients with love.

Nageswari, for example, is not much of a learned person. She learned to read and write when some social activists conducted a year-long adult literacy program in her village. And her medical competence? She attended a week-long training program on home remedies conducted by the Rural Education and Development Centre at Bettiah, Bihar.

During the training, she told me that she wanted to learn just one medicine well and practice it. I suggested to her the preparation of the pill meant for stomach ailments like indigestion, lack of appetite, gastric problems, constipation and dysentery. The pill is prepared the following way:

> Take pepper, dry ginger, jeera (cumin seed), somph
> (aniseed) and black salt in equal amounts—say 100 grams

each. Take omum seed (ajwain) 50 grams, and asofoetida (hing) 25 grams. Grind each of these separately and strain through a fine cloth. Mix these powders well. Add the juice of drumstick bark (Bot. name *Moringa oleifera*) and lemon juice in equal proportion. Mix and knead it well. Make pills of the size of muttor (pea).

Nageswari gives this pill to anyone with stomach-related ailments. Often we can see a queue in front of her house for medicine. For people of her own village and neighboring villages, Nageswari is their doctor. People have great confidence in her, and they are liberated to a great extent.

To those interested, she willingly teaches how to make the pills. Good news and the liberation process thus take wings.

People-oriented and humane

Herbal practitioners among the tribal people are people-oriented and humane. For various reasons they may not reveal all their secrets, but they are ready, day and night, to serve the suffering. Treatment is not their bread-earning profession; effective and fast healing of the patient is their only aim. As a member of the village community, the *vaidya* (herbal doctor) has close personal ties with patients and their families. Vaidyas don't usually have any fixed fees. When the patient gets well, the family may pay either in kind or in cash.

We sometimes get surprised by the marvelous skills of the self-trained practitioners. Surki Mestry is an example. He too, like the one who saved me in my childhood, is a mason by trade. He was poor. Many people from far-off places came to him with complicated nervous system and bone problems. Some of these cases had been given up by specialists and surgeons of world repute. But our old Surki Mestry would easily put them right.

All Surki Mestry would receive were gifts offered by some of those who were healed. In spite of his skill and practice, he lived in a hut until the novices of the Jesuit Novitiate in Patna helped him put up a proper house.

Remedies according to season

God has provided remedies in nature according to the season when particular diseases are more prevalent. In India, for example, sunstroke is very common in summer. Summer is also the time when we have plenty of mangoes.

> Cook an unripe mango in ashes. (If electricity or gas is available, boil it well it in water.) Cool it well. Squeeze it out and make a sarbat (juice) by adding water. Add sugar. Have the patient drink as frequently and as much as possible. Apply part of the same mango paste all over the body and bathe in cold water. The patient will be all right.

Similarly the specific remedies for jaundice—*Phillantus niruri* or the tender leaves of the castor oil plant—are easily available at the seasons when the disease is most prevalent. .

Common, cheap and in variety

Some of the most effective remedies are at our doorstep, in our kitchen (like salt and pepper), and in the back yard.

The beautiful Sangeeta had blackhead pimples by the time she turned twenty-four. She tried a number of treatments, to no avail. She consulted a skin specialist while at Vienna for her postgraduate studies in medicine. The doctor prescribed the best medicine available. It gave her some relief whenever she used it. But when she stopped the medicine, the problem began again. Her whole face would be full of pimples. She resented looking ugly.

Back in India, when she was in charge of a hospital, a village lady suggested a simple treatment:

> Grind turmeric and the tender buds of guava plant (Bot. name *Psidium guava*), and apply the paste on the face before going to bed. Wash it off in the morning. The treatment is to be continued for about three weeks. A smooth paste of turmeric and red sandalwood also has the same effect.

Sangeeta did exactly as the lady suggested. After three weeks, not only the pimples but also the scars disappeared. Now Sangeeta is happy that she looks even more beautiful than before.

Clearing pimples is but only one of the many healing effects of turmeric. Many such simple herbs commonly found everywhere are very effective in curing a number of diseases. If we can master about fifty remedies found in our backyard, kitchen and fruit garden, we will be able to treat most of the common ailments.

Recently the Catholic Hospital Association of India organized a national consultation on herbal and home remedies. Scholars and experts from the field were present. The group selected 42 such medicines that will be enough to treat our common ailments. The tables include botanical, English and Hindi names of the essential medicines.

With the following 42 medicines, one will be able to manage practically all the common ailments. All are harmless drugs; one need not be afraid of any side effects.

I. Fourteen medicinal plants available from the flower garden and around.

Botanical Name	English/Hindi Name
1. Ocimum sanctum	Tulsi
2. Ricinus communis	Castor oil plant
3. Lawsonia inermis	Henna plant
4. Aloe vera, Aloe barbadensis	Indian alces - ghrit kumari
5. Vinca rosea	Periwinkle
6. Euphorbia hirta	Chitrapala (Mal.); Dudhi (Hindi)
7. Andrographis paniculata	King of bitters, chiretta
8. Hibiscus rosea	Hibiscus or shoe flower
9. Centella asiatica	Indian penny wort
10. Cynodon dactylon	Lawn grass, dog grass; Dhub grass (Hindi)
11. Adhatoda vasika	Arus or adhatoda
12. Anacyclus pyretrum	Pellitory - Akarkara (Hindi)
13. Acorus calamus	Sweet flag - vacha
14. Azadsachta indica	Neem

II. Fourteen medicinal plants with food value

Botanical Name	English/Hindi Name
15 Moringa oleifera	Drum stick tree
16 Mangifera indica	Mango
17 Punica granatum	Pomegranate
18 Carica papaya	Papaya
19 Emblica officinalis	Goosebeery - Amala
20 Musa sapientum	Banana
21 Psydium guajava	Guava
22 Tamarindus indica	Tamarind tree
23 Citrus bergamia	Lemon
24 Momordica charantia	Bitter gourd
25 Agati grandifolia	Agastya
26 Amaramthus spinosa	Kata bhaji
27 Mentha arvensis	Mint
28 Boerhavia diffusa	Punarvava

III. Medicines that are in the kitchen

29	Common salt
30 Curcuma longa	Tumeric
31 Zingiber officinale	Ginger
32 Piper nigrum	Black pepper
33 Piper longum	Long pepper
34 Cuminum cyminum	Jeera
35 Ptychotis ajwain	Bishop's weed or omum seed
36	Melted butter, Ghee
37 Allium cepa	Onion
38 Allium sativum	Garlic
39 Myristica fragrans	Jaiphal, Nutmeg
40 Coriandrum sativum	Coriander seeds
41	Rock salt
42	Black salt

Philosophy of the herbal system of medicine

The underlying philosophy and principle of the herbal system is the same as that of Ayurveda, though in traditional practice it is not systematized or formulated. But they speak a language and represent a concept entirely different from the principles that govern modern medicine or the allopathic system.

The five elements

According to Ayurveda and herbal system, the human body is composed of five elements or *mahabhutas*: *pritwi* (earth), *ap* (water), *agni* (fire), *vayu* (air) and *akash* (ether).

Three humors or elementary substances

In addition to the five elements are three factors called humors: *vata, pitta and kapha*. The predominant elements for vata are air and ether; for pitta, fire; and for kapha, water and earth.

Causes of disease

According to Ayurveda and the herbal system, disease is caused by the imbalance—excess or shortage—of any one or more of these humors.[5] Vata (air and ether) governs all the movements and the nervous system. Imbalance of vata will lead to about 80 diseases, including all sorts of pain, paralysis, stiffness, and heart disease.

Pitta (fire) governs the functioning of the enzymes and hormones. Thus it controls digestion, pigmentation, body temperature, thirst, sight and courage. Its imbalance can lead to some forty diseases such as fever, jaundice, and skin and liver problems.

Kapha (water and earth) regulates both vata and pitta. It is responsible for joints, sustenance, sexual power, strength and patience. Its imbalance can cause twenty diseases, such as laziness, mucus, hardening of vessels, obesity and poor digestion.

The nature of herbs and other substances

Herbs and even substances like salt are endowed with rasa (taste) and virya (potency). There are six rasas: sweet, sour, pungent, bitter, saline and astringent. One or more mahabhutas (elements) will be predominant in each rasa. For example, sweetness has earth and water; water and fire predominate in sour taste; saline consists of earth and fire; pungency, air and fire; bitterness has air and ether; and astringency has air and earth. As for potency (virya), there are two qualities—heat and cold.

Principles underlying the selection of a herb for treatment
A particular herb is selected for a disease based on both the nature of the plant (its rasa and virya) and the area of imbalance (whether vata, or pitta or kapha) that caused the disease. A particular rasa or virya is capable of regulating the deranged vata, pitta or kapha, and thus reestablishing the equilibrium. When equilibrium is reestablished, health is restored.

Herbal system and germ theory
The herbal system, like Ayurveda, accepts the existence of germs, which allopathy sees as the cause of disease. However, we consider that one can be quite at home with the germs in the body if the system is healthy and balanced. Germs cannot dominate and do harm.

In the treatment process in Ayurveda and the herbal system, drugs have no direct action on the disease (except in high-potency drugs for such uses as antidotes to poison). When the body's equilibrium is reestablished, the body itself will take care of the germs and viruses.

This type of bodily action enables the same medicine to cure disorders of opposite nature. Thus, for example, tender and green drumstick leaves bring down blood pressure, if it is high, and raises it, if it is low. Bael fruit (Bot. name *Aegle marmelos*) is useful both for constipation and diarrhea. Soymida febriguga as well as shoe flower (hibiscus) cure both amenorrhea and menorrhagia.

Due to this process of healing, herbal treatment is sometimes slow, especially in chronic cases. When the equilibrium of the system is reestablished, treatment uproots the disease rather than suppressing it. Uprooting takes longer time than just cutting the tip.

The herbal system and empowerment

One of the concepts in community health care is to empower the people to manage their health problems by themselves. The simple herbal medicines could help in this process.

People in Kapoori Village in North India can now manage diarrhea and dysentery cases by themselves. Three years ago, I was conducting a training program for village health workers. A child suffering from dysentery was brought to the dispensary.

Sr. Freda examined the case and found that the child was in a critical condition. I told the father of the child to take five leaves of periwinkle (Bot. name *Vinca rosea*), grind and make a paste, and give it two or three times a day. As a last resort, the sister collected some leaves and gave them to the child's father. The next day he came to tell us that the child was quite all right. He said that he had the same plant in his home. He gave the preparation three to four times a day and the child recovered.

The news of the child's recovery with a few periwinkle leaves spread throughout the area. Now, people on their own use this herb in cases of diarrhea and dysentery. Many people have planted this herb in their homes.

An organized effort toward empowerment
Vana Mulika Samrakshana Sangham (an organization to protect medicinal plants) is a registered body at Sitamoun, Kerala, India. It pursues systematic efforts toward enabling many people at deep and wide levels.

The organization shows how ordinary poor people can be brought together into a beautiful caring and cooperating community. Fr. Joseph Chittoor, the pastor of Sitamoun church, is the inspiration behind this people's movement. At present it is in its infancy.

The core group consists of a dozen people, seven women and five men, mostly daily laborers. Fr. Chittoor trained these health volunteers in the use of simple, ordinary herbs for curing common ailments. Each of the twelve was entrusted with a dozen families to care for their health problems. The twelve arrange for the systematic health education and curative treatment of the families under their care.

The process met with some resistance in the beginning. One day, a man suffering from acute tonsillitis was to be taken to the hospital. But transportation was not easily available. Meanwhile the group offered to treat him with an herb. They prepared a paste of *Emilia sonchifolia*, garlic and salt. Part of it they gave him to eat and a part was applied externally. Certain improvements were noticed in just a few hours. He became perfectly all right in a couple of days. Such irrefutable and convincing experiences helped to build up positive attitudes toward the movement.

"Today at least 70 percent of diseases in the area are being treated with herbal remedies only," says Kumaran, the secretary of the organization. "The incidence of disease also has come down by at least 25 percent," says Thresiamma, one of the members. "The reason is that people now have started eating more vegetables. Every family now cultivates one vegetable or another." The group also promotes school health programs. Children are taught and encouraged to plant vegetables.

The process of promoting herbal medicine has also resulted in greater unity and cooperation among the people. In fact, the herbal program has been a launching pad for people to get organized. Their unity and organization have given them greater self-confidence. Though the whole group is of poor people, the organization has helped them enhance their self-respect. The core team comes together often and works as a group to prepare medicine for the whole area. This process helps build up mutual concern and cooperation not only among the core group, but also in the whole area of their activity. Another very interesting aspect of this group is that it is inter-faith—Hindu and Christian.

Built around the use and promotion of the simple herbal remedies, the Vana Mulika Samrakshana Samiti of Sitamoun has become an agent of change, helping people gradually evolve into a community where cooperation, sharing, equality and dignity of all prevail. All these are aspects of an integral, holistic health program that one cannot overlook. Health today is looked upon not just as a

313

curative and preventive venture, but also as a promotive one. Building attitudes in the people that make them more humane, more interrelated, more empowered to fight factors that oppress them, enslave them and condemn them to inhuman existence are all part of integral promotive health action today.

Conclusion

Experiments like those of Fr. Chittoor in Sitamoun link low-cost, easily available herbal medicines in a context of people's unity, organization and empowerment. They are steps in the right direction. We need more such ventures of people's action. I would like to invest myself in building a network of more such groups. As a priest I believe this is a way of realizing the kingdom of God, which is to begin already here on earth.

Notes

1   The specific descriptions of herbal treatments, based upon resources in the author's library, are offered as information rather than medical advice. For additional discusion of Ayurvedic medicine and related concepts, see chapter four—ED.

2   "History of Medicine and Surgery," *Encyclopedia Britannica.*

3   Vaidya Bhagavan Das, *Fundamentals of Ayurvedic Medicine.* New Delhi: Konak Publishers, p.11 ff.

4   Dr. C. Satyamala et al., *Taking Sides.* Madras: Anitra, p. 87 ff.

5   Vaidya Bhagavan Das and Acarya M. Junius, *A Handbook of Ayurveda*, New Delhi, 1988, p. 10 ff.

21

Homeopathy: A different approach to health

François Choffat

The homeopathic theorist Georges Vithoulkas
defines health as creativity. This fits in with the
Judeo-Christian concept of God making man in
his own image: a creator within the creation.

C hess and droughts (checkers) differ more by their rules than
by the shape of their pawns. In the same way, traditional and
homeopathic medicine do not differ so much, as is believed, by
their forms of medicines as in their varying concepts of illness and
healing. The "rules" of medicine are those of the Western culture.
But it is not easy to understand homeopathy when you have a classic scientific training, since its very basis is a system of thought
quite foreign to leading concepts today.

Medicine is based on a materialist view of man, sickness
and death. Homeopathy is part of a universal concept wherein the
body and mind are inseparable.[1] In order to explain homeopathy
we must first understand the historical background for these differences.

The origins of materialism

In the Middle Ages it would have been inconceivable to consider
the universe as simply material. One spoke of "Creation," implying
that visible reality was the manifestation of the Creator's will. The
phenomena of nature and life were possible only because God

renewed them constantly. The church claimed to know the truth, which encompasses both the spiritual and the material. They could not be separated.

Descartes developed the basis of rationalism, sidestepping the church's dogma. He claimed that the mind or spirit exists independently of matter, and vice versa. This is the historical basis for modern-day dualism. According to this school of thought, man's mind may consider matter objectively. Matter no longer obeys the divine Spirit. It functions in relation to its own laws, the first of which is the law of causality or determinism.

Man has been able to dominate nature by the knowledge and application of these laws. This stand has increased our control over matter and led our civilization inappropriately to esteem material values such as accumulation of wealth, production, consumption and material gain. Correspondingly, the humanities are now the poor relations of our culture. Cartesian dualism has led us to extremes of materialism.

To grasp such a complex reality, we have reduced problems to a number of elementary questions. This is reductionism. Our modern view tells us that the universe has no need of God for its continuing existence and neither does man need God in order to go on living. God is dead for our society. We have assumed power over reality, but at the same time we have lost our reason for living.

The death of vitalism

Medicine has resisted dualism for two centuries. The phenomena of life seemed to bypass the rules of determinism, because of their fantastic nature. It was thought that every living being was inhabited by a "vital energy" that prevented the matter itself from following its own laws and returning to a mineral state. This concept is called vitalism.

It was not until the 19th century that Claude Bernard proved through experimenting one function at a time on a living being, without altering any other vital constant factors, that life itself could be governed by the laws of cause and effect. Once medicine and biology was based on experiments carried out on animals, Claude Bernard was able to apply the laws of matter to natural phenomena. The discovery of Pasteur that microbes caused infectious diseases seemed to confirm this theory.

Medicine has thus gained great power over disease. But this step forward led medicine toward excessive materialism: the body alone is treated, considered as a machine. Reductionism has led to compartmentalizing knowledge and a plethora of specialists. Though it has gained in technical efficiency, medicine has lost its image of man as a whole. Above all, it has neglected man's spirit. Health and life have been reduced to mere engineering problems. If a living being is nothing more than an assemblage of molecules, any breakdown in the machine means a return to nothingness. One corollary to the materialist concept of life is that death becomes something to be feared.

Four principles

Homeopathy came before Claude Bernard and the introduction of dualism in biology. It was born during the French Revolution. Samuel Hahnemann (1755-1833), a German doctor, set out principles in his *Organon of Homeopathy*, published for the first time in 1810. This work covers twenty years of research and experiments. It describes in detail the theoretical and experimental foundations of a discipline that was to revolutionize early 19th-century medicine.

Homeopathy has never contested the vitalist's views. On the contrary, it presupposes the existence of the vital energy that modern science denies. Homeopathy is neither dualistic, materialistic nor reductionistic. As in all well-known traditional medicines like acupuncture, the human being is taken as a whole, neither singling out any one organ from the others nor separating mind from body. These medicines are called "holistic." Homeopathy questions the leading concepts of our materialistic civilization. For this reason it can only remain backstage and rather obscure.

There are four principles of homeopathy. The principle of *integrity* means that each patient is an integral whole. Considering each human being as a physical and psychic whole means that there is no such thing as two identically ill patients. This is the principle of *individualization*. Treatment is not applied to the disease but to the patient's way of reacting. The same illness will be treated differently in each patient. In fact, it is not the illness that gets the treatment, but the patient. The principle of *similitude* and the principle of *infinitesimal doses* will be described below in some detail.

Similitude

The principle of similitude, which gave homeopathy its name, is defined as follows: "A toxic substance that produces certain symptoms in a well patient in experimental circumstances is able to cure the same symptoms diagnosed in a sick patient." These symptoms form an indistinct part of the psychic and physical nature of the patient and are not taken into account separately.

We know, for example, that belladonna produces an extremely high temperature, dryness in the mouth, dilation of the pupils, congestion in the head, irritability and lethargy alternating with bouts of deliriousness and convulsions. Thus will belladonna be picked for the treatment of some convulsive fevers. The term homeopathy, created by Hahnemann, means that the remedy has an effect on the organism similar to that of the sickness itself.

Infinitesimal doses

The fourth principle is that of infinitesimal doses. To reduce the toxic effect of his remedies, Hahnemann tried prescribing weaker and weaker dilutions. After much research he discovered that each level of dilution, after a hard shaking, became more powerful. The therapeutic effect was sustained in the aqueous extract even when all traces of the original molecules disappeared. He went so far as to use dilutions of 10^{-60}. But even stronger dilutions are also used.

It is the absence of molecular activity in each remedy that causes the most surprise today, even though people are more equipped to understand it now than in Hahnemann's time. The remedy is no longer a chemical one, but rather a physical intermediary or messenger. The remedy might be compared to a computer program, whose message is recorded by the physical arrangement of molecules on a magnetic medium, with no chemical changes.

318

Medicine has become so imbued with the materialistic model of the 19th century that until now it has always rejected any suggestion of a theory of life dominated by physics. However, such a theory has been the subject of comment by numerous researchers in physics and biology. [2]

A different approach to cure

In medicine, health is established when sickness is not manifest; the vital organs remain quiet. This way of thinking conforms to the mechanical vision of life. But in homeopathy, health is a dynamic process, a constant oscillation of functions regulated like cybernetic systems, ever seeking a new balance that is never achieved. When an outside attacker upsets this balance, the body reacts by trying to adapt with a new balance, giving off symptoms—symptoms not of illness, but those of a patient trying to find a new balance. In a case of influenza, for example, the fever is a means of fighting the virus. To remove this reaction by prescribing aspirin is to undermine this means.

Homeopathy will therefore attempt to work alongside the patient's symptoms and not against them, respecting the natural forces of the healing process. That is why it is considered as a "natural medicine." This is fundamentally different from the conventional approach, which has a pharmacopeia mostly comprised of anti- or counter-medicines: against fever, analgesic, anti-inflammatory, antibiotics, antidepressants. Homeopathic cures alleviate only in exceptional circumstances; general management cures are rarely prescribed.

Sickness is the sign of a missing link

In a chronic illness, the process of healing is interrupted in its natural course by a lack or loss of information. The body reacts in a repetitive and inadequate way. The illness is a loss of information; the body no longer knows how to reestablish normal functions. Chronic symptoms are only signals of lost information. Medical therapy of a suppressive type can only serve to alleviate symptoms temporarily.

The homeopathic remedy acts like corrective software in a computer whose program has lost some information, through a computer "virus." Homeopathy works on the sum of a body's pathological reactions through one remedy that is, in fact, a complex message. The remedy, which holds the contents of the message, will be repeated or altered only after a sufficient period of observation.

Homeopathy goes against the material interests of the medical system; its aim is cure, not dependency of the patient. Homeopathy is an antidote to the escalation in health costs. Homeopathy will not replace medicine in all areas of pathology, but it is certainly well placed to give lasting relief to the many sick people for whom medicine can offer neither diagnosis nor treatment. It is also effective in numerous organic or functional disorders, allergies, psychic disturbances, digestive and neurological ailments, and infectious diseases such as AIDS. The "human computer" is able to regulate itself and preserve its own health, a life memory. It is the object of the vital principle which has been contested since Claude Bernard, but which modern research seems to be restoring.[3]

Toward good health

Homeopathy in principle does not work with palliatives. The therapy involves a long process of substitution and evolution, by which it tries to transform chronic symptoms—or inadequate reactions—into either less serious symptoms or acute symptoms that become spontaneously curable. A navigator must know in which direction his port of call lies and use navigational instruments to know his position at any moment. For the therapist, the goal is health; the instruments are the laws of healing. And so we have to know what good health consists of—apart from the quiet functioning of the vital organs—how to move toward such a state, and how to chart the course.

There is no absolute, universal definition for good health. It is a subject for metaphysical conjecture with no definite conclusion; we all have an essentially subjective idea of what health is. If man is only a machine, health may be reflected in the good functioning of his parts, when there is no breakdown in any organs. To repair a machine, one should first find out how it works. But medicine repairs any breakdown without exactly knowing what the machine is for, or even whether it has any use at all. People may show no physical symptoms in cases of depression or senility, for example, but their lives may have no meaning and nobody would say they are well. A tree is recognized by the quality of its fruits. In the same manner, the way a man works indicates whether or not he is in good health.

For a person to accomplish his function, we need to establish what that function is and understand where it differs from that of an animal, vegetable or mineral. This function is fused with our reason for living which, as we have already seen, has been lost in our materialist culture. Although greatly simplifying, I myself favor the definition given by one of my mentors, Georges Vithoulkas: "Health is creativity."[4] This definition fits in with the Judeo-Christian concept according to which "God made man in his own image," that is, a creator within the creation.

Creativity requires more than just the smooth running of the body, which may even become secondary. Severely ill or handicapped patients can even be more creative than many others who are fit and well. One advantage of this definition is that death is not the opposite of health; one can be creative up until death independently of the disintegration of the body.

The laws of healing

Homeopathy is the art of substituting one set of symptoms with another. It is important, then, to know whether the new condition is preferable to the first and whether it means a step forward in the cure. Hering, a homeopath from the last century, put forth three natural laws of health that apply to all healing processes or arts.[5] A change in the sick person is a step forward if:

1. Symptoms are displaced from inside to the outside. Example: If asthma is replaced by skin eruptions, or if migraine turns into diarrhea.

2. Symptoms become displaced from the upper parts to the lower parts. Example: If a cough is replaced by intestinal problems, or if periarthritis of the shoulder becomes pain in the wrist.

3. Current symptoms are replaced by symptoms experienced long before. Example: If adult rheumatism gives way to chest infections that the patient had as a child.

The essence of homeopathy is contained in these three short formulae. They can only be applied to a patient taken as a whole and as an individual. They have practically unlimited extensions in terms of practical use and as subjects for reflection.

Man is three-dimensional

From the holistic point of view, Hering's laws are incomplete since they are only to be applied explicitly to the physical being. They are dualistic and do not help address the relation between physical and psychic symptoms. Georges Vithoulkas has applied Hering's laws to the whole person by considering three levels: physical, emotional and mental.[6] Vithoulkas sees these three levels as a stack of cones. The mental, at the center, has priority over the physical, on the outside; the emotional is between the two.

- On the physical level, a succession of symptoms from the upper parts of the lower shows positive evolution.

- The emotional level corresponds to the soul in the Judeo-Christian concept of man. Here lies our mood, sadness or gladness, love and hate, self-image, confidence and inadequate feelings, the lust for life or lack of it.

- The mental or spiritual level is the home of our conscience and consciousness (in French, one word: *conscience*). Added to our consciousness is our ability to think clearly, our lucidity and memory. Our moral conscience is a looking upwards, transcending our consciousness. This implies a vision of good and evil and an intuitive perception of the meaning of life.

If the emotional level is part of our life instinct, the search for a meaning, aspiring to perfection and an absolute belong to the mental level. The highest and noblest functions are central; symptoms affecting the mental field are the most serious.

A sick person usually suffers from symptoms on all three levels. The relative intensity of symptoms marks out a kind of gravitational center of the sickness. One may evaluate the temporary state of health within a non-dualist perception by using a graded hierarchy of physical, emotional and mental symptoms.

This holistic conception is not easy to accept today. The interdependence of physical and nonphysical signs and the subsequent replacement by other symptoms is not a pattern that conforms to our cultural interpretation of disease. Here we are a long way from the psychosomatic diagnosis that doctors may use as an excuse for not finding the cause of an ailment, telling the patient to look inward for the answers.

To be able to regulate health, with all its readjustments, implies that there is a model of "good health" and an organizing force external to the body. In the same way, the coherent succession of symptoms according to Hering's laws and the transposition of symptoms from one level to another as in Vithoulkas' concept indicate that a human being is yielding to a superior organizer able to coordinate the three levels. An organizing principle must be responsible for both normal and healing functions of a person, since there are only quantitative differences between them. Here lies the concept of the vital principle.

The myth of immortality

In a frenzied search for quantity, our materialistic society has lost all reason for living and becomes bewildered in the face of death. Man's expiry date is seen as annihilation. If our spiritual values have been lost, medicine has become the last barrier against death, with the implicit but impossible mission to discover the secret of immortality. The principal criterion of health has become long life. Doctors devote a large portion of their efforts to delay the fatal termination date. Medicine makes little effort to improve the quality of life, so death is considered as a failure. In this state of affairs, health—assimilated to survival—has no price, which explains why our society refuses nothing to benefit medicine, and health care costs soar in consequence.

Homeopathy does not subscribe to this myth of immortality. As medicine of the mind as well as the body, it does not consider death as an enemy. It concentrates more on restoring the quality of life rather than fighting death. It may be more important to help a sick person die well rather than to keep him alive at all costs.

Thus homeopathy calls into question the principles and practice of a medicine excessively biased towards materialism. It places the whole individual at the center of its foundational concepts. It is

Implicit principles of medicine and homeopathy

Medicine	Homeopathy
Good health is a state	Health is a dynamic balance
Sickness is a sign of bad health	Sickness is a process of readaptation
Every symptom affects the part of the body in which it is manifest	Every symptom affects the whole body
Symptoms are to be eradicated	Symptoms are an attempt by the body to heal itself and need to be supported and directed
Determine symptoms in order to eliminate them	Determine the patient's ways of reacting in order to correct them
For every symptom there is a specific remedy	For every patient there is a different remedy
Strategy of suppression	Strategy conducted by substitution and evolvement
The mind is a manifestation of matter	The matter of human beings is inspired by an immaterial vital principle
Death is the conclusion of a human being and a failure for medicine	Death is a necessary passage to a continuing life
The goal of medicine is to stop humans from suffering and dying.	The goal of homeopathy is to assist man to live better and die well.

an alternative and a possible remedy to the materialist concept of our culture and medicine. Homeopathy is not reserved to believers in God, but any Christian who cares about coherence in seeking good health should take some interest in it. Moreover, homeopathy can be a factor in personal development and can back up the process of inner healing.

Notes

1   For convenience, the author uses the terms "medicine" for conventional medicine and "homeopathy" for homeopathic medicine.

2   Fritz Popp, *The Biology of Light*.

3   See, for example, *The Theory of Morphogenetic Fields* by Rupert Sheldrake.

4   Georges Vithoulkas, *The Science of Homeopathy*.

5   *Ibid.*

6   Only a brief outline of Vithoulkas' thinking is given here. The interested reader is referred to *The Science of Homeopathy*—ED.

References

Capra, Fritjof. *The Turning Point*. Bantam, 1987.

Choffat, François. L'homéopathie au chevet de la médecine? Essai pour un nouveau débat. Paris: Ed. du Cerf, 1993.

Coulter, Harris L. *Homoeopathic Science and Modern Medicine*. North Atlantic, 1991

Hahnemann, Samuel. *Organon of medicine*. Translated by Boericke, 6th ed., Delhi: Jain Publisher, 1980.

Poop, Fritz A. *Biologie de la Lumière, bases scientifiques du rayonnement cellulaire ultra-faible*. Liège, Marc Pietteur, coll. "Résurgence," 1989.

Sheldrake, Rupert. *The Presence of the Past: Morphic Resonance and the Habits of Nature*. Random, 1989.

Vithoulkas, Georges. *The Science of Homeopathy*. Grove-Atlantic, 1980.

22
Pranic healing

Eliza Kuppozhackel

Test everything in the light of reason and
experience—Mahatma Gandhi.

Before the colonizers brought Western or allopathic medicine to
India some 400 years ago, Indians exclusively practiced indigenous forms of medicine that evolved over thousands of years. Even
today, more than 85 percent of all Indians rely on indigenous systems of medicine. Early Buddhist monks from India took
Ayurvedic medicine—including their concepts of acupuncture,
acupressure, herbal medicine, yoga and pranic healing—to other
parts of Asia. These medical arts are currently practiced, in one
form or another, in India, China, Vietnam, Japan, Thailand, the
Philippines and elsewhere in Asia.

In recent years, Christians in India have adopted allopathic,
homeopathic, Ayurvedic and other systems of medicine to their
calling to be God's agents of healing. Currently pranic healing is
once again becoming popular in India, not only among Christians
but among people of all religions, castes and professions.

Practitioners of pranic healing believe that by itself the practice is neither Hindu, Buddhist, Christian nor Muslim. Moreover,
pranic healing is not intended to replace orthodox medicine but
rather to complement it. It can be combined easily with other systems of health care for faster and quicker results in healing.

People in the East typically believe that God has placed a
basic vital energy in the human body. This energy is responsible for

the maintenance of health. In this view, vital energy fields are as much a part of the body as are the immune, respiratory, circulatory, reproductive, and digestive systems. The body is seen as having its own healing mechanism, which needs to be nurtured and strengthened.

The World Health Organization, along with other groups, has made a sustained effort to revive indigenous systems of medicine where they exist. This has given Indians a new boost and faith in their own indigenous system of medicine.

Health as holistic well-being means harmony and integration of all interconnected systems. Healing restores harmony and integration within persons, community and society. If health is to be a reality for all people, harmony and balance must become a reality in each person by integrating physical, mental and spiritual dimensions. And in the society it means harmonizing all interwoven systems, be they social, political, economic, cultural or environmental.

Healing power from Jesus

One well-known Bible passage illustrates healing power or energy going out from our Lord Jesus. A woman who had suffered greatly for twelve years touched the cloak of Jesus.

> "Who touched me?" Jesus asked. ". . . Someone touched me; I know that power has gone out from me." Then the woman . . . told why she had touched him and how she had been instantly healed. Then he said to her, "Daughter, your faith has healed you. Go in peace" (Luke 8:45-48).

As Jesus went about teaching and proclaiming the new commandment of love, he healed many people. He relieved their physical suffering and restored their mental peace and inner harmony. They received new hope and new life. Jesus had no elaborate diagnostic procedures. He used ordinary, simple things like mud, water and comforting words. His compassion and healing touch brought about total transformation in people's lives.

What is pranic healing?

The Sanskrit word *prana* means life force, vital energy, breath of life. In many of the Indian languages, when a person dies it is said his prana has left him. The concept is found in various other languages. In Greek it is called *pneuma*, in Polynesian *mana*, in Hebrew *ruah* or breath of life, and in Chinese *chi*.[1]

Rishis (Hindu yogis) of ancient India were healers who used a form of pranic healing. They believed that vital energy from a stronger and healthier person can bring healing to a weaker or sicker person. The healer receives prana or vital energy and projects it to the patient and to bring about healing.

People who are healthy and have more prana in them make others around them feel better. On the other hand, people with less prana unconsciously tend to absorb prana from others. This is why sometimes we feel tired and drained of energy after encountering some persons.

Certain places are believed to be beneficial because they have abundant prana. When we go to a healthy place for holidays, we return full of vitality. Walking in the countryside where the air is fresh or resting under old and healthy trees gives a lot of prana or even healing. People who are weak and lethargic can revitalize themselves by consciously absorbing prana from air and ground.

When performing pranic healing, the practitioner begins by using a technique called scanning to identify problem areas. Many ailments are linked with problems in specific *chakras*, or energy centers. After sweeping or cleansing the affected area, the practitioner energizes the area and the appropriate chakra.

The chakras are seen as interpenetrating and extending beyond the visible physical body. They absorb, digest and distribute prana to the different parts of the body. The chakras control, energize and are responsible for the proper functioning of the whole physical body and its different parts and organs.

These concepts are questioned in the West because there is no total scientific proof for them. But Eastern sages and healers have long affirmed the existence of the vital body, which is also known as the aura. Exponents of the practice known as Kirlian photography have even produced color images of this phenomenon.

First-hand examples

A young mother rejoices

Anu, a young mother of two children, was suffering from constipation for three days. She asked me whether I had any treatment for her discomfort. I treated her for constipation. I also could feel that she was having headaches. I knew she had a history of migraine. So I treated her for that, as well. Half an hour later, she went to the toilet and returned to report she felt relieved and at ease. She later wrote to me saying that she had not had a recurrence of migraine.

She and her husband rejoiced when she also experienced relief from knee joint pain, which troubled her and for which they consulted several doctors and had allopathic and Ayurvedic treatments. It is one and a half years since she had the pranic healing and the knee joint pain and migraine never recurred so far. Every time I visit her, several of her neighbors approach me for healing.

An infant cries

During a healing training program in northeast India, I visited a village clinic. While I was there a woman brought a one-month old infant to the clinic. He was having severe chest congestion and had not cried for three days. The nurse tried to make him cry by hitting the sole of his feet, but there was no movement or sound from the child. The nurse advised the mother to take the child to the government health center for immediate treatment, as her clinic had only minimum facilities. She asked me whether I could help the child.

Since they were talking in the Garo language, I did not understand the extent of the problem. I sensed the chest congestion of the child, so I moved my hand over the chest of the child in a cleansing motion. When I did three sweepings the child made a small sound. At the fifth sweeping he started crying. The faces of the mother and the nurse lit up. I asked the mother to quiet the child, but both the nurse and the mother encouraged him to cry. Only then did I realize the extent of the problem. The child was treated with pranic healing two more times and became perfectly healthy.

A mother's agony

Sushma, another young mother, had a different problem. For two years, she could not do any work due to pain in her shoulder and back. She could not even lift or move her hand. She was entirely dependent on her husband and in-laws. The mental agony that she could not do anything for her husband and child made her sad and discouraged. The X-ray showed an extra growth of bone on the right shoulder. The doctors suggested surgery but were not confident about the result. Physiotherapy was suggested as an alternative. She tried it for a few months but it did not help her much.

Then she heard about pranic healing from a magazine and came for treatment. After two sessions the pain was much relieved and she could lift and turn her hand. With three more sessions she started doing normal work at home. The treatment was terminated after seven sessions, with the condition that she report back in a month. Six months since the pranic healing, Sushma is now a happy woman taking care of her family.

A girl on the bus

Pranic healing can be done at any time and at any place. I was traveling in a crowded bus from our center to a nearby town. Many were standing, including school children. The students were struggling to keep their balance while the bus was zigzagging through the villages. One girl almost fell on me. I made little space for her to sit down. The girl had burned herself that morning and had a large blister on her hand. Her pain was so severe that she was unable to stand holding her school bag and lunch box.

I asked her if she would like me to do something to reduce her pain. She readily agreed. While she kept her hand on her knee I did pranic healing on her hand. After about five minutes of healing, the pain disappeared along with the blister. The girl was very happy and had a grand smile of good-bye when she got off the bus near her school.

A carpenter returns to work

Often a problem gets worse because medical facilities are not easily available. If help can be provided at the crucial moment, many complications can be avoided. A carpenter was repairing our roof and started to climb, when a nail made a deep wound in his palm. He came to me to apply herbal medicine to stop bleeding. Instead, I offered pranic healing.

After twenty minutes of pranic healing, not only had the bleeding and pain stopped but his whole wound healed completely. He was happy and soon got back to his work. He said that without the pranic healing he would have had to take leave for at least three days before he could work with his hand again.

Distance healing

Healing can be done also at a distance. Ravi, a 36-year-old man with total paralysis below the neck following an accident, was brought by a social worker to our order's Ayusha Clinic. An appointment was made over the telephone, but I had not realized the extent of his problem. When I learned that he was about to be carried to the treatment room, I asked that he remain in the car. I called the social worker and the man's friends to the clinic and explained the process of pranic healing. I asked them to sit and pray for healing.

I did distance healing for Ravi. After the healing process I went outside and asked Ravi what he felt. He said that he felt some energy flowing through his benumbed hand. I asked him to lift his hand, and he raised it. The hand trembled, but he could hold it up at the shoulder level. Everyone had a sense of awe and wonder on their face. Ravi was full of happiness and quoted Bible words to me. "I was like the paralytic at the pool for the last eleven years," he said. "But this good social worker had pity on me and brought me here." Ravi is continuing treatment. He is now able to lift both his arms and legs but is not yet able to walk.

Pranic healing in India

In India today, pranic healing is a boon to many, especially in the villages where most of our people live and for whom adequate medical care is often not available. There is a heavy concentration on drugs, doctors and hospitals in the cities, but the poor can hardly afford them. The competition and profit-making drive of the multinational companies keep even the lifesaving drugs beyond the reach of the poor. Not only that, what is available is often substandard and spurious. The side effects of many drugs are also not to be underestimated.

Pranic healing has created a lot of interest in India. Many people are healing all kinds of ailments with marvelous results. Anyone with average intelligence and common sense, a compassionate heart and the good will to help others can learn and practice it.

Sometimes people demand scientific proof for its effectiveness. It is not easy to do so. In some cases all we know is that the person was suffering but after treatment there is no more pain and suffering. As Mahatma Gandhi once said, "The Golden Rule is to test everything in the light of reason and experience, no matter from where it comes."

Pranic healing is done usually by both the healer and patient asking for God's guidance, protection and healing. It makes the healing faster if healer and patient are receptive to prana or vital energy and above all, to the source of all energies, God himself. For those who believe in God, we ask them to pray. Those who do not are asked to be open and receptive to the healing energy. But God's power can heal everyone, whether or not they are believers. After every healing patients are encouraged to praise and thank God.

Here in India people believe that all healing is of God and that God uses many different methods to heal people. Pranic healing is another technique we in India have adopted as a way to provide healing to many people in need and for the service and glory of God. We believe that God is using many of us to erect signposts for his kingdom through the use of this indigenous system of healing. In our cultural setting, this is an appropriate thing to do, since the gospel can best be presented in the context of the culture.

Note

1   See Chapter 4 for a cross-cultural survey of prana and related
concepts. The interested reader may wish to consult *The Ancient
Science and Art of Pranic Healing* by Choa Kok Sui. The book is
published by Institute for Inner Studies, Inc., Evekal Building, 855
Passay Road, Corner Amorsolo St., Makati j, Metro Manila,
Philippines. Second edition, 1990.

23

Growing plants without soil

Miller Fabio Villalobos Florez

Hydroponic techniques can produce food where
soil and environmental conditions are not adequate for traditional agriculture.

Hydroponics, the growing of plants without soil, has developed from experiments carried out to determine the composition of plants and what substances make them grow. Such work
on plant constituents dates back to 1600 A.D. However, plants were
being grown in soil-less culture far earlier than this. The hanging
gardens of Babylon and the floating gardens of the Aztecs of Mex-
ico and those of the Chinese are examples of hydroponic cultivation. Egyptian hieroglyphic records dating back to several hundred
years B.C. describe the growing of plants in water.

Before the time of Aristotle, Theophrastus (372-287 B.C.)
undertook various experiments in crop nutrition. Botanical studies
by Dioscorides date back to the first century A.D.

The earliest recorded scientific approach to discover plant
constituents was in 1600 when Jan van Helmont showed that plants
obtain substances for growth from water. In 1699, an Englishman,
John Woodward, grew plants in water containing various types of
soil, and found that the greatest growth occurred in water that contained the most soil. He concluded that plant growth was a result
of certain substances in water derived from soil, rather than simply
a result of water itself. In 1804, de Saussure proposed that plants
are composed of chemical elements obtained from water, soil and

air. This proposition was verified later by Boussingault, a French chemist, in experiments with plants grown in sand, quartz and charcoal, to which were added solutions of known chemical composition.

Various research workers had demonstrated by that time that plants could be grown in an inert medium moistened with a water solution containing minerals required by the plants. The next step was to eliminate the medium entirely and grow the plants in a water solution containing these minerals. This was accomplished by two German scientists, Sachs (1860) and Knop (1861). These early investigations in plant nutrition demonstrated that normal plant growth can be achieved by immersing the roots of plants in a water solution containing salts of nitrogen, phosphorus, sulfur, potassium, calcium and magnesium, which are now defined as the macronutrients. With further refinements in laboratory techniques and chemistry, scientists discovered seven elements required by plants in relatively small quantities—the microelements or trace elements. These include iron, chlorine, manganese, boron, zinc, copper and molybdenum.

In subsequent years, researchers developed many diverse basic formulas for plant nutrition. Some of these workers were Tollens (1882), Tottingham (1914), Shive (1915), Hoagland (1919), Trelease (1933) and Robbins.

Interest in practical application of this so-called "nutriculture" did not develop until about 1925, when the greenhouse industry expressed interest in its use. Greenhouse soils had to be replaced frequently to overcome problems of soil structure, fertility and pests. As a result, research workers became aware of the potential use of nutriculture to replace conventional soil cultural methods. Between 1925 and 1935, extensive development took place in modifying the laboratory techniques of nutriculture to large-scale crop production.

In the early 1930s, W. F. Gericke of the University of California put laboratory experiments in plant nutrition on a commercial scale. In doing so he called these nutriculture systems *hydroponics*. The word was derived from two Greek words, *hydro* (water) and *ponos* (labor)—literally "water working".

Justification

Hydroponics can be defined as the science of growing plants without use of soil, but by use of an inert medium, such as gravel, sand, peat, vermiculite, pumice or sawdust, to which is added a nutrient solution containing all elements needed by the plant for normal growth and development. Since many hydroponic methods employ some type of medium it is often termed "soil-less culture," while water culture alone would be true hydroponics.

The use of this alternate process for food production is justified in the following situations:

1. In regions were a soil matrix is not available:
   a. urban agriculture
   b. in courtyards, internal areas

2. Due to limiting factors such as:
   a. physical—physical conditions that hinder the cultivation process such as sandy or hard soil, excessive clay
   b. chemical—soil with toxic compounds or elements such as aluminum or complete absence of key elements
   c. biological—presence of nematodes or fungus in the soil, detrimental to plant growth, such as fusarium, which leads to plant tissue destruction

3. When it represents an advantage:
   a. at the scientific level—nutritional studies and evaluation of elements
   b. at the educational level—agronomical studies and vegetal physiology
   c. in therapeutics

4. When it offers financial advantages:
   a. by production—in hydroponic culture, under excellent conditions, productivity of about 18 kilograms per square meter has been achieved. Financial advantages occur especially with tomatoes, cucumbers and green peppers.

b. by quality—sanitary level and composition

c. opportunity—taking advantage of the availibility of products out of season, which increases product value and marketing opportunities

d. localization—growing close to centers of consumption and planning crops that are not usually produced in the region.

Developing hydroponic cultivation

To start a system of hydroponic cultivation, one should consider:

1. Site conditions

A grower should try to meet as many of the following siting requirements as possible, to reduce the risk of failure:

- Full east, south and west exposure to sunlight with wind-break on north

- Level area or one that can be easily leveled

- Good internal drainage with minimum percolation rate of 1 inch per hour

- Availability of natural gas, three-phase electricity, telephone and good quality water capable of supplying at least one half gallon of water per plant per day

- On a good road close to a population center for wholesale market and retail market at greenhouses if you choose to retail

- Close to residence for ease of checking greenhouse during extreme weather

- North-south oriented greenhouses with rows also north-south

- A region with a maximum amount of sunlight

- Lack of excessively strong winds.

Specific variables to be taken in consideration are as follows:

a. Temperature can be a limiting factor to the hydroponic cultures. Both maximum and minimum values should be taken into account. The influence at extreme values is as follows:

- from warm to cold: a longer vegetative cycle; fruits produced are hard, with higher fiber content
- from cold to warm: softening of fruits, physiological problems (cabbage not included), decrease of vegetative cycles and higher incidence of disease

b. Radiation--plants with narrow leaves need more radiation than plants with large leaves. When light is not sufficient, the plants degrade.

c. Humidity—if higher than 70 percent, fungus may develop. Ventilation is an important factor to reduce humidity.

d. Wind—soft winds contribute to humidity control. Plastic barriers can be utilized for wind control. Wind velocity should not be higher than 50 km/hour.

e. Rain—complete control can be achieved by covering the cultures or by keeping them in greenhouses.

2. Hydroponic media

    a. Water
- of good quality, without toxic compounds
- readily availabile
- close to the cultivation area
- temperature between 18 and 22 degrees centigrade.

    b. Substrate

The substrate substitutes for the soil used in traditional agriculture. It should have :
- a depth between 5 cm and 10 cm
- good capacity for moisture retention
- good capillarity, meaning the horizontal displacement of the water through the substrate
- light weight to facilitate handling
- good price; in some regions a mixture of rice shell and sand can be obtained free.

A good example of a substrate is a mixture of rice shell and sand in the proportion of 4 to 1. The rice shell has a structure made of silica which remains an organic material and which decomposes during the culture development. This is a good substrate, but it must be previously disinfected. It can be used with hot water to avoid fungal development or the formation of toxic substances.

Other types of substrate are a mixture of brick and roof tile, pumice stone, packing foam material and some polyurethanes, which may show favorable conditions but are expensive (see Table 1, Properties of Substrates).

c. Nutrient solution

Experiments made in Colombia have utilized a liquid solution called *coljap* made of a *major* nutrient and a *minor* nutrient.

The *major* nutrient is so named because it contains the elements that plants need in large quantities. It contains:

Nitrogen	N	$Ca\,(NO_3)_2$
Phosphorus	P	$NH_4\,H_2\,PO_4$
Potassium	K	NO_3
Calcium	Ca	Included in $Ca\,(NO_3)_2$

The solution is colorless.

The *minor* nutrient includes the elements that plants need in smaller quantities. The solution is yellowish and contains:

Iron	Fe	Fe-CIT
Magnesium	Mg	$Mg\,NO_3$
Sulphur	S	$Mg\,SO_4$
Manganese	Mn	$Mn\,SO_4$
Copper	Cu	$Cu\,(NO_3)_2$
Zinc	Zn	$Zn\,SO_4$
Boron	B	$H_3\,BO_3$
Molybdenum	Mo	Mo-A
Cobalt	Co	$Co\,SO_4$
Chlorine	Cl	$K\,Cl$

d. Dosage

The concentration of the hydroponic nutrients depends on the specific crops as well as on other basic variables associated with vegetal nutrition. In experiments made in Colombia with tomatoes, cucumbers and green peppers, application was made per square meter of a *"full"* solution composed of 2.5 cm³ per liter of *major* and 1.0 cm³ of *minor*. The solution was applied once a day before 9 A.M., and in the afternoon only water was applied.

In a period of 30 days, during plant growth, flowering and fruit formation, application was made in the same way of a *full* solution composed of 5 cm³ per liter of *major* and 2 cm³ of *minor*.

A system for solution recovery can be used to avoid nutritional deficiencies and system contamination. This particular measure can greatly reduce operational costs.

e. Drainage

It is very important to provide the system with a drain for excess solution. In open systems drainage will also help to avoid contamination.

f. Types of systems

There are several types of hydroponic systems. The choice will depend on local conditions such as availibility of water and economic aspects. The following types can be considered :

- Naked roots—a sophisticated technique
- Roots in water—a closed system where the roots float supported by materials such as packing foam (polystyrene)
- Cultivation with substrate—the method used in experiments done in Colombia. Called popular hydropony, this technique can be applied in poor communities.

The methodology to follow when cultivating with substrate is as follows:

Boxes A wooden box, 1 to 2 m long, 1.20 m wide and 10 cm deep, is lined with a plastic sheet to form a slight slope toward the drain. The box is filled with substrate composed of rice shell and washed river sand in a proportion of 4 to 1. The box should be protected against heavy rain by such means as a plastic cover. One of the advantages of this system is the ease with which it can be moved from one place to another.

Seeding   Small pots with one hole in the bottom and three holes on the sides to allow for the passage of water can be utilized for seeding. They should be filled with the same substrate as above. The seeding is made at a depth of about 0.5 cm. Only water is utilized during the germination period up to the formation of small leaves. After that, the plants should be transported to wooden boxes according to the distances shown in Table 2.

Protection   The wooden boxes should be protected against heavy rain and excessive light by covering with black plastic sheets or other suitable material.

Types of seeds   When dealing with vegetables, one should work with certified seeds. In Colombia it is possible to get seeds directly from tomatoes and cucumber *"cohombro"* and have them conveniently prepared for seeding.

Plant support   Each plant should be tied with polyester fibre to small rods stuck into the substrate. This procedure is particularly important when planting tomatoes, cucumbers and green peppers.

Conclusion

This technology can be a good option to produce food in many parts of the world, such as Latin America, where the soil and environmental conditions are not adequate for the development of traditional agriculture. The cost of the nutrient solution and the availibility of water are key elements for the development of this promising option for food production.

TABLE NO. 1 - PROPERTY OF SUBSTRATES

SUBSTRATE	GRAIN SIZE	PHYSICAL	CHEMICAL	BIOLOGICAL	RETENCION X AERATION	DENSITY TON/M3	COST 0-15
river sand	2.0	excellent	good	?	M-M	2.0	6
rock sand	0.5	excellent	very bad	good	E-D	2.0	3
gravel	10	excellent	good	good	D-E	2.0	6
pumice stone	10	good	median	excellent	M-M	0.8	?
brick	10	median	median	excellent	M-M	0.8	?
charcoal	10	good	median	excellent	M-M	0.8	2
coke	10-25	good	excellent	excellent	B-A	0.6	10
rock charcoal	5-10	?	?	excellent	?	0,5	?
saw dust	4-6	median	good	good	A-B	0.3	1
rice shell	3-6	median	median	median	B-A	0.15	0.6
coffee shell	5-8	very bad	very bad	?	A-?	0.15	-
clay	6-15	excellent	excellent	excellent	M-M	0.25	15

D - Defficient
B - low
M - medium
A - High
E - excessive

Cost - arbitrary scale from 0 to 15, in Bogota, Colombia.

TABLE No.2 - SPECIES, VARIETIES AND SEEDING DENSITY OF THE MAIN
VEGETABLES TO CULTIVATE AT HOME.

NAME	VARIETY	DISTANCE (cm)	
		COLUMN	ROW
Lettuce	Grandes Lagos	20	20
Carrot (*)	Chantenay	10	20
Tomato	Chonto y Milano	50	1 row
Cabbage	Copenhagen Market	50	50
Red beet	Crosby's Egyptian	15	25
Caully flower	Bola de Nieve	30	50
Radisch (*)	Rojo	10	20
Spinach (*)	Viroflay	20	30
Coriander (*)	Comun	40	40
Onion C.	Yellow Granex	10	18

(*) For direct seeding. All the others for transport.
Source : Manual de Hortalizas of the ICA.

**MARC**

Bringing you key resources on the world mission of the church

MARC books and other publications support the work of MARC (Mission Advanced Research and Communications Center), which is to inspire fresh vision and empower Christian mission among those who extend the whole gospel to the whole world.

Recent MARC titles include:

▶ *Survival of the Fittest: Keeping Yourself Healthy in Travel and Service Overseas*, Dr. Christine Aroney-Sine. An informative guide to help you maintain your physical, emotional and spiritual well-being while traveling internationally.
$ 9.95

▶ *Health, Healing and Transformation*, A. Allen, K. Luscombe, B. Myers, E. Ram, editors. Explores discipleship as a way to bring about health, healing and wholeness.
$ 7.95

▶ *God So Loves the City: Seeking a Theology for Urban Mission*, Charles Van Engen and Jude Tiersma, editors. Experienced urban practitioners from around the world explore the most urgent issues facing those who minister in today's cities.
$ 21.95

▶ *Healing the Children of War*, Phyllis Kilbourn, editor. A handbook for Christians who desire to be of service to children who have suffered deep traumas as a result of war.
$ 21.95

▶ *The Changing Shape of World Mission* by Bryant L. Myers. Presents in color graphs, charts and maps the challenge before global missions, including the unfinished task of world evangelization. Also available in color slides and overheads—excellent for presentations!

Book..$ 5.95
Slides..$ 99.95
Overheads.......................................$ 99.95
Presentation Set *(one book, slides and overheads)* $175.00

Order Toll Free in USA: 1-800-777-7752
Visa and MasterCard accepted

MARC A division of World Vision International
121 E. Huntington Dr. • Monrovia • CA • 91016-3400

Ask for the MARC Newsletter and complete publications list